Michelle Gibson
Deborah T. Meem
Editors

MW01054435

Femme/Butch:
New Considerations
of the Way We Want to Go

Femme/Butch: New Considerations of the Way We Want to Go
has been co-published simultaneously as *Journal of Lesbian
Studies*, Volume 6, Number 2 2002.

Pre-publication
REVIEWS,
COMMENTARIES,
EVALUATIONS . . .

"**D**ISRUPTS THE FICTIONS OF
HETEROSEXUAL NORMS. . . .
A much-needed examination of the
ways that butch/femme identities
subvert both heteronormativity and
'expected' lesbian behavior."

Patti Capel Swartz, PhD
Assistant Professor of English
Kent State University

Harrington Park Press

Femme/Butch:
New Considerations
of the Way We Want to Go

Femme/Butch: New Considerations of the Way We Want to Go has been co-published simultaneously as *Journal of Lesbian Studies*, Volume 6, Number 2 2002.

The *Journal of Lesbian Studies* Monographic "Separates"

Below is a list of "separates," which in serials librarianship means a special issue simultaneously published as a special journal issue or double-issue *and* as a "separate" hardbound monograph. (This is a format which we also call a "DocuSerial.")

"Separates" are published because specialized libraries or professionals may wish to purchase a specific thematic issue by itself in a format which can be separately cataloged and shelved, as opposed to purchasing the journal on an on-going basis. Faculty members may also more easily consider a "separate" for classroom adoption.

"Separates" are carefully classified separately with the major book jobbers so that the journal tie-in can be noted on new book order slips to avoid duplicate purchasing.

You may wish to visit Haworth's website at . . .

http://www.HaworthPress.com

. . . to search our online catalog for complete tables of contents of these separates and related publications.

You may also call 1-800-HAWORTH (outside US/Canada: 607-722-5857), or Fax 1-800-895-0582 (outside US/Canada: 607-771-0012), or e-mail at:

getinfo@haworthpressinc.com

Femme/Butch: New Considerations of the Way We Want to Go, edited by Michelle Gibson and Deborah T. Meem (Vol. 6, No. 2, 2002). *"Disrupts the fictions of heterosexual norms. . . . A much-needed examination of the ways that butch/femme identities subvert both heteronormativity and 'expected' lesbian behavior." (Patti Capel Swartz, PhD, Assistant Professor of English, Kent State University)*

Lesbian Love and Relationships, edited by Suzanna M. Rose, PhD (Vol. 6, No. 1, 2002). *"Suzanna Rose's collection of 13 essays is well suited to prompting serious contemplation and discussion about lesbian lives and how they are–or are not–different from others. . . . Interesting and useful for debunking some myths, confirming others, and reaching out into new territories that were previously unexplored." (Lisa Keen, BA, MFA, Senior Political Correspondent,* Washington Blade*)*

Everyday Mutinies: Funding Lesbian Activism, edited by Nanette K. Gartrell, MD, and Esther D. Rothblum, PhD (Vol. 5, No. 3, 2001). *"Any lesbian who fears she'll never find the money, time, or support for her work can take heart from the resourcefulness and dogged determination of the contributors to this book. Not only do these inspiring stories provide practical tips on making dreams come true, they offer an informal history of lesbian political activism since World War II." (Jane Futcher, MA, Reporter,* Marin Independent Journal, *and author of* Crush, Dream Lover, *and* Promise Not to Tell*)*

Lesbian Studies in Aotearoa/New Zealand, edited by Alison J. Laurie (Vol. 5, No. 1/2, 2001). *These fascinating studies analyze topics ranging from the gender transgressions of women passing as men in order to work and marry as they wished to the effects of coming out on modern women's health.*

Lesbian Self-Writing: The Embodiment of Experience, edited by Lynda Hall (Vol. 4, No. 4, 2000). *"Probes the intersection of love for words and love for women. . . . Luminous, erotic, evocative." (Beverly Burch, PhD, psychotherapist and author,* Other Women: Lesbian/Bisexual Experience and Psychoanalytic Views of Women *and* On Intimate Terms: The Psychology of Difference in Lesbian Relationships*)*

'Romancing the Margins'? Lesbian Writing in the 1990s, edited by Gabriele Griffin, PhD (Vol. 4, No. 2, 2000). *Explores lesbian issues through the mediums of books, movies, and poetry and offers readers critical essays that examine current lesbian writing and discuss how recent movements have tried to remove racist and anti-gay themes from literature and movies.*

From Nowhere to Everywhere: Lesbian Geographies, edited by Gill Valentine, PhD (Vol. 4, No. 1, 2000). *"A significant and worthy contribution to the ever growing literature on sexuality and space. . . . A politically significant volume representing the first major collection on lesbian geographies. . . . I will make extensive use of this book in my courses on social and cultural geography and sexuality and space." (Jon Binnie, PhD, Lecturer in Human Geography, Liverpool, John Moores University, United Kingdom)*

Lesbians, Levis and Lipstick: The Meaning of Beauty in Our Lives, edited by Jeanine C. Cogan, PhD, and Joanie M. Erickson (Vol. 3, No. 4, 1999). *Explores lesbian beauty norms and the effects these norms have on lesbian women.*

Lesbian Sex Scandals: Sexual Practices, Identities, and Politics, edited by Dawn Atkins, MA (Vol. 3, No. 3, 1999). *"Grounded in material practices, this collection explores confrontation and coincidence among identity politics, 'scandalous' sexual practices, and queer theory and feminism. . . . It expands notions of lesbian identification and lesbian community." (Maria Pramaggiore, PhD, Assistant Professor, Film Studies, North Carolina State University, Raleigh)*

The Lesbian Polyamory Reader: Open Relationships, Non-Monogamy, and Casual Sex, edited by Marcia Munson and Judith P. Stelboum, PhD (Vol. 3, No. 1/2, 1999). *"Offers reasonable, logical, and persuasive explanations for a style of life I had not seriously considered before. . . . A terrific read." (Beverly Todd, Acquisitions Librarian, Estes Park Public Library, Estes Park, Colorado)*

Living "Difference": Lesbian Perspectives on Work and Family Life, edited by Gillian A. Dunne, PhD (Vol. 2, No. 4, 1998). *"A fascinating, groundbreaking collection. . . . Students and professionals in psychiatry, psychology, sociology, and anthropology will find this work extremely useful and thought provoking." (Nanette K. Gartrell, MD, Associate Clinical Professor of Psychiatry, University of California at San Francisco Medical School)*

Acts of Passion: Sexuality, Gender, and Performance, edited by Nina Rapi, MA, and Maya Chowdhry, MA (Vol. 2, No. 2/3, 1998). *"This significant and impressive publication draws together a diversity of positions, practices, and polemics in relation to postmodern lesbian performance and puts them firmly on the contemporary cultural map." (Lois Keidan, Director of Live Arts, Institute of Contemporary Arts, London, United Kingdom)*

Gateways to Improving Lesbian Health and Health Care: Opening Doors, edited by Christy M. Ponticelli, PhD (Vol. 2, No. 1, 1997). *"An unprecedented collection that goes to the source for powerful and poignant information on the state of lesbian health care." (Jocelyn C. White, MD, Assistant Professor of Medicine, Oregon Health Sciences University; Faculty, Portland Program in General Internal Medicine, Legacy Portland Hospitals, Portland, Oregon)*

Classics in Lesbian Studies, edited by Esther Rothblum, PhD (Vol. 1, No. 1, 1996). *"Brings together a collection of powerful chapters that cross disciplines and offer a broad vision of lesbian lives across race, age, and community." (Michele J. Eliason, PhD, Associate Professor, College of Nursing, The University of Iowa)*

Femme/Butch:
New Considerations
of the Way We Want to Go

Michelle Gibson, PhD
Deborah T. Meem, PhD
Editors

Femme/Butch: New Considerations of the Way We Want to Go has been co-published simultaneously as *Journal of Lesbian Studies*, Volume 6, Number 2 2002.

Harrington Park Press
An Imprint of
The Haworth Press, Inc.
New York • London • Oxford

Published by

Harrington Park Press®, 10 Alice Street, Binghamton, NY 13904-1580 USA

Harrington Park Press® is an imprint of The Haworth Press, Inc., 10 Alice Street, Binghamton, NY 13904-1580 USA.

Femme/Butch: New Considerations of the Way We Want to Go has been co-published simultaneously as *Journal of Lesbian Studies*, Volume 6, Number 2 2002.

The development, preparation, and publication of this work has been undertaken with great care. However, the publisher, employees, editors, and agents of The Haworth Press and all imprints of The Haworth Press, Inc., including The Haworth Medical Press® and The Pharmaceutical Products Press®, are not responsible for any errors contained herein or for consequences that may ensue from use of materials or information contained in this work. Opinions expressed by the author(s) are not necessarily those of The Haworth Press, Inc. With regard to case studies, identities and circumstances of individuals discussed herein have been changed to protect confidentiality. Any resemblance to actual persons, living or dead, is entirely coincidental.

Cover design by Jennifer M. Gaska

Library of Congress Cataloging-in-Publication Data

Femme/butch : new considerations of the way we want to go / Michelle Gibson, Deborah Meem, editors.
     p. cm.
     "Femme/Butch: new considerations of the way we want to go has been co-published simultaneously as Journal of lesbian studies, volume 6, Number 2, 2002."
     Includes bibliographical references and index.
     ISBN 1-56023-300-1 (cloth : alk. paper) – ISBN 1-56023-301-X (pbk. : alk. paper)
     1. Lesbians. 2. Lesbians–Identity. 3. Gender identity. 4. Lesbianism. I. Gibson, Michelle.
II. Meem, Deborah.
HQ75.5 .F459 2002
305.48'9664–dc21

2002008453

Indexing, Abstracting & Website/Internet Coverage

This section provides you with a list of major indexing & abstracting services. That is to say, each service began covering this periodical during the year noted in the right column. Most Websites which are listed below have indicated that they will either post, disseminate, compile, archive, cite or alert their own Website users with research-based content from this work. (This list is as current as the copyright date of this publication.)

(continued)

*Special Bibliographic Notes related to special journal issues
(separates) and indexing/abstracting:*

- indexing/abstracting services in this list will also cover material in any "separate" that is co-published simultaneously with Haworth's special thematic journal issue or DocuSerial. Indexing/abstracting usually covers material at the article/chapter level.
- monographic co-editions are intended for either non-subscribers or libraries which intend to purchase a second copy for their circulating collections.
- monographic co-editions are reported to all jobbers/wholesalers/approval plans. The source journal is listed as the "series" to assist the prevention of duplicate purchasing in the same manner utilized for books-in-series.
- to facilitate user/access services all indexing/abstracting services are encouraged to utilize the co-indexing entry note indicated at the bottom of the first page of each article/chapter/contribution.
- this is intended to assist a library user of any reference tool (whether print, electronic, online, or CD-ROM) to locate the monographic version if the library has purchased this version but not a subscription to the source journal.
- individual articles/chapters in any Haworth publication are also available through the Haworth Document Delivery Service (HDDS).

Femme/Butch: New Considerations of the Way We Want to Go

CONTENTS

ABOUT THE EDITORS

Michelle Gibson, PhD, is Associate Professor of English and Women's Studies in the University College of the University of Cincinnati, where she teaches courses in writing, literature, and LGBT studies. Her work focuses on theorizing about gender and identity, particularly as they apply to the teaching of writing. Her articles have appeared in the *Journal of Teaching Writing*, *Feminist Teacher*, *Writing on the Edge*, and *Studies in Popular Culture*.

Deborah T. Meem, PhD, is Professor of English and Women's Studies in the University College of the University of Cincinnati, where she teaches courses in writing, literature, and LGBT studies. She publishes in the areas of popular culture, composition studies, lesbian studies, and Victorian literature. She is currently editing Eliza Lynn Linton's 1880 novel *The Rebel of the Family* for Broadview Press.

Together, Drs. Gibson and Meem have co-authored articles on butch/femme and on lesbian literature in *College Composition and Communications*, *Studies in Popular Culture*, and *Feminist Teacher*.

Femme/Butch

Shaira Holman

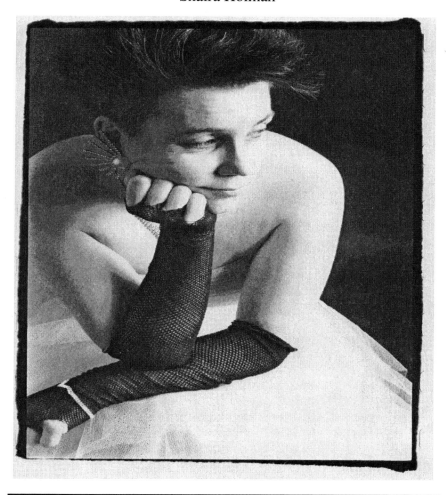

[Haworth co-indexing entry note]: "Femme/Butch." Holman, Shaira. Co-published simultaneously in *Journal of Lesbian Studies* (Harrington Park Press, an imprint of The Haworth Press, Inc.) Vol. 6, No. 2, 2002, pp. 1-2; and: *Femme/Butch: New Considerations of the Way We Want to Go* (ed: Michelle Gibson, and Deborah T. Meem) Harrington Park Press, an imprint of The Haworth Press, Inc., 2002, pp. 1-2.

Shaira Holman
© 2000

Shaira Holman's artistic background includes performance, photography, mixed media, video production, art-activism (Vancouver Association for Non-Commercial Culture), and collective collaborations, from Artropolis to Television. She can be reached at <shaira@vcn.bc.ca>.

Introduction:
The Way We Want to Go

Michelle Gibson
Deborah T. Meem

For over a century, butch-femme lesbian gender has represented contested territory. Even the terms themselves are cloudy. "Butch" seems to have originated first, having gained currency by the 1890s referring to a female butcher, "a hard-fisted woman of the people" (Linton 598). This makes sense, since lesbian identity first coalesced around the figure of the "mannish invert" who dressed and acted in ways previously considered reserved for men. The sexologists, and lesbians themselves, were slower to focus on the femme *as* a lesbian, originally seeing her only as "the pick of women whom the average man would pass by" (Ellis 220), a "womanly woman" who settled for a female lover for lack of anything better.

By the Second World War, lesbians in the United States had adopted the idea of butch-femme to the extent that lesbian community in large cities was often organized around clearly understood butch and femme roles. In the

---

Michelle Gibson and Deborah T. Meem are Professors in the University College of the University of Cincinnati. They work side by side (their offices are even right next door to each other) as teachers of writing, women's studies, and lesbian studies. They also work together as scholars. Together, they have published work on butch-femme in *Feminist Teacher, Studies in Popular Culture, and College Composition and Communication*. They are also a real-life butch-femme couple, which means, of course, that femme Michelle is definitely in charge, though she allows butch Deb the occasional power fantasy.

Address correspondence to Michelle Gibson or Deborah T. Meem by e-mail: <michelle.gibson@uc.edu> or <deborah.meem@uc.edu>.

[Haworth co-indexing entry note]: "Introduction: The Way We Want to Go." Gibson, Michelle, and Deborah T. Meem. Co-published simultaneously in *Journal of Lesbian Studies* (Harrington Park Press, an imprint of The Haworth Press, Inc.) Vol. 6, No. 2, 2002, pp. 3-8; and: *Femme/Butch: New Considerations of the Way We Want to Go* (ed: Michelle Gibson, and Deborah T. Meem) Harrington Park Press, an imprint of The Haworth Press, Inc., 2002, pp. 3-8. Single or multiple copies of this article are available for a fee from The Haworth Document Delivery Service [1-800-HAWORTH, 9:00 a.m. - 5:00 p.m. (EST). E-mail address: getinfo@haworthpressinc.com].

3

1950s and 1960s, butch-femme behavior so imbued working-class lesbian bar culture that many women perceived their primary identity as butch or femme, rather than female or lesbian (Kennedy and Davis 5).

The advent of second-wave feminism in the late 1960s and 1970s drove many butches and femmes underground, as the new movement scorned butch-femme as an unhealthy, not to mention politically incorrect, imitation of sexist male-female power relations. After a decade or so of invisibility, butch-femme gender roles resurfaced as part of the "lesbian sex wars" of the 1980s. This time, however, lesbian gender was academically theorized as feminist theory, deconstruction, and postmodernism merged to produce queer theory. The pioneering work of Sue-Ellen Case, Judith Butler, and others introduced the concept of butch-femme gender as lesbian erotic play.

As you read the articles in this collection, you will notice that a number of them introduce their subject matter with a rehearsal of background information on butch-femme similar to the above three paragraphs. It is important information, to be sure–and helpful for newcomers to the subject. It occurs to us in writing this general introduction, however, that lesbian studies scholarship may very well be reaching the point where this information is no longer necessary as introductory material for individual articles. The standard, widely available lesbian histories–Kennedy and Davis, Faderman, Newton et al.–include considerable discussion of butch-femme dynamics within lesbian communities. Recent work on lesbian gender–by Nestle, Feinberg, Prosser, Halberstam, and others–has deepened the analysis of butch-femme and expanded the scope to include transgender individuals. And the queer theoretical approach generally presupposes reader familiarity with the history and contemporary practice of butch-femme. So perhaps the impulse to include substantial introductory material before every article is just about obsolete–a testament to the wide circulation of lesbian studies scholarship.

Having begun with a nod toward the history of the butch-femme phenomenon, we need to make clear that this collection represents an attempt to bring together a number of theoretical approaches to butch-femme–only one of which is queer theory. Frankly, we believe that an anthology of queer theoretical approaches to butch-femme would be interesting, but would not necessarily add much to the scholarship on butch-femme lesbian gender because queer theory has positioned itself in opposition to more woman-centered approaches like lesbian feminism. We would like to see lesbians work toward an inclusive scholarship–one that simultaneously marks itself as woman-centered and resists limitations on the way woman, lesbian, gender, sexuality, etc. are defined. What we have attempted to do as we have selected articles and worked with their authors is to encourage an examination of various compelling questions:

- Can theory about butch-femme exist in the electric realm of sex and sexuality, or does theory necessarily neutralize sexuality? Melanie Maltry and Kristin Tucker's article speaks to this issue; it conflates theory and practice, using the intellectual apparatus of queer theory to analyze specific sex acts associated with butch/femme.
- What role does popular culture play in helping us to theorize about lesbian gender? Rebecca Kennison's piece on Marlene Dietrich and Lori Rifkin's discussion of women in suits both take up issues of dress, performance, fame, and influence. In different but related ways they consider the connections among cultural artifacts, cultural icons, cultural representations, and cultural studies.
- What are the relationships between history and butch-femme lesbian gender? Here we turn to Liberty Smith's analysis of elided femme experience in eighteenth-century "passing woman" stories. Smith's article critiques the common societal perception of butch women as the only "real" lesbians, by examining the earliest roots of this perception and recovering lost femme lives from literary and historical obscurity. Helen Hok-Sze Leung's article on Chinese women and Monika Pisankaneva's on the emerging lesbian community in Bulgaria both consider the related idea of what role butch-femme identification plays in cultures which lack cohesive and recognizable lesbian institutions.
- Is lesbian identity development a phenomenon requiring certain discrete "stages" or does it involve a more free-flowing process? Certainly in the US rigid butch-femme roles defined lesbian experience until cultural feminism repudiated them, and their eventual re-emergence in the form of erotic play seems to represent yet another stage. But will this pattern obtain in China? In Bulgaria? Elsewhere?
- What relationship exists between social class and contemporary thinking about butch-femme lesbian gender? Sara L. Crawley's socio-literary examination of Leslie Feinberg's semi-autobiographical novel *Stone Butch Blues* assumes a particular working-class orientation. In addition, Crawley explores the tenuous relationship between stone butch and transgender identification, thereby interrogating the role of the idea "woman" as it relates to female masculinity.
- Crawley's piece contrasts interestingly with Heidi M. Levitt and Sharon G. Horne's work in raising the question of who studies lesbian cultural patterns, how, and for what purpose. Though both articles fit under the broad social science umbrella, Crawley sets out deliberately to blur disciplinary and methodological boundaries (sociology/literary study, fiction/nonfiction, etc.). Levitt and Horne, on the other hand, remain firmly anchored in the field of psychology, their stated goal being to add a spe-

cific piece to the body of literature on lesbian psychology, to introduce a new variable into the ways scholars and psychotherapists approach lesbianism. To add yet another dimension to the issue of (inter)disciplinarity, we see Rachel Epstein melding ethnography and theory into a discussion of butch motherhood that does not "fit" neatly into any methodological category.

- How about the relationship between race and butch-femme? Here a difficulty arose for us. Even though we sent out two calls for papers and let the project span approximately eighteen months, we received no articles that fully interrogate issues of race as they are related to lesbian gender. As two white women, we acknowledge that the problem might well have been some kind of oversight in the call for papers, or perhaps our way of representing the discussion revealed our limitations. We simply don't know why we were not able to encourage more women writing about race to submit articles; what we do know is that it didn't happen and we regret that–partly because the lack of discussion of race diminishes this collection, but perhaps more important, also because we believe that examination of the relationship between race and lesbian gender is a project that needs to be pursued.

We have observed that there are several strengths to the approach we have taken, not the least of which is that we were fortunate enough to receive articles from lesbians living outside the US. There is, we believe, an international flavor to this collection that highlights important questions about the relationship among politics, culture, and lesbian gender. Another of the strengths of our approach has been that it has allowed us to de-emphasize distinctions between "high" and "low" culture and between "popular" and "academic" culture. As a reader, you will notice fairly quickly that we have included visual art by Shaira and by Yohah Ralph, and a playful poem by Lesléa Newman; perhaps you will be more surprised, though, by our inclusion of pictures of lesbian performers who either identify as butch or femme, or whose work focuses on the sexual play of those gender markers. The process of collecting the photographs and the quotations that accompany them began when we attended the 2001 National Women's Music Festival in Muncie, Indiana and listened as performers like C. C. Carter, Vickie Shaw, and Jamie Anderson spoke with electrifying pride about the sexuality of their femme lesbian gender, a move that would probably not have been possible even thirty years ago when femmes were considered "passing" lesbians or "sell-outs" to popular images of feminine beauty.

Parts of this collection also inhabit the borderland at the edge of previously "acceptable" scholarship. Robin Maltz and Laura A. Harris explore the links between consensual butch-femme sex and "taboo" subjects like child sexual abuse and incest. Maltz and Harris question what it means when we enact in our sexual lives situations and experiences usually associated with abuse. Certainly, their discussions of "Mommy" and "Daddy" play lie outside the traditional limits of feminist content. The Catherine Mackinnon anti-porn school has historically frowned on in-your-face expressions of what it perceived to be outrageous lesbian sexuality. As a result, it is possible that some readers will experience discomfort as they read these pieces, but as scholars whose work and lives have been deeply touched by our thinking and feeling about butch-femme lesbian gender, we value discomfort.

As feminist-identified middle-class white lesbians, the two of us have inherited a knee-jerk tendency toward Political Correctness. For us, though, this involves more than lip service and liberal guilt—we believe in what have historically been feminist values of inclusiveness, consideration, and (can we say it?) empowerment. Our scholarship in the area of lesbian gender, however, causes us to question the way that approach turns back onto itself until the very notion of inclusion becomes exclusive. Take the example of Lea DeLaria, for instance; by her own admission, people find her "horribly offensive" (5). As far as we can tell, almost nothing that comes out of her mouth (or her mind, for that matter) is PC. In fact, in *Lea's Book of Rules for the World*, she says quite a bit that we find personally offensive—but damn it, when either of us picks up that book and begins to read, we laugh like hell and insist on reading passages aloud to one another. What's this all about? It's about pushing the envelope. It's about resisting the impulse to relegate some of our most basic impulses to the realm of the "improper," thereby denying ourselves the potential to wallow (and even delight) in our own sometimes complex and often offensive humanity. After all, who gets to decide what is proper and improper? Lesbian sexuality has been deemed "improper" by conservative straights, and butch-femme gender has been deemed "improper" by conservative lesbians. We would like our work to transcend the idea of propriety.

Returning to Lea DeLaria, we observe how our reaction to her no-holds-barred humor partakes of curiously opposed impulses: the hilarity inspired by crossing over into forbidden space ("Is it a law in Texas that you have to weigh three hundred ninety-five pounds to be a lesbian?" [7]); and the uncomfortable laughter born of recognizing one's alliance with conservative social forces (which have always dictated how women should appear and behave). We see how resistance and conformity seem to set off in opposite directions; but we also see how resistance and conformity meet each other at the closing of the circle. In short, the blade cuts both directions. Puritans come in all shapes and sizes, in all colors, and with all sexual inclinations. As soon as we start "purifying" our impulses, we become the very Puritans who would deny us the sex and sexuality that is, in the end, the only totally necessary component of our scholarship on lesbian gender.

And so it's not a drive to be inclusive that makes us so sorry that we were not able to elicit more discussion about race and butch-femme; it's our feeling that analyses of race push the envelope in much the same way as do analyses of "outrageous" expressions of sexuality. What we have happily observed as we have received work from the authors and artists included in this collection is that they all seem to be in the process of re-vising, re-seeing, re-thinking. Some are reshaping their disciplines, some their nations, some their sexualities, some their lives–but all insist that we open ourselves to new intellectual, emotional, or sexual possibilities. In spite of the editors' tendency toward political correctness, this is the way we want to go, in every aspect of our lives. Feminism as a movement has always assumed that process is at least as important as product. This collection freezes a point in the ongoing process of butch-femme practice–and scholarship–and performance. We are glad to feel that our feminist roots jibe with the continuing evolution of butch-femme in its various incarnations.

WORKS CITED

Butler, Judith. *Gender Trouble: Feminism and the Subversion of Identity*. NY and London: Routledge, 1990.

_____. "Imitation and Gender Insubordination." *inside/out: Lesbian Theories, Gay Theories*. Ed. Diana Fuss. NY and London: Routledge, 1991. 13-31.

Case, Sue-Ellen. "Toward a Butch-Femme Æsthetic." *The Lesbian and Gay Studies Reader*. Ed. Henry Abelove, Michèle Aina Barale, David M. Halperin. NY and London: Routledge, 1993. 294-306.

DeLaria, Lea. *Lea's Book of Rules for the World*. NY: Dell, 2000.

Ellis, Havelock. *Studies in the Psychology of Sex*. Vol. II. Philadelphia: Davis, 1918.

Faderman, Lillian. *Odd Girls and Twilight Lovers: A History of Lesbian Life in Twentieth-Century America*. NY: Columbia UP, 1991.

Feinberg, Leslie. *Stone Butch Blues*. Ithaca: Firebrand, 1993.

_____. *Transgender Warriors: Making History from Joan of Arc to Dennis Rodman*. Boston: Beacon, 1996.

Halberstam, Judith. *Female Masculinity*. Durham: Duke UP, 1998.

Kennedy, Elizabeth Lapovsky, and Madeline Davis. *Boots of Leather, Slippers of Gold: The History of a Lesbian Community*. Harmondsworth: Penguin, 1993.

Linton, Eliza Lynn. "The Wild Women As Social Insurgents." *Nineteenth Century* Oct. 1891. 596-605.

Nestle, Joan. *The Persistent Desire: A Femme-Butch Reader*. Boston: Alyson, 1992.

Newton, Esther. "The Mythic Mannish Lesbian: Radclyffe Hall and the New Woman." *The History of Homosexuality in Europe and America*. Ed. Wayne R. Dynes and Stephen Donaldson. NY: Garland, 1992. 217-235.

Prosser, Jay. *Second Skins: The Body Narratives of Transsexuality*. NY: Columbia UP, 1998.

Dark Chocolate

Jamie Anderson

(From a Femme to her Butch)

The way to a woman's heart is through her lips
Through the shudder of her sighs and the motion of her hips
Through the softness of her thighs, to that place between her shoulders
And if a woman wants her, do you wanna hold her back?

Are you think' 'bout a woman you might like to see?
Look her deep in the eyes and say, slow dance with me
You know what you're wanting, you might ask now
You can show her so she'll know how

Jamie Anderson is a nationally touring singer-songwriter and workshop leader in the areas of performance, songwriting, and music business. She writes for *Acoustic Guitar* and is featured in their book *Songwriting and the Guitar*. The founder of Tsunami Recordings, she has written and performed her own songs on tour for over ten years.
Address correspondence to Jamie Anderson by e-mail: <tsunamiinc@aol.com>.

[Haworth co-indexing entry note]: "Dark Chocolate." Anderson, Jamie. Co-published simultaneously in *Journal of Lesbian Studies* (Harrington Park Press, an imprint of The Haworth Press, Inc.) Vol. 6, No. 2, 2002, pp. 9-10; and: *Femme/Butch: New Considerations of the Way We Want to Go* (ed: Michelle Gibson, and Deborah T. Meem) Harrington Park Press, an imprint of The Haworth Press, Inc., 2002, pp. 9-10.

That the way to your heart is through your lips
Through the shudder of your sighs and the motion of your hips
Through the softness of your thighs to that place between your shoulders
And if she wants you, do you wanna hold her back?

I'm think' 'bout a woman who might just take me home
Feed me dark chocolate and other sugar that she owns
I know what I'm wantin', I'm asking now
I can show you, so you'll know how

(That) The way to my heart is through my lips
Through the shudder of my sighs and the motion of my hips
Through the softness of my thighs to that place between my shoulders
And if you want me, I won't hold back
I won't hold back

Prioritizing Audiences:
Exploring the Differences
Between Stone Butch
and Transgender Selves

Sara L. Crawley

SUMMARY. In Leslie Feinberg's novel, *Stone Butch Blues*, the main character, Jess, can be read as either stone butch or transgendered, suggesting that stone butch and (female-born) transgender presentations are similar. Yet, with similar behaviors and expectations, it seems unclear what makes these two identifications distinct. In this paper, I suggest that one significant difference between these categories is the audience that is

---

Sara L. Crawley is a butch dyke and a PhD Candidate in Sociology and Women's Studies at the University of Florida. She is currently Visiting Instructor in the Women's Studies Center at Florida International University. Ms. Crawley is having fun finishing a dissertation based on focus group, couple and individual interviews with all sorts of lesbians which suggest that butch and fem are narrative resources for constructing lesbian selves.

Author note: I would like to acknowledge my mentors, Tace Hedrick and Kendal Broad (as always), and the editors of this volume for helpful reviews of this manuscript. Additionally, I would like to thank Kim Emery for having the gumption to offer lesbian literature and queer theory courses in conservative north Florida. Without Kim's cogent theoretical analyses, kind and careful reviews, and one great lunch meeting that sparked my interest in the notion of audience, this paper would not have existed. This paper is dedicated to Barbara Bonanno, who rocks my world just as femme as she wants to be.

Address correspondence to Sara L. Crawley, Florida International University, Women's Studies Center, University Park, DM212, Miami, FL 33199 (E-mail: crawleys@fiu.edu).

[Haworth co-indexing entry note]: "Prioritizing Audiences: Exploring the Differences Between Stone Butch and Transgender Selves." Crawley, Sara L. Co-published simultaneously in *Journal of Lesbian Studies* (Harrington Park Press, an imprint of The Haworth Press, Inc.) Vol. 6, No. 2, 2002, pp. 11-24; and: *Femme/Butch: New Considerations of the Way We Want to Go* (ed: Michelle Gibson, and Deborah T. Meem) (Harrington Park Press, an imprint of The Haworth Press, Inc., 2002, pp. 11-24. Single or multiple copies of this article are available for a fee from The Haworth Document Delivery Service [1-800-HAWORTH, 9:00 a.m. - 5:00 p.m. (EST). E-mail address: getinfo@haworthpressinc.com].

11

foregrounded in developing presentations of self. I suggest that stone butch identification prioritizes a lesbian, specifically butch and fem, audience in developing self, whereas transgender identification prioritizes a heterosexual audience, specifically people invested in the dominant paradigm of a rigid gender system (as a critique to that paradigm). Using Feinberg's character Jess as a prototype of both stone butch and transgender selves, I discuss the theoretical and political implications of foregrounding audiences. *[Article copies available for a fee from The Haworth Document Delivery Service: 1-800-HAWORTH. E-mail address: <getinfo@haworthpressinc.com> Website: <http://www.HaworthPress.com> © 2002 by The Haworth Press, Inc. All rights reserved.]*

KEYWORDS. Butch, transgender, self, audience, performance

Several months ago on an Internet list for stone butches and admiring fems, I observed and participated in several discussions concerning how similar stone butch identification and (female-born) transgender identification are. Although "stone butch" and "transgender" are distinct labels that one could wear, the practitioners of these categories are quite similar in their gender expressions and in their ambivalence towards their female bodies. Indeed, in the course of several on-line discussions, no one on the list was able to definitively determine what the differences are between stone butches and trans men, although list members (including myself) seemed committed to acknowledging that there is a difference. But in Leslie Feinberg's (1993) semi-autobiographical novel *Stone Butch Blues,* I read several clues as to what might be missing in previous theories of gender and sexuality.

In this essay, I will suggest that the divergent labels, stone butch and transgendered, are a result of the audiences for which each identification creates its self-presentation. I argue that stone butches are most concerned with constructing and presenting self to a butch and fem audience, while transgender people are most concerned with constructing and presenting self to a heterosexual audience as a critique to the rigid gender binary. Choosing to foreground one audience over the other has various theoretical and political implications, which I address. I also attempt to borrow theories across disciplinary boundaries to re-conceptualize notions of selves outside the binaries of gender (masculine/feminine), sexuality (hetero/homo) and subjectivity (subject/object).

PRIORITIZING AUDIENCES

Gender and sexuality are not just "done"; they are "done" for particular audiences. Although West and Zimmerman's (1987) paradigmatic article on "doing" gender clearly argues that gender cannot be escaped because sex categories (and their ensuing gender norms) are always applied *by others*, theories of gender and sexualities have often ignored or underplayed the importance of audiences in the construction and performance of identities. The important contribution of West and Zimmerman's argument is that gender is understood as not just something that one wishes to imitate or something that one can participate in arbitrarily, but that others know the rules of gender and hold individuals accountable to them. That is, gender is not just what each individual "does" but also what is done to each of us by others based on our presumed biological sex. Hence, if we know we will be held accountable for our gendered and sexualized presentations, how might we take into account those audiences when we construct our presentations of self?

I would like to think of gender and sexuality as projects in which we engage in constructing our selves. In doing so, we take into account *audiences* for whom we are presenting our selves and communities in which we interact. Focusing on audience allows us to understand how specific performances are tailored to fit situations as well as how individuals construct the selves by which we live. Throughout this article I refer to the notion of social selves that relies on the work of Erving Goffman (1959). In Goffman's work, selves are created in response to social expectations about roles in which both the person "doing" self and the group for whom self is performed (the audience) are working together to make sense of any situation. [For a cogent reading of the literature on social selves and an important new direction in the theories of social selves, see Holstein and Gubrium (2000).] It may seem that I tend to discuss audiences as relatively simplistic, undifferentiated groups (e.g., "straight people," "butches and fems like us," "lesbian/gay/bisexual/transgender people," etc.). It is not my intention to oversimplify the diversity of individuals who may read an individual's performance of self. I wish to be clear that, in this paper, the audiences to which I refer are *the performer's* preconceived notion of groups, not necessarily "real" groups. While I think it is reductionist to unproblematically conceive of unitary, undifferentiated groups, I do think that in practice many people imagine social groups as unitary and well defined. Hence, the audiences to which I refer are not representative populations in the U.S. but, rather, social groups that live in the everyday imaginations of lay persons. They may be what Feagin and Vera (1995:13-14) refer to as "sincere fictions"–"personal mythologies that reproduce societal mythologies at the individual level."

As a central theme for this paper, I argue that stone butch and transgender selves are created similarly but for different audiences. The stone butch project is one that prioritizes audience as its own community–other butches and fems. The transgender project, however, prioritizes an oppositional audience of people invested in the dominant, heterosexual paradigm as a critique to the simplicity of that paradigm. That is, the transgender project specifically attempts to address the audience that believes in distinct, binary biological sex categories in an attempt to disrupt the neatness of those categories. From the start, let me be clear on two points. First, I am suggesting that stone butch and transgender people *prioritize* one audience as more important in constructing self more often than other audiences. I am not suggesting that only one audience actually views that presentation or that in different contexts the audience may be altered for a period of time. I am merely suggesting that individuals pick one label–stone butch or transgendered–as a general theme about one's self in which one audience is more specifically targeted. Second, I am not suggesting that either the transgender or stone butch project should be seen as more transgressive than the other. Rather, it is more important to note how the differences between these projects inform us of the importance of audience in our own gender and sexuality projects.

UNDISCIPLINING METHODOLOGY

Shortly, I will use Leslie Feinberg's character Jess from *Stone Butch Blues* to support my argument regarding audience. But first, as a sociologist, I feel compelled to address my use of a fictional character as "data." I justify this unconventional methodology on four important points. First, using feminist content analysis, I suggest that it is permissible for me to read fiction as part of an overall scientific endeavor because fiction can be read as a *cultural artifact* (Reinharz 1992:142-8). As such, fiction is not read as "true" and representative of populations of "real" people, but as products of people within a particular culture that are worthy of scientific attention *as texts*. In this essay, I am not embarking on a literary criticism or an empirical study. I am attempting to theorize the existence of two identity categories. For this purpose, I believe it is quite defensible to use a fictional character since my argument is intentionally theoretical and political.

Second, much like Radclyffe Hall's (1928 [1956]) relationship to Stephen in *The Well of Loneliness*, *Stone Butch Blues* is commonly viewed as Leslie Feinberg's semi-autobiographical expression of her own experiential knowledge–theorizing her experiences in a fictional format (Prosser 1995:489). So, while Jess may be a prototype of either stone butches or transgender people at various points in her life course, this prototypical character is intended to express Feinberg's own experiential knowledge of these issues.

Third, Jess's gender expression is as real or authentic as any gender expression. Borrowing from Butler (1991:185), "gender is a kind of imitation for which there is no original." Though it is easy to become accustomed to thinking of heterosexual men and women as owning masculinity and femininity, in fact there is no true, original masculine or feminine form that is being replicated. Hence, any coherent gender expression (i.e., a performance that is recognizable as gender) is as valid as any other.

Fourth, and potentially most important, dykes read *Stone Butch Blues* as real and historical and use it in practice. This novel received such critical acclaim because there was nothing like it previously in print. *Stone Butch Blues* is regularly asserted as documentation of stone butch and transgender experience–as a book that describes and speaks to "us." Thus, I embark on reading fiction as informative to the scientific endeavor of theorizing gender and sexuality.

FEINBERG'S JESS:
STONE BUTCH AND TRANSGENDER AS DISTINCTLY SIMILAR

In Leslie Feinberg's novel, *Stone Butch Blues*, the narrator and main character describes her fictional biography as a stone butch and, later, as a person who, after having breast reduction surgery and taking male hormones, passes as a man largely to gain regular employment and avoid violent encounters with homophobic, heterosexual men, especially the police. In Feinberg's account of Jess's life, the young Jess statedly identifies as stone butch. It is never clear whether Feinberg is purposefully choosing to portray Jess as transgendered later in Jess's life during the period of time in which Jess passes as male (Prosser 1995).

Throughout the novel, Jess as stone butch or as transgendered wears the same kinds of clothes (chinos and a T-shirt, a suit jacket and tie, a black leather jacket), engages in similar types of male-dominated professions, and enacts the same kinds of masculine mannerisms. Jess also maintains consistent sexual interests: attraction for fems. Both the young, stone butch Jess and the older, transgendered Jess express that their only viable attraction is for fem women.

The characters themselves express hesitation about accurately labeling their own subjectivities. During a discussion among Jess and three butch friends (Grant, Ed and Jan) of the implications of another passing butch who apparently identified himself as transsexual, several butches expressed ambiguity about their own identification as follows:

Jan put her beer bottle down on the table. "Yeah, but I'm not like Jimmy. Jimmy told me he knew he was a guy even when he was little. I'm not a guy."

Grant leaned forward. "How do you know that? How do you know we aren't? We aren't real women, are we?"

Edwin shook her head. "I don't know what the hell I am." (Feinberg 1993:144)

What is striking about Feinberg's development of Jess is the fluidity of Jess's physical body presentation concurrent with the consistency of her gender expression. [I recognize that not all stone butch or transgender people would use feminine pronouns to describe Jess. I use them because Feinberg uses feminine pronouns to describe the butch characters in *Stone Butch Blues*.] Throughout the physical changes that Jess undergoes, she maintains that she is still herself on the inside. Referring to her emotional response to passing as a man, Jess states, "I was still me on the inside, trapped in there with all my wounds and fears" (Feinberg 1993:173). She had altered the body but not the butch. Over time, her gender expression does not change, only the body that enacts it. As a result of the physical changes she undergoes, Jess can be read as either stone butch (as the title implies) or as transgendered according to Prosser's (1995: 489-90) interpretation.

Noting the consistency of her gender and the various presentations of Jess as stone butch and as transgendered, how are the categories of stone butch and transgender identification to be differentiated? The simple solution is to suggest the difference is the intention of passing or the physical alteration of one's body to attain that goal. But that explanation fails upon the realization that women have been passing as men without physical alterations for centuries, for various reasons that may or may not coincide with Jess's reasons for wanting to pass (Feinberg 1996; Wheelwright 1989).

THE IMPORTANCE OF AUDIENCE

Feinberg does implicitly establish the simple difference between stone butch identification and transgender identification as the audience to whom she is intentionally presenting her identification. Jess indicates that her reasons for abandoning stone butchness in favor of passing is the social acceptance (and safety) that follows from not being visibly different from heterosexuals. Jess is not changing who she "is," she is only changing *to whom* she is directing her gender expression—the audience that she is prioritizing as most important. Whereas she was prepared to be raped and beaten to present herself to the butch and fem community as a young stone butch, she developed her interest in passing as a man when the butch and fem community was no longer readily available for her as a refuge–broken apart by economic need and by feminism's political opposition to butch/fem interaction. After passing as a man, Jess developed her transgender identification (more implicitly than statedly) by refusing to erase the person she felt she had been–a person who was neither male nor female. The focus of her gender expression changed from a revolutionary, visible figure developed for a butch and fem audience to an anonymous gender refugee hiding from a violent heterosexual audience, and later, a revolutionary, visible transgender person to both a lesbian and heterosexual audience.

STONE BUTCH SELVES AND POLITICAL TRANSGRESSIONS

In stone butch identification, (a gendered) sexuality is foregrounded. The definition of stone butchness–one who is always the sexual actor and is herself untouchable to her partner–calls up references to sexuality, especially butch/fem sexual interaction. Whether stone butches are, in fact, not ever touched sexually is immaterial. (Feinberg gives several cues that imply that even she doubts the accuracy of the definition in practice.) Stone butch identification is primarily created and maintained by butches for fems and monitored by both. According to historical accounts, butches, as women with masculine gender expressions, created public attention to lesbian community by their visibility, but butches and fems maintained the boundaries of that community by establishing their sexual relationships to each other (Kennedy and Davis 1993:151-4). Hence, stone butches created and presented selves to a butch and fem audience.

Kennedy and Davis describe how creating stone butch selves can be seen as politically transgressive. They report on the importance of sexual prowess for butches in early lesbian communities in Buffalo, New York, as follows, "For the tough butches, being able to please a woman more than a man could was as important in the defense of the community as were their skills in fighting" (Kennedy and Davis 1993:195). Stone butch sexuality defended the possibility of lesbian community. And lesbian community monitored that stone butch sexuality such that, when two lovers were engaged in sexual acts, the interaction took place not only between two people but under the social sanctioning of the entire community. Feinberg addresses this directly when the young, stone butch Jess goes home with an older, experienced fem for the first time and then becomes too scared to have sex with her. Jess expresses awareness of the importance of how others would receive the news of her sexual hesitation as follows: "But back at the bar, I couldn't escape the consequences" (Feinberg 1993:32). Butch and fem sexual interactions were part of community interaction. Stone butch identification helped to build sexual communities and those communities greatly impacted the creation and maintenance of stone butchness as a viable sexual subjectivity. It is the audacity of females to create selves that are sexually competent at satisfying their female partners that is the transgressive project of stone butchness (Halberstam 1998:128). In Goffman's (1959) terms, stone butches are asserting a moral self which demands that others grant it legitimacy. (Here, I am not suggesting that fem subjectivity did not also build butch and fem communities. I believe it did. But my focus in this essay is the comparison of stone butch identification with transgender identification. Hence, my focus is on stone butch contributions.)

The political implications of building communities based on female desire for females is nothing short of subversive of patriarchal proscriptions of sexuality. For as de Lauretis (1994) theorizes, communities based on female desire for other females comprise what she terms sexual difference, a breaking away from heterosexual, male-centered notions of sexual subjectivity. I suggest that butch and fem communities are based on just such a possibility of female sexual subjectivity. (In suggesting this, I do not wish to align myself with "sexual difference" theorists. I simply want to borrow from their political project. While I agree that masculinity among lesbians does not signify the wish for a penis, I question the lifelong "psychic" impact of early childhood interactions with one's mother or father either developmentally or symbolically. Instead, I am much more concerned with the ongoing impact of gender and sexuality constructs on the possibility of women's sexual agency in our everyday definitions of self. Nonetheless, I agree with de Lauretis' general notion that lesbian sexual subjectivity is not a replication of male sexuality. See Foster (1999) for a cogent discussion of sexual difference theory as opposed to feminist sociological theories of gender.)

Further, agentic sexual selves could be open to other relational possibilities beyond butch/fem, such as butch/butch or fem/fem. Feinberg opens the possibility of various kinds of attractions via the character Frankie, a butch who is attracted to butches, and via Jess's relationship with Ruth, a (biological male) high fem, drag queen. But, these potentialities are not fully explored by Feinberg or accepted by Jess. Even though Jess suggests that it is high fem and not biological sex that attracts her, when given the chance to have sex with Ruth whom Jess admits she loves, Jess rejects the possibility even though she expresses extreme loneliness to the point of sensory deprivation. Feinberg's theorizing falls short of actively pursuing these kinds of potentialities. This may be because Feinberg's notions of female sexuality are still patrolled, if only in Feinberg's discretion, by the communities in which Feinberg became involved in butch/fem sexuality. Thus, community continues to define and reinforce the available subjectivities.

But if communities were to organize around and support various definitions of butch and fem, the notion of multiple subjectivities provides endless possibilities of sexualities that move beyond binary notions of hetero/homo or subject/object binaries. Indeed, one concern about theorizing lesbian sexuality as sexual difference to heterosexual (in)difference is that this notion is itself essentializing and dichotomizing. The notion of "male" sexuality and "female" sexuality reinforces essential sexual dichotomies (i.e., females develop one set of interests, males another). Is it necessary to "economize" heterosexual sexual subjectivity as an organization in which one participant enjoys subjectivity and the other must, by definition, not? Given the argument that I have been making thus far, is it not also possible (however difficult, given the current cultural mandate of heterosexual, male dominance) to envision heterosexual female desire and subjectivity? It would seem hypocritical to suggest that butch masculinity is adaptable to political necessity while heterosexual (male) masculinity is not also malleable.

TRANSGENDER SELVES AND POLITICAL TRANSGRESSIONS

Transgender identification foregrounds gender over sexuality and also over biological sex itself. (Although as a non-normative gendered subjectivity, transgender identification is also implicitly sexualized.) As such, transgender identification is created for a heterosexual audience, specifically people invested in the dominant paradigm of a rigid gender system as a critique to that paradigm. As females who embody "masculinity" as well as (presumed) biological males, the existence of transgender people creates a purposeful critique to the rigidity of the binary gender paradigm that attempts to determine gender, sexual orientation, status, subjectivity (or the lack thereof), and identity at birth based on presumed biological sex. Gender expression that supersedes both sexuality and biological sex engages a heterosexual audience by implicitly problematizing the "naturalness" of the dominant gender system.

Prosser (1995:508) interprets Feinberg as defining "the transgendered community as one centered around gender, not sexuality" and suggests that "this is surely what distinguishes it from the queer community (and places it in an unintentional but significant alliance with feminism)." Prosser argues that Jess exemplifies not a transsexual person, a person who wishes to change from one sex to the other, but rather a transgender person. Jess is not attempting to cross from one sex to another, but is attempting not to be placed in either male or female categories. Jess only passes as a man for a period of time and, while Jess has breast reduction surgery and takes male hormones to grow a beard, Jess never completely reassigns her sex. For Jess, passing as male is a form of survival, not a psychic homecoming. Ultimately, Jess remains not quite male and not quite female. At the point when Jess decides to discontinue taking male hormones, she explains her ambiguous feelings about biological sex and transgender identification as follows: "Who was I now–woman or man? That question could never be answered as long as those were the only choices; it could never be answered if it had to be asked" (Feinberg 1993:222).

Jess's character consistently argues against being placed in the realm of the transsexual. In saying, "I don't feel like a man trapped in a woman's body. I just feel trapped" (Feinberg 1993:158-9), Jess implies that she has not felt that the problems she experiences are internal. Throughout the novel, Feinberg makes it quite clear that all of Jess's troubles are external–lack of social acceptance, not lack of comfort or familiarity with herself. Indeed, in those settings in which Jess does seem to receive social acceptance, Feinberg renders Jess as overjoyed with herself–almost boastful of her physical appearance, her comfort on a motorcycle, her prowess as a butch dancer, her success at "fitting in" in butch and fem communities. Feinberg has created Jess as simple and likable largely by locating her problems as the result of supremely unfair treatment from others–the companies she works for, the school systems that allow boys to rape her on campus, her co-workers who do not understand her, the sexist homophobes who blame her for taking their jobs and who destroy her motorcycle. All these problems occur because the gender expression which Jess seems unable and unwilling to give up is inconsistent with patriarchal social requirements. Jess is not looking for a gender (which seems comfortably consistent for her) or a sex (which she seems comfortable altering without "reassigning"), but a space of social acceptance–a community, a partner or family, a job that allows her to pursue personal success. Lamenting the loss of Theresa, the partner whom Jess speaks of as the equivalent of her estranged wife, Jess narrates, "The moments she pulled my head onto her lap and stroked my face were all I knew of refuge and acceptance" (Feinberg 1993:223).

My concern is not whether Jess is "really" transgendered, but the political implications of a gender expression that situates itself as more determined than biological sex. Jess's character, a person with no distinct sex, falsifies the construction of sex as dichotomous. It is this interest in not being located to a biological sex that is truly transgressive (Stone 1990:297).

MULTIPLE SELVES AND CHANGING AUDIENCES

Discussing the implications of selecting an audience–that is, selecting either stone butch or transgender selves–opens the possibility of implying that one identification is more subversive than the other. This is not my intention, for that creates yet another hierarchy, a hierarchy of radical-ness in which one may be seen as less transgressive than the other–not working as hard for political change. This direction is wholly destructive to the political usefulness of gender or sex subversion and is antithetical to either of the stone butch or transgender projects. In order to short circuit any possible reading of my argument that allows one to create such a hierarchy, I wish to remind the reader, in fact, how similar stone butchness and transgenderedness remain.

While stone butchness directs itself toward a butch and fem audience and emphasizes sexuality, stone butch presentation is not completely lost on the heterosexual audience. If stone butchness is not disrupting notions of biological sex, it certainly creates a similar visible presentation to what Jess pursues in her unsexed body–a socially unrecognizable gender expression, a "he-she." The creation of self for a butch and fem audience is still an uncomfortably "different" gender presentation to the watchful although not targeted heterosexual audience. If this were not the case, Jess would not have been so concerned for her physical safety as a stone butch.

Similarly, if transgender identification foregrounds gender expression and presents self to a heterosexual audience, are transgender selves not participating in creating communities of sexual agency? Indeed, in Jess's relationship with Annie, a heterosexual woman who believes that Jess is a heterosexual man, Feinberg positions Jess as having proven herself a more caring, intimate and proficient lover than heterosexual men, which is often argued as a stone butch trait. One might argue that any sexual activity engaged in by the unsexed self is by definition creating alternative sexual subjectivities–sexuality that is not centered on heterosexual maleness. It is difficult to imagine how the purposefully unsexed self could participate in sexual (in)difference (i.e., by de Lauretis' definition, heterosexual, male-centered sexuality). Does transgender identification not also provide other sexual possibilities beyond butch/fem, such as trans/butch? Feinberg creates a potentiality which she fails to fully explore in the characters of Ethel and Laverne, two co-workers of Jess and Duffy who have masculine appearances but who are married to men. When Duffy asks Jess whether the two are in a sexual relationship, Jess rejects the possibility saying, "Well, they're he-she's but they're not butches" (Feinberg 1993:86). Even without satisfying the sexual content of butch identification, the two women can be interpreted as "he-she's" or gender outlaws. What kind of subjectivity is created by masculine women who participate in heterosexual relationships? Jess adds a social implication with, "Jeez, Duffy, it's not like they're getting off much easier by being married–they're still he-she's" (Feinberg 1993:87).

Returning to the e-mail list in which I participated, this may be why the list members could not define stone butch differently from transgender. Because they can both play to different audiences, they effectively inhabit multiple selves. This is to be expected in the complex social context of late capitalism. Selves almost require variability. They can change audiences, making difficult the possibility of thinking of a unitary coherent self. A singular-defined, strictly-enforced, static self is nearly impossible.

Thus, suggesting that either stone butch or transgender identification is more transgressive than the other is to miss the many similarities between the two identifications and to overemphasize the shades of meaning which separate them. Whether consciously constructed to different audiences as multiple selves or not, the effect of a multiple and varied transgressive self is accomplished.

Rather than asking which self is more transgressive, I believe a better question is asking why an individual chooses one project (or audience) over the other: that is, what are the factors in determining which audience becomes foregrounded over the other? Are the factors simply related to whether an individual foregrounds either gender or sexuality? Similar to the character Jess, many individuals who have claimed stone butch identification have later come to identify as transgendered. For these individuals, when and why did the audience change?

I want to avoid providing a glib, catchall explanation and merely propose some possible relationships not only between individuals and audiences, but also between individuals and communities and between audiences and communities. As I argued earlier, during the development of stone butch identification audiences were also often communities. Stone butch presentation was created for and reinforced by butch and fem communities. The presentation was created for the place of acceptance, refuge or "home" (Prosser 1995:489-90). Feinberg's Jess illustrates for us how the audience that Jess dressed for as a stone butch was the community of butches and fems in which she felt some of the highest levels of acceptance throughout Jess's fictional biography. But, audience and community for a transgender person, as I have framed it here, are clearly different groups. The audience is perceived to be adversarial. But, what is the community of a transgender person? Particularly in this current historical moment, where does a transgender person find acceptance, refuge and "home"?

Feinberg seems to imply that Jess and Ruth created community with each other and among Ruth's drag queen friends. Was this Jess's community? Could lesbian or butch and fem communities also be community for transgender people? Feinberg implies that the communities might overlap, but that butch and fem communities do not necessarily accept transgender people. Although Feinberg leaves us with the hope that Jess will be able to restore the friendships of her youth with her former butch and fem community, the hope is tenuous, vague and distant at best. But in speaking at the lesbian and gay rally near the end of the novel, Jess seems to be working on the project of creating an emerging transgender community (which I believe is also Prosser's and Stone's and, of course, Feinberg's project). Given the importance of community to butches and fems, the necessity of community for transgender people seems beyond idealistic. It seems to be a necessity with real effects. If community to butches and stone butches (and fems) is a place of acceptance, refuge or "home," then it is a space for butch survival. Certainly, Feinberg argues that this is not only a survival of identity but also a physical survival.

To conclude, I want to focus not just on what this paper suggests about stone butches or transgendered people, but more broadly on how it informs our understanding of gender and sexuality in all people. What this work emphasizes is the incredible importance of audience in the development of individuals' understandings of self–the importance of others in allowing us to claim a particular gender or sexuality. If others refuse to see us as anything other than the physical bodies into which we are born, then there is no possibility of nonstandard gender or sexual subjectivity. That is, no matter who you think you are, if others only see you as male or female and proceed to assign the requisite gender and sexuality, then the gender binary will be impossible to overcome. This is an exceedingly limiting vision of human possibility and a project in whose deconstruction we can all participate. We must begin to broaden our own understandings of gender and sexuality. We must break down the conceptual binaries that impede the development of our multiple selves. We must begin to read others as they choose to be read if we hope to deconstruct rigid, dichotomous notions of gender and sexuality.

WORKS CITED

Butler, Judith. 1991. "Imitation and Gender Insubordination." Pp. 180-192 in *The Material Queer:A LesBiGay Cultural Studies Reader*, edited by Donald Morton, 1996. Boulder, CO: Westview Press.

De Lauretis, Teresa. 1994. *The Practice of Love: Lesbian Desire and Perverse Desire.* Bloomington, IN: Indiana University Press.

Feagin, Joe R. and Hernan Vera. 1995. *White Racism.* New York: Routledge.

Feinberg, Leslie. 1993. *Stone Butch Blues.* Ithaca, NewYork: Firebrand Books.

_____. 1996. *Transgender Warriors: Making History from Joan of Arc to Dennis Rodman.* Boston: Beacon Press.

Foster, Johanna. 1999. "An Invitation to Dialogue: Clarifying the Position of Feminist Gender Theory in Relation to Sexual Difference Theory." *Gender & Society* 13:431-456.

Goffman, Erving. 1959. *The Presentation of Self in Everyday Life.* New York: Anchor Books.

Halberstam, Judith. 1998. *Female Masculinity.* Durham, NC: Duke University Press.

Hall, Radclyffe. 1928[1956]. *The Well of Loneliness*. New York: Quality Paperback
  Book Club.
Holstein, James A. and Jaber F. Gubrium. 2000. *The Self We Live By: Narrative Iden-
  tity in a Postmodern World*. New York: Oxford.
Kennedy, Elizabeth Lapovsky and Madeline D. Davis. 1993. *Boots of Leather, Slip-
  pers of Gold: The Making of a Lesbian Community*. New York: Penguin.
Prosser, Jay. 1995. "No Place Like Home: The Transgendered Narrative of Leslie
  Feinberg's *Stone Butch Blues*." *Modern Fiction Studies 41*:483-514.
Reinharz, Shulamit. 1992. *Feminist Methods in Social Research*. New York: Oxford
  University Press.
Stone, Sandy. 1991. "The Empire Strikes Back: A Posttranssexual Manifesto." In *Body
  Guards: The Cultural Politics of Gender Ambiguity*, edited by J. Epstein and K.
  Straub. New York: Routledge.
West, Candace and Don Zimmerman. 1987. "Doing Gender." *Gender & Society*
  1:125-51.
Wheelwright, Julie. 1989. *Amazons and Military Maids: Women Who Dressed as Men
  in the Pursuit of Life, Liberty and Happiness*. London: Pandora.

Explorations of Lesbian-Queer Genders:
Butch, Femme, Androgynous or "Other"

Heidi M. Levitt
Sharon G. Horne

SUMMARY. The purpose of this study was to explore the influence of gender expression on queer women's experiences of identity, social interaction and discrimination. This article presents the results of a questionnaire, completed by 149 queer women involved in a southeastern U.S. women's community in which interactions and norms are strongly influenced by butch-femme gendering. Questionnaires ascertained participants' age of first awareness of their queer orientation and their gender expression. In relation to their gender expressions, their experience of discrimination, from both the general population and the lesbian com-

Heidi M. Levitt, PhD, is Assistant Professor of Clinical Psychology at the University of Memphis. Her research concentrates on processes of personal change. Within this broad rubric, she studies processes of significant moments, metaphor, narrative, and silence within psychotherapy. She is also interested in gender identity and has conducted research on eating disorders, lesbian gender identity, and butch-femme community. She is an experiential psychotherapist and her approach to both therapy and research is rooted within humanistic and constructivist traditions.

Sharon G. Horne, PhD, is Assistant Professor of Counseling Psychology at The University of Memphis. She has presented her research on gay, lesbian, bisexual, and transgender issues and identity at conferences and as an invited speaker at university colloquia. She also conducts international research and consultation on issues pertaining to trauma and violence against women. Her teaching includes graduate-level courses on gender, on couples, and on counseling gay, lesbian, and bisexual clients.

The first author gratefully acknowledges the support of the Social Science and Humanities Council of Canada while conducting this research project.

[Haworth co-indexing entry note]: "Explorations of Lesbian-Queer Genders: Butch, Femme, Androgynous or 'Other.'" Levitt, Heidi M., and Sharon G. Horne. Co-published simultaneously in *Journal of Lesbian Studies* (Harrington Park Press, an imprint of The Haworth Press, Inc.) Vol. 6, No. 2, 2002, pp. 25-39; and: *Femme/Butch: New Considerations of the Way We Want to Go* (ed: Michelle Gibson, and Deborah T. Meem) Harrington Park Press, an imprint of The Haworth Press, Inc., 2002, pp. 25-39. Single or multiple copies of this article are available for a fee from The Haworth Document Delivery Service [1-800-HAWORTH, 9:00 a.m. - 5:00 p.m. (EST). E-mail address: getinfo@haworthpressinc.com].

munity, was assessed. Participants were asked to specify the degree to which their gender expression was important in their social interactions and to assess the impact of butch and femme identities upon the identifying women and the lesbian community. Results indicated that gender expression may relate to butch and femme women's age of first awareness of sexual orientation and gender expression; experience of discrimination and social interaction; and valuing of butch-femme identification within the queer community. *[Article copies available for a fee from The Haworth Document Delivery Service: 1-800-HAWORTH. E-mail address: <getinfo@haworthpressinc.com> Website: <http://www.HaworthPress.com> © 2002 by The Haworth Press, Inc. All rights reserved.]*

KEYWORDS. Gender, butch, femme, identity, androgyny, transgender, sexual orientation, lesbian

Butch-femme gender expressions emerged within the American lesbian culture of the 1950s and 1960s, and thrust lesbians into public visibility for the first time (Lapovsky-Kennedy & Davis, 1993). These expressions were quickly submerged, however, as emerging feminist groups in the 1970s construed these expressions to be an aping of traditional gender roles, and prescribed for lesbian culture an androgynous feminist aesthetic and non-gendered social interaction (Case, 1989; Nestle, 1992). Since this time, some lesbian communities have begun to reclaim butch and femme gender expressions and identities (Faderman, 1991). These post-feminist identities differ from their earlier incarnations as they have arisen within social contexts that allow for a complexity of gender roles that was not permissible in the 1950s, and within queer communities influenced by second-generation feminism (Aston, 1996; Burch, 1998; Butler, 1991; Healey, 1996; Nestle, 1996: Walker, 1993).

Over the last decade there has been a flurry of theoretical and fictional writing on "lesbian genders" (e.g., Aston, 1996; Halberstam, 1998; Harris & Crocker, 1997; Munt, 1998), some indicating that these genders have generalized to bisexual and queer culture (Butler, 1991; Nestle, 1996). Queer butch and femme women have described struggles to claim their identities within larger feminist-lesbian cultures that still may misunderstand the postmodern meanings of their efforts for an atavistic or sexist recreation of heterosexual gender roles (Case, 1989; Nestle, 1992). Empirically, few studies have been conducted on modern butch-femme experience (e.g., Pearcey, Docherty &

Dabbs, 1986; Singh, Vidaurri, Zambarano & Dabbs, 1989), and fewer (i.e., Weber, 1996) contextualize findings within a broader lesbian community.

Historically, women have been underrepresented in the study of sexual identity (Chung & Katayama, 1996). Increasingly, research is showing that the processes of coming out, self-identification, and self-labeling are complex for lesbian and bisexual women and may differ from their male counterparts (Bart, 1993; Brown, 1995; Diamond, 1998; McCarn & Fassinger, 1996; Rust, 1993). Several theorists have studied the lesbian coming out/lesbian self-identification process as well as the relationship to community affiliation (Cass, 1979; Chapman & Brannock, 1987; McCarn & Fassinger, 1996). Although these theories shed light upon developmental and psychological factors important to healthy self-identification and affiliation within the lesbian community, these models have yet to factor in gender expression and its possible impact on sexual identity and orientation.

Many questions have been asked about the developmental process of queer women, but the role of gender expression in this development is unclear. Gender awareness is present as early as age three (Ruble & Martin, 1998), but a sense of gender atypicality has not been explored. In the process of child development, the terminology of butch, femme, androgyny that is particular to queer culture, of course, is not often present. Yet, many butch women report having early experiences of feeling uncomfortable in feminine clothing, or of wanting to be boy-like, so a sense of preferred gender expression likely exists (e.g., Halberstam, 1998). The question remains, therefore, as to how awareness of gender expression and sexual orientation relate.

Gender expression may influence later social interactions in many ways. Identities based upon gender expression (e.g., butch or femme) can allow a queer community to recognize and value women's preferred styles of interaction and expression. These gender expressions, however, may influence experiences of rejection or discrimination as well. Gays, bisexuals, and lesbians experience discrimination and prejudice that impacts their psychological well-being (Herek, 1995; Herek, Gillis & Cogan, 1999). Herek (1995) suggests that people who balk traditional gender-defined characteristics may be more susceptible to harassment and discrimination. One might question, therefore, whether butch women would experience greater discrimination than other queer women due to their gender atypicality, yet little is known about the relationship between gender expression and discrimination for queer women. The purpose of this exploratory study was to examine gender expression within the context of a queer community and learn more.

METHOD

Participants

Participating in this study were 149 queer women residing in a Southeastern U.S. university town. As a past member of this community, the primary author would describe it as holding feminist and separatist values. This description is used to mean that most women identified as feminist, and that men were excluded from community events, which occurred on a near-daily basis. Activism was prized within the community and members were involved in the organization of numerous lesbian national and regional events.

Members' identities and the intra-community interactions were heavily influenced by butch-femme gendering, although women who did not identify in these terms were equally valued within the community. Many of the women who did not adopt these identities, however, appeared to find it useful to describe their gender and sexuality in reference to these terms (e.g., "I am a 6 on the butch-femme scale" or "I am a femmey-androgynous lesbian and I like to date butches."). The community appeared to hold a presumption of butch-femme coupling but also supported couples that did not fall into this framework. Community expectations for androgynous women's partnering seemed to be based upon the romantic histories of those women.

This sample was composed mainly of lesbians (87%, n = 131) but included some women who identified as bisexual (8%, n = 12) and "other" (3%, n = 4). Most of the women in the community identify as feminist (76%, n = 114) and 9% (n = 13) said they were uncertain of their feminist status while 13% (n = 20) indicated that they were "not feminist." In terms of gender expression, 16% (n = 24) of the women identified as butch, 31% (n = 47) identified as femme, 31% (n = 47) identified as androgynous, and 15% (n = 22) identified as "other." The modal income range endorsed in this group was $30-40,000 per year. The women were predominantly white (88.1%), but included seven Latina and two Black women. This distribution appeared to be representative of this relatively racially homogeneous lesbian community.

Procedures

This survey was distributed at the community's largest annual lesbian event, and was enclosed in the community newsletter. Self-addressed stamped envelopes were included with each newsletter to facilitate the process of responding. The response rate approached 50%.

The ongoing involvement of the primary author in this community equipped her with an extensive ethnographic experience of the meanings of butch and femme within this group. In this process, she conducted interviews with twelve butch and twelve femme women about their gender identities. Although these interviews were not the focus of the present analysis, the present measure was developed on the basis of these experiences, which provided this author with a rich context from which to base questions relevant to this community.

Measure

The authors developed a 15-question survey. As this instrument represents a novel inquiry into experiences of gender expression within queer culture, the questionnaire was developed for the purposes of this study. Questions were designed to check the commonly held beliefs of community members about their experiences of butch-femme-androgynous identities.

This survey asked women to identify their gender expression (butch, femme, androgynous or "other"), sexual orientation (lesbian, bisexual, heterosexual or "other"), feminist identity status (feminist, not a feminist, uncertain), origin of gender expression (choice, innate, part choice-part innate, uncertain), and age of first awareness of their sexual orientation and gender expression. In this article, women who identified as "bisexual," "lesbian," or "other" will be described using the adjective "queer" to recognize their non-heterosexual status. The authors felt that an "other" sexual orientation category was necessary as some women identify their sexuality in personal or idiosyncratic ways (e.g., "I'm a femme-dyke"), do not experience any one mode of queer gender expression as dominant (e.g., "I'm a femmey-butch") or actively resist the labelling of sexuality or gender expression. The questionnaire included items about the participants' experiences of discrimination based upon sexual orientation (Cronbach alpha = .74) and gender expression within heterosexual contexts and lesbian contexts (Cronbach alpha = .79). As well, participants were asked to indicate the importance of their gender expression in their social and romantic relationships within the lesbian community. These same questions were not asked of heterosexual relationships as these lesbian-derived gender identities often are not recognized or understood outside of queer contexts and, therefore, may not influence relationships in a direct way. Finally, women were asked to indicate if they felt the effect of butch and femme identities was positive or negative. Androgynous or "Other" gender expressions were not asked about as they are not constructed as personal identities in this community in the same way as butch and femme identities. As well, participants were asked about the impact of these identities upon lesbian community only, as this is the subculture most affiliated with these identity types.

RESULTS

Development of Sexual Orientation and Gender Expression

Women in this study were asked to indicate when they first felt that they were aware of their sexual orientation and gender expression and to indicate the degree to which they felt their gender expression was innate (see Table 1). The mean age reported for first awareness of sexual orientation was 19. An ANOVA was conducted that indicated that there is a marginally significant difference in this age, F (3, 98) = 2.6, p = .056, when considering women of different gender expressions. Utilizing a Tukey HSD posthoc analysis, the difference between butch (M = 14.6) and femme (M = 21.9) ages appeared to be most significant, p = .07.

Participants reported the age at which they first were aware of their gender expression (M = 13). In written descriptions, women who identified their gender expression as "other" appeared, either, to reject the labelling of gender expression (e.g., "don't really like having a label") or to view their gender expression as not fixed in either a butch or femme identity (e.g., "strongly butch in some ways, strongly femme in other ways"). Using a univariate analysis, there were no significant differences, F (3, 74) = .20, p = .90, evidenced in this data when examining women of all reported gender expressions with regard to age of first awareness of butch, femme, androgynous, or other gender expression.

Using a repeated measures ANOVA to examine the participants' ages of awareness of sexual orientation as compared with their recognition of their gender expression, a significant difference between these two ages was found, F (1, 69) = 12.9, p = .001. Employing paired sample T-tests, age of sexual orientation awareness appeared to be significantly later than gender expression awareness only for femme women, t (25) = 2.51, p = .02.

TABLE 1. Mean Age of First Awareness of Gender Expression and Sexual Orientation

Gender Expression	Gender Expression Age	Sexual Orientation Age
Butch	10.9 (9.8)	14.6 (11.0)
Femme	13.8 (14.7)	21.9 (10.6)
Androgynous	13.5 (10.5)	16.5 (9.5)
Other	12.4 (13.7)	19.9 (11.8)
Total	13.0 (12.3)	18.6 (10.8)

When asked whether their gender expression is experienced as innate or as a choice, 48% of the respondents indicated that their gender expression seemed innate, 42% indicated that it resulted from a combination of chosen and innate factors, 6% percent indicated that it was purely choice and 2% percent were uncertain. Using a hierarchical log-linear analytic procedure, χ^2 (9, $N = 139$) = 12.6, $p = .18$, no differences were found among gender expressions with regard to the belief that gender expression is experienced as innate, a choice, both or neither.

Gender Expression and Social Interactions

Participants were asked to report on their experiences of discrimination and to indicate how important their gender expression was in their social interactions within their own community. In terms of discrimination, women were asked to indicate the frequency at which they have these experiences in heterosexual culture due to their sexual orientation as well as their gender expression. They were also asked to indicate how often they experienced discrimination due to their gender expression within lesbian communities (see Table 2).

When asked about experiences of discrimination based upon their sexual orientation in heterosexual society, a significant difference was shown in the ratings of women of different gender expressions, using an analysis of variance (ANOVA) procedure, F (3, 133) = 4, $p = .01$. Utilizing a Tukey HSD posthoc test, results indicated a significant difference between butch and "other" ratings ($p = .02$) and a borderline significant difference between butch and femme ratings ($p = .06$).

TABLE 2. Reported Frequencies of Discrimination by Gender Expression

Gender Expression	Within Heterosexual Interactions, Discrimination Based Upon		Within Lesbian Interactions, Discrimination Based Upon
	Sexual Orientation	Gender Expression	Gender Expression
Butch	3.5 (1.0)	3.4 (1.1)	2.2 (1.1)
Femme	2.9 (1.3)	1.9 (1.1)	2.2 (1.4)
Androgynous	3.2 (1.0)	2.8 (1.1)	1.7 (1.1)
Other	2.5 (1.1)	2.0 (0.9)	1.6 (0.8)
Total	3.1 (1.2)	2.5 (1.2)	1.9 (1.2)

Note: Results are from ratings upon a 5-point scale where 1 = never and 5 = often. Standard deviations are indicated in parentheses.

Ratings of the frequency of discrimination experiences due to gender expression in heterosexual society also indicated significant differences between participants of different gender expressions, F (3, 136) = 13.7, p = .001. Butch women reported facing the most discrimination, followed by androgynous women, "other" women and femme women (see Table 2). Significant differences were found between butch and femme (p = .001), butch and other (p = .001), femme and androgynous (p = .001), and androgynous and other women (p = .012) when ratings were analyzed with a Tukey HSD test. Ratings of discrimination within the lesbian community as opposed to the larger heterosexual community were not significantly different across gender expression categories, F (3, 134) = 2.24, p = .09.

Participants were asked to indicate the importance of their gender expression in their romantic and social interactions within the lesbian community (see Table 3). When examined using an ANOVA analysis, it appeared that women of differing gender expressions rated their importance within both romantic contexts, F (3, 129) = 3.3, p = .02, and social contexts, F (3, 132) = 3.5, p = .02. Tukey HSD posthoc analyses revealed that, when considering social contexts, only the ratings of butch and "other" women were significantly different (p = .012). Within romantic relationship ratings, a trend appeared, showing that butch women found their gender expression to be more important than either androgynous or "other" women, but not more than femme women (p = .06 for both differences).

Affects of Butch-Femme Identification

Women in this study were asked to indicate if they feel there are affects of identifying as butch or femme upon the identifying women, then upon the les-

TABLE 3. Reported Importance of Gender Expression in Romantic and Social Interactions

Gender Expression	In Romantic Relationships	In Social Interactions
Butch	2.2 (1.1)	4.0 (1.2)
Femme	2.2 (1.4)	3.6 (1.5)
Androgynous	1.7 (1.1)	3.0 (1.4)
Other	1.6 (0.8)	2.6 (1.7)
Total	1.9 (1.2)	3.3 (1.5)

Note: Results are from ratings upon a 5-point scale where 1 = never and 5 = often. Standard deviations are indicated in parentheses.

bian community (see Table 4) and, finally, if the general affects of these identities were positive or negative. None of the respondents, within any group of queer women, checked that gender expression has "no affect" in relation to either the identifying women or on the lesbian community. All of the means fell upon the positive side of the scale (i.e., > 2.5), indicating that, on average, the general affects of these identities are seen as more positive than negative by women of all gender expressions within this community.

In terms of the effects of femme and butch identities on the identifying women, ratings by women of different gender expressions did not appear significant, $F (3, 123) = .97, p = .41$. When comparing the ratings of impact of establishing a femme identity for femmes and butch identity for butches, using a multivariate repeated measures ANOVA, a significant difference was found, $F (1, 123) = 47.0, p = .001$, indicating that queer women felt that femme identities had more positive affects ($M = 3.64$) for identifying women than butch identities ($M = 3.02$).

There were no significant differences found between ratings of the perceived affects of butch and femme identities on the lesbian community, using a multivariate repeated measure multivariate analysis, $F (1, 113) = .69, p = .41$. Neither were differences in these scores evidenced when comparing the ratings of women of differing gender expressions, $F (3, 113) = .63, p = .60$.

DISCUSSION

Results of this study provide evidence that queer women have developmental and social experiences particular to their gender expression. Of note, ninety

TABLE 4. Perceived Affects of Identifying as Butch or Femme upon the Identifying Women and the Lesbian Community

Gender Expression	Upon the Identifying Women		Upon the Lesbian Community	
	Butch	Femme	Butch	Femme
Butch	3.35 (.98)	3.68 (.65)	3.59 (.50)	3.60 (.60)
Femme	2.96 (.82)	3.74 (.58)	3.55 (.87)	3.46 (.77)
Androgynous	3.00 (.74)	3.62 (.66)	3.33 (.61)	3.41 (.63)
Other	2.75 (.79)	3.60 (.86)	3.17 (.86)	3.41 (.71)
Total	3.01 (.83)	3.67 (.65)	3.43 (.74)	3.46 (.69)

Note: Results are from ratings upon a 5-point scale where 1 is "very negative" and 5 is "very positive." Standard deviations are indicated in parentheses.

percent of the participants felt that their gender expression was, at least partially, an innate characteristic. The average age of recognition of one's gender expression (13) was found to precede that of sexual orientation (19) for butch, femme, androgynous, and "other" women. Significant differences were found between butch and femme women's first awareness of sexual orientation, with butch women reporting a mean age of 14.6 and femme women a mean age of 21.9. Butch women, perhaps due to the perception of their gender atypicality, may have an awareness of "feeling different" at a young age that leads to an earlier recognition of their sexual orientation. Many butch interviewees described the difficulties of growing up and resisting traditional gender roles but having no way to label their experiences. One interviewee described the experience of being butch *"throughout my life, as a young child I was the toolbox kid, always in my dad's toolbox, always helping him do stuff, . . . It took an act of Congress to get me to wear a dress."*

Only femme women first became aware of their sexual orientation significantly later than their gender expression, and significantly later than butch women became aware of their sexual orientation. A number of femme women interviewed described only being able to identify as lesbian after contact with a butch-femme community. This contact was needed for them to realize their erotic attractions, as butch aesthetics aren't popularly represented in mainstream culture. One interviewee said, *"It's that process of figuring it out because it's a subculture. It's not visible."* The traditional constriction of gender which makes butchness invisible in mainstream culture, in combination with femme women's similarity to the gender expression of heterosexual women, may make it more difficult for femmes who may be attracted to butch women to realize their sexual orientation at an early age.

The gender expression of queer women was related to reports of discrimination within heterosexual society, with butch women reporting the most discrimination based on both sexual orientation and gender expression. These findings are congruent with theories of discrimination based on gender atypicality (Herek, 1995). Butch women defy heterosexual gender norms and thus are at greater risk for discrimination in this context, while femme women, by their very existence, challenge traditional feminist-lesbian aesthetics and may be discriminated against within these butch-androgynous contexts. One butch interviewee described that this occurred to butch women more because *"they are identifiable as lesbian . . . (and it comes) from people who don't know you. . . . Once people get to know you they kind of treat you in one way, but . . . harassment has come more like when you go to a gas station or a public bathroom. . . . They don't know you're an executive. . . . That you do this or the other. . . . I find (harassment) coming more from strangers, like when you are walking down the street."* They faced unique challenges when being raised in a homophobic society.

The importance of gender identity appeared to interact significantly with gender expression in romantic contexts as well as lesbian social contexts. Butch and femme women indicated that their gender expression was more important at a trend level than androgynous or "other" women, perhaps because their gender expressions function as important markers for romantic and sexual attractions, desires and behaviors within butch-femme communities (Case, 1989). One femme interviewee described the importance of her identity in her romantic and sexual life by labeling her own *"femme hunger–it is that kind of umm, being able to be femme and not have to hold it back does allow me to be, uh, to express myself sexually in a whole different way, in a way that is umm, just really powerful and um . . . just being able to be more true to myself."* With regard to social contexts, butch and "other" women appeared to significantly differ, with butch women reporting that their gender expression was more important to them. It remains to be seen whether androgyny will remain the feminist-endorsed gender expression as, judging from the recent productivity in butch-femme writings, interest is increasing in the reconstruction of butch-femme queer genders.

Finally, in terms of the perceived affects of gender expression upon identifying women and upon the lesbian community, women of all lesbian-queer genders felt, on average, that butch and femme identifications were positive. Participants of this study unanimously felt that gender expression does have an effect on both the community and individual level. Participants felt that femme identification had significantly more positive effects upon femme women than did butch identification upon butch women. It may be that femme women are thought to be advantaged by having a gender expression that may be similar to heterosexual women or that women misunderstand the rewards and strength that butch women can receive through butch-identification. Additionally, the recent positive depictions of femme-androgynous lesbians on popular TV shows like *Friends, ER, Ellen,* and *Ally McBeal,* in contrast with media images of butch women as negative or "humorous" stereotypes of lesbians, may increase this confusion about butch experience and perpetuate myths about femme women having heterosexual privilege.

Limitations and Strengths

One reason why there has been little other empirical research on gender expression may be that it is so difficult to access sizable queer samples that identify butch-femme gendering. Although strength of this study is that sufficient participants of different gender types responded to the survey, one corresponding limitation of this exploratory survey is its restriction to one queer community. This community is quite diverse, however, as it is located in a university town, and as such, members come from all over the southeastern U.S. As well, the community has a high level of extra-community interaction and is known for its activity in regional and national lesbian events. Future researchers, however, should seek to validate the present findings within broader based studies.

A further limitation was the necessary brevity of this exploratory study. As this survey was brief and not intended for the development of a measure of gender expression, questions did not easily allow for the assessment of reliability. Many further questions remain to be asked about developmental and social experiences and about gender expression identity. As well, gender expression should continue to be examined using a variety of empirical methodologies. Although surveys allow individuals to report their own experiences, and consequently are a good place to begin inquiry into phenomena, they necessarily include the hazards of self-report and retrospection. The first author's qualitative inquiries into gender expression will lend to this methodological plurality (e.g., Levitt & Bigler, in press).

The major contribution of this study is that it offers empirical evidence that gender expression is important in the development and social experiences of queer women. These findings indicate that gender expression is a variable to consider in many areas of future research, including studies of coming out, lesbian identity formation, childhood development, and social policy surveys of discrimination and violence.

REFERENCES

Aston, C. (1996). Getting hold of the phallus: Post-lesbian power negotiations. In N. Godwin (Ed.), *Assaults on convention* (pp. 158-177). UK: Cassell.

Bart, P. B. (1993). Protean women: The liquidity of female sexuality and the tenaciousness of lesbian identity. In S. Willkinson & C. Kitzinger (Eds.) *Heterosexuality: A feminism and psychology reader.* (pp. 246-252). London: Sage.

Brown, L. S. (1995). Lesbian identities: Concepts and issues. In A. R. D'Augelli & C. J. Patterson (Eds.), *Lesbian, gay, and bisexual identities over the lifespan: Psychological perspectives* (pp. 3-23). New York: Oxford University Press.

Burch, B. (1998). Lesbian sexuality/female sexuality: Searching for sexual subjectivity. *Psychoanalytic Review*, *85*, 349-371.

Butler, J. (1991). Imitation and gender insubordination. In D. Fuss (Ed.), *Inside/out: Lesbian theories, gay theories.* New York: Routledge.

Case, S. E. (1989). Toward a butch-femme aesthetic. In L. Hart (Ed.), *Making a spectacle* (pp. 282-299). Ann Arbor: University of Michigan Press.

Cass, V. C. (1979). Homosexual identity formation: A theoretical model. *Journal of Homosexuality*, *4*, 219-235.

Chapman, B. E. & Brannock, J.C. (1987). Proposed model of lesbian identity development: An empirical examination. *Journal of Homosexuality, 14*, 69-80.
Chung, Y. B. & Katayama, M. (1996). Assessment of sexual orientation in lesbian/gay/bisexual studies. *Journal of Homosexuality, 30*, 49-62.
Diamond, L. M. (1998). Development of sexual orientation among adolescent and young adult women. *Developmental Psychology, 38*, 1085-1095.
Faderman, L. (1991). *Odd girls and twilight lovers: A history of lesbian life in twentieth century America.* New York: Columbia University Press.
Halberstam, J. (1998). *Female masculinity.* Durham: Duke University Press.
Harris, L. & Crocker, E. (1997). *Femme: Feminists, lesbians and bad girls.* New York: Routledge.
Healey, E. (1996). *Lesbian sex wars.* UK: Virago Press.
Herek, G. (1995). Psychological heterosexism in the United States. In A. R. D'Augelli & C. J. Patterson (Eds.), *Lesbian, gay, and bisexual identities over the lifespan: Psychological perspectives* (pp. 321-346). New York: Oxford University Press.
Herek, G., Gillis, R. J., & Cogan, J. (1999). Psychological sequelae of hate crime victimization among lesbian, gay, and bisexual adults. *Journal of Consulting and Clinical Psychology, 67*, 945-951.
Lapovsky-Kennedy, E. & Davis, M. D. (1993). *Boots of leather, slippers of gold: The history of a lesbian community.* New York: Penguin.
Levitt, H. M. & Bigler, M. (In press). Facilitating lesbian gender exploration. In J.S. Whitman and C. J. Boyd (Eds.), *The therapist's notebook for lesbian, gay and bisexual clients: Homework, handouts and activities for use in psychotherapy.* Binghamton, NY: The Haworth Press, Inc.
McCarn, S. R. & Fassinger, R. F. (1996). Revisioning sexual minority identity formation: A new model of lesbian identity and its implications for counseling and research. *The Counseling Psychologist, 24*, 508-534.
Munt, S. (1998). *Butch/femme: Inside lesbian gender.* Washington: Cassell.
Nestle, J. (1992). *The persistent desire: A femme-butch reader.* Boston: Alyson.
Nestle, J. A. (1996). *A restricted country.* New York: HarperCollins.
Pearcey, S. M., Docherty, K. J., & Dabbs, J. M. (1996). Testosterone and sex role identification in lesbian couples. *Physiology & Behavior, 60*, 1033-1035.
Ruble, D. N. & Martin, C. L. (1998). Gender development. In W. Damon (Ed.), *Handbook of child psychology*, (pp. 933-1016). New York: Wiley.
Rust, P. (1993). "Coming out" in the age of social constructionism. *Gender and Society, 7*, 50-77.
Singh, D., Vidaurri, M., Zambarano, R. J., & Dabbs, J. M. (1999). Lesbian erotic role identification: Behavioral, morphological, and hormonal correlates. *Journal of Personality and Social Psychology, 76*, 1035-1049.
Walker, L. (1993). How to recognize a lesbian: The cultural politics of looking like what you are. *Signs: Journal of Women in Culture and Society, 18*, 866-890.
Weber, J. C. (1996). Social class as a correlate of gender identity among lesbian women. *Sex Roles, 35*, 271-280.

APPENDIX
Community Survey

1. I consider my **sexual orientation** to be: Lesbian__; Bisexual__; Straight__;
   Other (describe) _____ I felt I was this orientation since age: _____

2. I consider my **gender expression** to be Butch: __; Femme__; Androgynous__;
   Other (describe)_____ I felt I was this gender expression
   (Butch/Femme/Andr/etc.) since age: _____

3. From a scale of 1-10 where 1 = Butch, 0 = Neutral, and 10 = Femme, I rate
   myself as _____

4. I consider myself to be: A feminist _____ ; Not a feminist ___; Anti-feminist ___;
   Uncertain ___

5. My gender expression *(as indicated in #2)* feels like it is dominantly:
   A choice ____; Innate _____; Part choice and part innate _____;
   Uncertain _____

6. My gender expression is important in aspects of my social interactions within the
   lesbian community:
   Often _____; Sometimes _____; Occasionally _____; Rarely _____;
   Never _____

7. My gender expression is important in aspects of my relationship with my part-
   ner/lover(s):
   Often _____; Sometimes _____; Occasionally _____; Rarely _____;
   Never _____

8. I face discrimination in the straight world because of my sexual orientation:
   Often _____; Sometimes _____; Occasionally _____; Rarely _____;
   Never _____

9. I face discrimination in the straight world because of my gender expression:
   Often _____; Sometimes _____; Occasionally _____; Rarely _____;
   Never _____

10. I face discrimination in lesbian communities because of my gender expression:
    Often _____; Sometimes _____; Occasionally _____; Rarely _____;
    Never _____

11. I'd guess the percentages of gender expression types in my community to be:
    Butch _____%; Androgynous _____%; Femme _____%;
    Other (write) _____%

12. What do you think are the affects of identifying as butch for butch women?
    Very Positive ___; Generally Positive ___; Mixed ___; Generally Negative ___;
    Very Negative __; No Effect___

13. What do you think are the affects of identifying as femme for femme women?
Very Positive ___; Generally Positive ___; Mixed ___; Generally Negative ___;
Very Negative __; No Effect___

14. What do you think are the affects of women identifying as butch on the lesbian community?
Very Positive ___; Generally Positive ___; Mixed ___; Generally Negative ___;
Very Negative __; No Effect___

15. What do you think are the affects of women identifying as femme on the lesbian community?
Very Positive ___; Generally Positive ___; Mixed ___; Generally Negative ___;
Very Negative __; No Effect___

Age: _____; Race: (However you describe yourself: white, latina, black, etc.)_____

Annual Income: < 10,000 ___; 10-14___; 15-19___; 20-29___; 30-39 ____;
40-49____; 50+____

Butches with Babies:
Reconfiguring Gender and Motherhood

Rachel Epstein

SUMMARY. This article is about butches who get pregnant and become mothers. It suggests that butch motherhood might widen the range of both maternal and butch subjectivities by linking a queer masculinity and sexuality to the attachments of the female body. A butch confrontation with the stigma that comes with the territory of femininity may also draw her in new ways to feminist struggles to provide social supports to those who mother. *[Article copies available for a fee from The Haworth Document Delivery Service: 1-800-HAWORTH. E-mail address: <getinfo@haworthpressinc.com> Website: <http://www.HaworthPress.com> © 2002 by The Haworth Press, Inc. All rights reserved.]*

KEYWORDS. Butch, motherhood, maternal, pregnancy, parenting, gender, sexuality, masculinity/femininity, feminism

---

Rachel Epstein has an MA in Sociology and is working on a PhD in Education. She is currently taking a break from the PhD process to coordinate a project on LGBT parenting. She works also as a mediator of community, organizational, and relationship conflicts and is especially keen to assist queer folk who are parenting together to work out their conflicts, thus avoiding painful court processes (E-mail: rachelep@fsatoronto.com).

The author would like to thank Lorna Weir and Paul Anzte for reading an earlier version of this article, and Lois Fine and Rebecca Raby for reading and commenting on this version. A special thanks to Lois Fine for the joys of parenting with her.

[Haworth co-indexing entry note]: "Butches with Babies: Reconfiguring Gender and Motherhood." Epstein, Rachel. Co-published simultaneously in *Journal of Lesbian Studies* (Harrington Park Press, an imprint of The Haworth Press, Inc.) Vol. 6, No. 2, 2002, pp. 41-57; and: *Femme/Butch: New Considerations of the Way We Want to Go* (ed: Michelle Gibson, and Deborah T. Meem) Harrington Park Press, an imprint of The Haworth Press, Inc., 2002, pp. 41-57. Single or multiple copies of this article are available for a fee from The Haworth Document Delivery Service [1-800-HAWORTH, 9:00 a.m. - 5:00 p.m. (EST). E-mail address: getinfo@haworthpressinc.com].

This article is about butches who get pregnant and become mothers. It is written in the context of current discussions and debates within feminist and queer studies that deconstruct, destabilize and denaturalize the connections between anatomical sex, social gender, sexual identification, gender identification, gender performance, sexual object choice and sexual practice. It grows from ten years of thinking about, writing about and practicing lesbian parenting, as well as informal and formal talks and interviews with other lesbian parents; during this period I have carried out research projects on the division of labor in lesbian parenting households, on nonbiological lesbian parenting, on the ways that "lesbian" and "feminist" mothers negotiate parenting, and on the experiences of the children of lesbians in schools. During interviews for these projects, several people raised issues of butch identity in relation to mothering. The quotes I draw on in this article are extracted from these interviews; in only one case did I do an interview specifically about "butch motherhood." From this long personal, academic and activist engagement with issues of concern to lesbian parents, combined with a love, appreciation and respect for butches, both specifically and generally, grew a fascination with the ways that butch-identified mothers describe their experiences of pregnancy and parenting. This paper reflects my attempt to pull together some of this material and to reflect on the potentialities embedded in this striking, and sometimes seemingly contradictory combination of "masculine" and "feminine." The quotes used in the text are extracted from interviews conducted over the past ten years.

My own identification is as a femme and as the biological mother of a nine-year-old girl whom I have co-parented since birth with her butch-identified other mother. I approach this subject with some trepidation, not only because I am writing about experience that is not mine, but also due to awareness that for some butch-identified lesbians the bodily experiences of pregnancy, childbirth and motherhood are neither aspired to nor desired. My hope is that these musings on how some butch-identified lesbians negotiate the terrain of motherhood will be taken as a contribution towards a deconstruction of the dualisms of masculine/feminine, sexual/maternal and queer gender outlaw/attached female and towards a widening of the range of both maternal and butch subjectivities.

Below I draw primarily on the work of Judith Butler and Biddy Martin to argue: (a) attention to the psychic constructions, interiorities, disavowals and exclusions upon which gender identity is built can allow for more fluid, unstable gender identities and practices. In this instance, it becomes possible to reconfigure "butch" to include the maternal, without loss of butch identity; (b) butch mothers might represent a possibility for a "queer maternal narrative," a narrative that refuses the separation of motherhood from sexuality, or queerness from the feminine and the family; and, finally, (c) that a butch confrontation with the stigma that comes with the territory of motherhood may draw her in new ways to feminist struggles regarding the conditions under which women mother.

BUTCH MOMS: A POSSIBILITY THAT ALREADY EXISTS

Most recent work on gender, and particularly on lesbian gender, is heavily influenced by Judith Butler's critique of dominant discourses of gender and sexuality and her claims regarding the constructed nature of sexual dualism and the fiction of gender coherence (Butler, 1990). Butler's work addresses the frequent accusation made towards lesbian butch/femme roles–that they mimic and recreate heterosexual gender roles. She complicates this picture by redescribing these practices/performances as reconfigurations of sex and gender that expose the fraudulence of all claims to authentic gender identity. To Butler, practices of gender parody such as drag and butch/femme, rather than embodying imitations of heterosexuality, actually illustrate the lack of an original to imitate; the parody is of the very notion of an original.

Within lesbian contexts, the "identification" with masculinity that appears as butch identity is not a simple assimilation of lesbianism back into the terms of heterosexuality. As one lesbian femme explained, she likes her boys to be girls, meaning that "being a girl" contextualizes and resignifies "masculinity" in a butch identity. As a result, that masculinity, if that it can be called, is always brought into relief against a culturally intelligible "female body." It is precisely this dissonant juxtaposition and the sexual tension that its transgression generates that constitute the object of desire. In other words, the object (and clearly there is not just one) of lesbian-femme desire is neither some decontextualized female body nor a discrete yet superimposed masculine identity, but the destabilization of both terms as they come into erotic interplay (Butler, 1990, 123). Butch/femme roles take place in the context of and are enabled by the hegemonic categories of heterosexuality, but their significance is the internally dissonant and complex way they refigure these categories.

Butler's work has been interpreted as suggesting that resisting gender is a voluntary affair, and that the goal of gender resistance fighters might be an escape from gender into a celebration of all difference. But, in fact, she emphasizes over and over that she is not interested in "celebrating each and every new possibility *qua* possibility," but in "redescribing those possibilities that already exist, but which exist within cultural domains designated as culturally unintelligible and impossible" (Butler, 1990, 148-49).

It is in this light that I pursue a discussion of butch motherhood–as a closer look at a "possibility that already exists" and what it may offer to understandings of gender, sexuality, and motherhood. Much of the early research on lesbian mothers aimed to prove that lesbian mothers are "the same as" and as good as heterosexual mothers, and was designed to assist lesbian mothers and their lawyers in developing arguments aimed at allowing mothers to maintain custody of their children. While child custody battles fueled by homophobia are by no means a thing of the past, there now exists a critical mass of lesbians who became mothers as lesbians, and the focus of research is shifting to "consider the diversity and transgressive potentialities of our lesbian maternal selves" (Gabb, 1999, 9). It is as a "transgressive potentiality" that I turn attention to butch mothers.

Also important to state at the outset is my rejection of the idea that there is a butch (or femme) psychic make-up or disposition. Once one breaks free from what Butler calls the "imaginary logic" of the heterosexual matrix, the mutual exclusivity of identification and desire, the notion that if one is a man one always desires a woman, and vice versa, then a whole range of complex interrelationships between identification and desire become intelligible (Butler, 1993, 239). And, just as butches differ in psychic disposition, so too do they differ in their relationship to motherhood, as witnessed by the following two quotations, both from butch mothers, the first non-biological, and the second biological:

> Well, I love children, but I actually don't think I could go through carrying them. It just doesn't seem me. (JB, 1994)

> Wanting to get pregnant, yes I did, yep, definitely. You know it's life. It offers you experiences, you going to turn that down? I didn't turn down LSD, I didn't turn down hyperventilating, why would I turn down pregnancy and childbirth? (BW, 1998)

While some butches become biological mothers, and others do not, butch motherhood itself is not a new phenomenon. As is clear in Kennedy and Davis' account of butch/femme roles in the 1940s and 1950s, while the recent "lesbian baby boom" might be opening up new cultural configurations within which to choose motherhood and making it more possible to integrate a lesbian life with motherhood, lesbians, and specifically butch-identified lesbians, have always had babies and been mothers. Kennedy and Davis describe much variation among their narrators when it comes to matters of children and family. In general, the ridicule, ostracism and hatred directed at butch women led them to make a "firm division between their social lives and their work and family lives. They moved out of their family homes and socialized in gay and lesbian bars only on weekends" (374). Some felt pressured to marry, and bore children within heterosexual mar-

riages, while others were committed to working and building independent lives outside of marriage. Some desired children but did not want to sleep with men in order to get pregnant; others did get pregnant by sleeping with men. While butches did have babies, there were not many opportunities to integrate a lesbian life with motherhood. Some women had siblings or other family members raise their children, others took great pains to keep their lesbian activity a secret from their children, while others refrained from having children because they did not feel a lesbian environment was good for children. In general, lesbianism and motherhood were viewed as incompatible and there were few attempts made to live openly as a lesbian and a mother.

On the Front Porch
Photo: R. Epstein

DISRUPTING BUTCH IDENTITY

In her 1993 book *Bodies That Matter*, Butler explores the notion that what is refused or repudiated in the formation of the subject, what the subject seeks to deny, is what compels it from the start (1991, 28). She explores the exclusions necessary for the body's boundaries to form, and the ways that abjected identifications "haunt that boundary as an internal ghost of sorts" (1993, 65). Abjected identifications are repeatedly repudiated in order to sustain the subject's boundaries. But the refusal to identify with any given position means that on some level an identification has taken place. In terms of sexuality, a rejection of heterosexuality is to some degree an identification with the rejected heterosexuality. And for the butch-identified lesbian:

> ... if butchness requires a strict opposition to femmeness, is that a refusal of an identification or is this an identification with femmeness that has

already been made, made and disavowed, a disavowed identification that sustains the butch, without which the butch qua butch cannot exist? (1993, 115)

Assuming that no subject can proceed without avowal and disavowal, Butler dismisses the idea that new and different identities can be taken on by a simple avowal of identifications that have been disavowed. She does, however, suggest the crucial nature of acknowledging the exclusions on which identifications are built and the "tacit cruelties that sustain coherent identity, cruelties that include self-cruelty" (115). She argues that unless these exclusions are acknowledged, they continue to enforce exclusionary principles on whoever is seen to deviate from a notion of coherent identity.

Sally Munt (1998) describes a similar process when she refers to the shame that occurs when we internalize an ideal we are not able to meet:

> [W]e become ashamed, punishing ourselves, and projecting this onto others whom we include in our failure. For example: butch baiting, especially from other butches, is a product of this failure ("You aren't a real butch, because . . ."). An aspect of this is the competitiveness shame produces, a measuring of oneself against an internalized and projected ideal, and a desire to make others fail in comparison to ourselves ("I'm butcher than you"). This does not promote butch diversity, it idealizes an impossible category. (6)

Impossible, because it does not recognize the disavowals that constitute identity. If heterosexuality is constituted through a disavowal of homosexuality, and butchness through a disavowal of femininity and/or the maternal, then, unless these disavowals are acknowledged, butches who mother run the risk of exclusion and degradation from both heterosexuals and lesbians who are invested in the notion of coherent identity.

Below a butch mom describes the reaction of her butch friends to her foray into motherhood:

> Among some of our butch friends there was confusion and a sense of wait and observe. People were watching. The butches were watching themselves, and everybody was watching them. How odd did this look? It scared them. Again, I think this is a lot of people's sex role stuff, heterosexism, etc. Not too much questioning or doubting about (the femme's) role and how she'll handle it. She wears a skirt, she gives birth, she's got tits, she'll breastfeed. Fine, great, no problem. But what's (the butch) going to do? (BW, 1992)

A pregnant butch deviates from what butch identity is supposed to entail. In some ways the reactions this butch received echo a life-long experience of what Halberstam (1998a, 61) refers to as the "intense liabilities of queer masculine embodiment . . . because butch girls are raised to understand their masculinity as a physical liability and a bodily defect" (60). Although she is now engaging in an ultra-feminine act, the reactions she receives lead her to wonder "what all was bad, wrong and ugly about me now? It was hard on me being a pregnant butch. Going to the bars or dances, social stuff, that was hard and the reception was not too great" (BW, 1998).

She observes that some of the negative reaction comes not only from butches who are disturbed by this gender-inconsistent behavior, but from other lesbians for whom contact with men and sperm, which are seen to also potentially bring AIDS, is inconsistent with lesbian identity:

> I did have a suspicion that some of it was that being pregnant was bad, being a lesbian who got sperm in them was really bad. And later I found out that that did exist . . . at lesbian/gay pride day this gaggle of preppy-looking drunk young white women saw the kids playing, saw my partner and started mouthing off about "these are the women who bring AIDS into the lesbian community." Young women who put it on the list of more things to prove why lesbians are the most bestest people in the world, cause we don't get AIDS. (BW, 1998)

Butch pregnancy and motherhood disrupt notions of coherent butch identity and butch mothers are subject to the cruelty that can result from a lack of willingness to see beyond these notions. At the same time, butch mothers are continually reconfiguring what it means to be butch and widening the range of butch experience.

RECONFIGURING BUTCH

> Reconfiguring gender requires reconfiguring the institutional and discursive conditions that structure and are structured by regulatory norms, but also reconfiguring interiorities, and, in particular, distributions of power, autonomy, attachment, and vulnerability. (Martin, 1996, 74)

Biddy Martin (1996) argues for a more complex inclusion of the psyche in analysis of gender. She suggests that butch and femme are both constrained by their frequent association with particular psychic constructions. Butch is associated with woundedness and defense structures, and femme with genuine vulnerability, empathy, receptivity, and emotionality. But, argues Martin, both butch and femme (or masculine and feminine) are defense structures: the femme's dependence masks not only her own aggressions, desires and autonomies, but also the butch's or man's dependence and limitation; the feminine association with victimization, vulnerability, loss and death allows the masculine or butch to defend against his or her own limits and wounds.

Her argument, similar to Butler's, is that acknowledgement of one's disowned parts, while possibly experienced as cross-gendered behavior or feelings, does not change gender identity. Rather it expands the affective and behavioral dimensions one might allow oneself to experience as part of a felt sense of gender. Motherhood for a butch, then, might expand what it means to be butch, without emptying butch of its meaning as an identification.

Ann Cvetkovich (1998), writing about butch emotional style, points out the apparent paradox of butch sexuality:

> . . . that the butch who "takes erotic responsibility" for her partner's sexual pleasure could, in her eagerness to tend to another's desires, as easily be considered feminine as masculine. (159)

Others, such as Judith Halberstam, describe the butch who prefers to give than to get as transforming "the mechanisms of masculinity," producing new constellations of embodiment, power and desire within female masculinity (1998b, 276). Whether one views the "giving" butch as masculine or feminine, in some ways butch identity is not antithetical to the giving required of mothers. As one butch mom puts it, "I certainly don't see mothering and butch as a conflict. You know, butch wants to take care of everything" (LRT, 1992).

On the other hand, in dominant cultural discourses, motherhood is defined as a central female experience and the attributes of "good mothers" are linked to femininity–caring, nurturing, softness, emotionality, openness and physical availability. In particular, the bodily experiences of pregnancy, childbirth, and breastfeeding are constructed as the ultimate in femininity. The butch whose words I quote below reconfigures butch masculinity as she describes the pleasure she incurred from pregnancy:

> I felt my ovulation and knew this was it. Hello, hello, knock, knock, I gotta go. I'm sorry I can't help it, it's not in my hands. And then six hours later I'm pregnant and about a couple of days later I know I'm pregnant, even though I have to wait some time to have the test. My body is starting to change. Tied to the earth, as if I could feel a tie with a little stone in the ground. And as if my blood was warming. Then a few days later my tits were starting to grow and my nipples were sensitive. I felt in the mystery area of my uterus, gravity, different gravity. I felt it. (BW, 1998)

Although she liked being pregnant, she also describes her difficulty in negotiating the "feminine" terrain of dependency and needing to ask for help:

> I liked pregnancy a lot. It seemed to put me on a more even keel. I really wanted to be pregnant and feel what that was like and experience every little bit of that. I had a fantastic appetite, which I was allowed to indulge and that was fun. But then when I got large and especially when my blood pressure started getting high, I had to start asking people for help. (BW, 1992)

> I have this image of myself, five o'clock on a cold March night, and it's blowing, it's snowing and I'm pushing a baby carriage and carrying six bags of groceries and a bag of laundry and the baby's crying and I have to lug everything up fourteen stairs to the first floor. And don't ask me if I need help! I cannot fucking stand asking people for help around physical things. I mean even when I'm real sick I can't stand it. And this wasn't even sick or injured, you know, this is: I'm ultra-female and asking for help. And I hate that. That's what it felt like. I'm asking for help *because* I'm a woman, goddamn it, it drove me nuts. (BW, 1992)

Pregnancy challenged this butch to reconfigure her pre-pregnancy identity as someone who is independent, self-reliant and does not need help. Interestingly, when she goes on to talk about breastfeeding, which is typically depicted as a quintessentially feminine experience of selflessness and giving, she describes it, not in those terms, but in terms of independence and "not needing anybody":

> My daughter breastfed for 13 goddamn months. She wouldn't take a bottle, so I couldn't get a break. I was being run by this little wee baby and my tits. It was quite a phenomenon. I liked the experience of it. Because you just don't know till you're there. There's something important about breastfeeding, it's about not needing anybody. This is all that needs to be. (BW, 1998)

This butch mom is not only reconfiguring "butch" to include the "feminine" experience of breastfeeding; she is reconfiguring "mother" to include her butch identification with self-reliance. Butches can be butch *and* be mothers, while at the same time they reconfigure and expand the psychic and material possibilities embedded in motherhood, femininity, masculinity, femme and butch. Allowing pregnancy and motherhood to remain in the realm of the feminine, limits and constrains both butch and femme.

SEXUALITY, QUEER DESIRE AND THE MATERNAL

Ellen Lewin (1995) notes the continued centrality of motherhood, both in dominant cultural discourses and within the discourse of feminism, in defining what women are and what they should be (104). Motherhood is viewed as something that naturally happens to women and that can be both the basis of their social, economic and political disadvantage, and/or a source of moral or spiritual rewards. In either case, motherhood and womanhood are "naturally" connected.

"Lesbian" and "mother" are terms which, until very recently, were seen as mutually exclusive. Motherhood is defined as taking place in the context of heterosexual relations, and lesbianism is commonly viewed as immutable. Thus, "motherhood and lesbianism simply cancelled each other out in the popular imagination" (103). As well, lesbians are "assumed to be creatures defined by their sexual appetites and thus . . . at odds with the kind of selfless devotion expected of mothers" (Lewin, 1995, 103). Lesbian mothers are not assumed to have the "natural" attributes expected of mothers, and, in custody situations, must demonstrate their maternal virtue. Part of what constitutes a "good" lesbian mother, in the eyes of institutional authorities, is her willing-

Getting Ready for School
Photo: R. Epstein

ness to deny or hide her active sexuality and her desire to live openly as a lesbian.

This separation and tension between lesbian desire/sexuality and motherhood is apparent too in popular discourse on lesbian mothers. Perhaps partly due to the defensive posture necessitated by the attack on our legitimacy as mothers, lesbian mothers, as Gabb (1999) points out, are typically "represented by images showing loving embraces, devoted smiles and wholesome values." While these images may heighten awareness and popular acceptance of lesbian mothers, they continue to obscure our sexuality beneath the shroud of selfless maternal love (16).

Just as motherhood discourse denies sexuality, and butch discourse denies motherhood, queer theory tends to separate queer sexuality from the maternal. Martin (1996), while acknowledging queer theory's important contribution to gender analysis, is critical of some queer theory that sees attachments to the feminine, to the maternal, and to that which represents home, family and what gets seen as the asexual realm of reproduction, as constraining and disciplining what should be mobile desires. As Susan Driver (1998) puts it, the "desiring moments of sexual outlaws" are seen in opposition to "the static embodiments of women's reproductive sexuality" (7). Martin argues that radical anti-normativity throws out a lot of babies with a lot of bathwater: "family, along with its normalizing and constraining functions and forms; concerns about children, along with the disidentification of sexuality from reproduction" (70).

Within both motherhood discourse and some queer theory, motherhood and sexuality are separated and dichotomized. "Butch," however, is a sexual subject position. As MacCowan argues: "butch and femme are gender constructions that arise from a sexual definition of lesbianism" (306). Joan Nestle, in the introduction to *The Persistent Desire* (1992), describes butch/femme as "a lesbian-specific way of deconstructing gender that radically reclaims women's erotic energy" (14). She refers to the "inherent eroticism of the subject," and acknowledges the public erotic connections created by the sexual ceremony and dialogue of butches and femmes from the 1930s through the 1960s (15). Butch (and femme) are about gender identification/presentation and sexual desire. Butch mothers, then, embody a complex and challenging relationship to the dualism of motherhood/sexuality and perhaps represent the potential for a queer maternal narrative that includes sexuality *and* motherhood. Butch motherhood can challenge depictions of lesbian motherhood as "safe, sanitized and conventional" (Gabb, 16) in favor of a portrayal of a more dangerous, non-conventional motherhood. Gabb calls for new and different portrayals of lesbian motherhood, for images that depict the complexity of our maternal and sexual identities and challenge the myth of the asexual family. Butch mothers can provide this challenge by combining the joys of a more "out there" sexuality with the joys of motherhood.

Of course, those invested in particular and coherent butch or maternal subjectivities will oppose this queer maternal narrative:

There's a lot of people out there (and this could be people in institutions like schools, other dykes, other so-called political people) who can accept this situation if it appears that we are trying to emulate the status quo. If we can't emulate the mom and dad and kids, we can at least emulate the middle class idea. We can at least be really proper, you know, and very good mothers. And they're really appalled when they find out that we're going to be who we want to be, who we please. We're going to dress the way we dress, we're going to have the kind of sex we want to have, and we're going to be blatant about that. A lot of people are very twisted and upset by that. That's really the big confronting thing to them. (JB, 1994)

Butch mothers live out the contradictions and tensions rising from their location within and between discourses that delineate what it means to be a mother and what it means to be butch. One butch mom describes the pressures on sexually transgressive mothers to conform to normative values and behaviors in order to maintain their inclusion in the "good mother" category:

There is such pressure on us, as dykes, as weirdos, as outsiders, and you know that anything that goes wrong with these children, somebody's going to blame it on your sexuality and how you're bringing them up. So that puts pressure on you to bring them up as perfectly fitting-in children. And you have to stop all the time and say "no, no, no, no, no" . . . and we're into pretty wild and raunchy sex and leather outfits and all this stuff and how do you go into the world and balance all this? For a while I think I decided, "OK, I'm going to give up that sex stuff, I'm going to become a nice, safe academician. I'm pretty good at this university stuff, couldn't I just get a PhD and I'd be a famous smarty cakes, right." And then I go, "No, no, this is the devil talking, you're about to make a really sick deal here. So put back on that leather jacket, get out to that dance, you know, and let the kids see all of that." (BW, 1992)

The same butch mother talks about the difficulty of maintaining butch identity in a pregnant state, including the style problems arising from the continued association of motherhood and femininity:

Not only are you big and pregnant, your clothes are shit. Everything that I was wearing didn't belong to me, right, and they don't make butch maternity wear. It's bad enough, they make the mother look like a baby and all that stuff . . . but even if they don't they at least try and make it look femme or feminine, so it was real hard to find good butch wear. (BW, 1992)

How do you keep looking butchy? By the time I'm pregnant I have another kid, a baby in diapers. So I'm tired, I'm pregnant and I'm a tired new mother as well. So the financial and the energy efforts to really do butch, find the best pair of pregnancy pants to do butch, and the suspend-

ers and the fedora . . . I should have said, "Honey, this is the time we need
to invest in the fedora, please, please, I beg you" . . . Where the fuck is
your identity going to go? You're not possibly going to look like yourself
or have anybody peg you right. (BW, 1998)

And butch moms, despite their sexual subject position, are not immune to
the potential negative impact on sexuality of pregnancy, childbirth, breastfeeding and the early years of parenting:

> I can't remember anything much, except the morning my milk came in af-
> ter the baby was born and I had these enormous tits and I made a joke out
> of that, before I broke down and cried . . . because the baby had slept
> through the night and the milk came in and my tits were enormous and
> hard and burning and in agony. Well, I guess my lack of memory leads to
> the conclusion that it wasn't a very stimulating time sexually. (BW, 1998)

BUTCH FEMINISM

Although it is critical to heed Halberstam's reminder that the butch experience of transgression is "often filled with fear, danger and shame rather than
heroic satisfaction" (1998a, 59), Martin raises another potential consequence
of queer theory's emphasis on gender non-conformity: the possibility that the
punishments that accrue from being feminine become less visible than the pu-
nitive consequences of failing to conform. As an example, Martin refers to Judith Butler's reading of the film *Paris Is Burning*. In the film, Venus
Xtravaganza, a transvestite, is murdered by a john. Butler imagines that Venus
is murdered because the john discovered she had a penis and had only pretended to be a woman. Martin, crediting one of her students, suggests another
narrative, i.e., that Venus Xtravaganza passed too successfully as a woman and
was murdered *as a woman*, a not uncommon occurrence. She argues that "in
the effort to highlight obvious sexual differences and defiance of norms, the
all-too-obvious and, thus, invisible difference that it makes to be a woman
drops out of view" (82).

I would suggest that butch motherhood can have the effect of bringing the
butch into confrontation with the feminine and with the complex experience of
womanhood. By this I do not imply that butch experience lies outside womanhood; as Inness and Lloyd put it:

> [B]y virtue of her female body, the butch will have different life experi-
> ences and expectations from a man's. For example, a man does not expe-

rience the social pressure to be feminine that a butch does. Men are not worried about being raped the way women, even butches, are. As women, butches are still often considered less intelligent and capable then their male co-workers. In sum, butches are raised to be women, are treated like women, and suffer the stigma of not looking and acting the way women are expected to. (19)

Halberstam, too, reminds us that

[B]utch does not essentially and necessarily partake in the privileges assigned to masculinity in a male supremacist society. Butches also suffer sexism, butches also experience misogyny; butches may not be strictly women but they are not exempt from female trouble. (1998, 64)

As these quotations imply, butches, in Martin's terms, "experience the pain of being cast as queer in the most negative possible terms," but may not experience fully the "punishments that accrue to femininity itself" (Martin, 73). Pregnancy and motherhood, then, might be double-edged for the butch. On the one hand, she may find herself less stigmatized as she is drawn into the fold of "natural" womanhood; on the other hand, she may experience more of the stigma that comes with the territory of femininity as she is confronted with the impact of external sources that continue to simultaneously pedestalize and devalue the work of motherhood. Roberta Hamilton (1990) argues that, despite a feminist revaluation of motherhood in the 1980s, based partly on lesbian custody cases and the lesbian baby boom, it remains crucial to keep a critique of full-time mothering in the feminist agenda:

The challenge posed to heterosexism by lesbian motherhood is real. But without an integrated challenge to the heterosexist, racist, patriarchal capitalism that informs *inter alia* the gendered wage gap–still more a chasm than a gap–it means that unpartnered lesbian mothers are as likely to live in poverty with their children as their single heterosexual counterparts. Nor does a discrete nuclear unit with two same-sexed parents counter the isolation of the continuing regime of socially unsupported motherhood, first identified publicly by countless women in consciousness-raising groups two decades ago. Transforming the circumstances in which children are raised, as feminist activists once insisted, involves taking on the whole catastrophe–on many fronts and with shifting contingents of allies. (30)

Butch mothers, then, in experiencing the impact of "socially-unsupported motherhood," may find themselves drawn into feminist struggles to change the conditions under which they mother.

CONCLUSION

Jewelle Gomez (1998) describes the erotic tension, interest and excitement she experiences when women "spill over into territory not deemed our own," bringing together the unexpected:

> For me the erotic tension of being a lesbian lives in that place where un-expected elements come together: the stone-butch woman who knows how to turn a hem, or looks like a little girl when she laughs. Or the high femme with her skirt hiked up as she changes a tire. The tension of when the unexpected comes together is what makes being a lesbian, and being a femme, interesting. It is also what makes being a lesbian a political act. That spilling over into the categories women are not meant to occupy is the transgressive behavior that can break down the barriers to personal and political liberation. (106)

Butch mothers perform the unexpected in many directions. Butches are not supposed to be mothers, and mothers are not supposed to be butch. When butches mother they denaturalize both terms and transform both subjectivities.

In this article I have attempted to articulate some of the possibilities contained in the particular combination of masculinity and femininity that is butch motherhood. Drawing on Butler and Martin I suggest that acknowledgement of the disavowals or disowned parts upon which gender identity is built can open up new qualities, experiences and behaviors within a particular gender identity. Motherhood for the butch can involve reconfiguring "butch" by nego-tiating new relations to vulnerability, dependence, and attachment, while at the same time reconfiguring motherhood by bringing a butch sensibility to the act of parenting. Butch motherhood also works to deconstruct the dualisms of sex-uality/motherhood and masculine/feminine by linking a queer masculinity and sexuality to the attachments of the female body. Finally, butch motherhood puts butches in a different relation to the social organization of mothering, per-haps shifting their relation to feminist struggles to provide social supports to those who mother.

In *Bodies That Matter*, Butler discusses the nature of political signifiers. She argues that political signifiers that designate subject positions are not de-scriptive. They do not represent pregiven constituencies, but are empty signs which come to bear phantasmatic investments of various kinds (191). The signifier "butch," like all political signifiers, produces the expectation of a coherent and unified subject, an expectation that can never be met because of the disavowals and exclusions upon which "butch" is built. To Butler it is the open-ended and performative function of the signifier that is crucial to what she calls "a radical democratic notion of futurity" (191). By this she means a future that remains open to the resignification and rearticulation of any given identity, that recognizes the exclusions upon which identifications are built, and in recognizing them, makes room for shifts in meaning and new identificatory possibilities. There can be no closure on any given identity, *nor should there be*. Butch mothers shift the meanings and the possibilities contained in motherhood, femininity, masculinity, femme and butch. Like Jewelle Gomez I await future resignifications and more of the unexpected.

WORKS CITED

Butler, J. (1990). *Gender Trouble: Feminism and the Subversion of Identity*. NY and London: Routledge.
_____. (1991). Imitation and Gender Insubordination. In D. Fuss (ed.), *Inside/Out: Lesbian Theories, Gay Theories*. NY and London: Routledge.
_____. (1993). *Bodies That Matter: On the Discursive Limits of Sex*. NY and London: Routledge.
BW. Personal interview, January 7, 1992.
BW. Personal interview, June 16, 1998.
Cvetkovich, A. (1998). Untouchability and Vulnerability: Stone Butchness as Emotional Style. In S.R. Munt (ed.), *Butch/Femme: Inside Lesbian Gender*. London: Cassell.
Driver, S. (1998). Feminist sublimations, queer disidentifications: Losing touch with maternal sexuality. Unpublished paper.
Gabb, J. (1999). Imag(in)ing the Queer Lesbian Family. *Journal of the Association for Research on Mothering*, Special Issue on Lesbian Mothering. 1(2), Fall/Winter.
Gomez, J. L. (1998). Femme Erotic Independence. In S.R. Munt (ed.), *Butch/Femme: Inside Lesbian Gender*. London: Cassell.
Halberstam, J. (1998a). Between Butches. In S.R. Munt (ed.), *Butch/Femme: Inside Lesbian Gender*. London: Cassell.
_____. (1998b). *Female Masculinity*. Durham and London: Duke UP.
Hamilton, R. (1990). Feminism and Motherhood, 1970s-1990: Reinventing the Wheel? *Resources for Feminist Research 19 (3&4)*.
Inness, S. & Lloyd, M. (1996). G.I. Joes in Barbie Land: Recontextualizing Butch in Twentieth-Century Lesbian Culture. In B. Beemyn & M. Eliason (eds.), *Queer Studies: A Lesbian, Gay, Bisexual and Transgender Anthology*. NY: NYU Press.
JB. Personal interview, December 30, 1994.

Kennedy, E. & Davis, M. (1993). *Boots of Leather, Slippers of Gold: The History of a Lesbian Community.* NY: Penguin.

Lewin, E. (1995). On the Outside Looking In: The Politics of Lesbian Motherhood. In R. Ginsberg & R. Rapp (eds.), *Conceiving the New World Order: The Global Politics of Reproduction.* Berkeley: U of California P.

LRT. Personal interview, January 12, 1992.

MacCowan, L. (1992). Re-collecting History, Renaming Lives: Femme Stigma and the Feminist Seventies and Eighties. In J. Nestle (ed.), *The Persistent Desire: A Femme/Butch Reader.* Boston: Alyson.

Martin, B. (1996). *Femininity Played Straight: The Significance of Being Lesbian.* NY and London: Routledge.

Munt, S.R. (ed.). (1998). *Butch/Femme: Inside Lesbian Gender.* London: Cassell.

Nestle, J. (ed.). (1992). *The Persistent Desire: A Femme/Butch Reader.* Boston: Alyson.

The Butch/Femme Tango

Mary C. Matthews

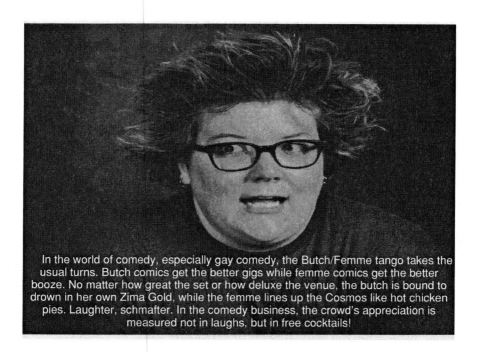

In the world of comedy, especially gay comedy, the Butch/Femme tango takes the usual turns. Butch comics get the better gigs while femme comics get the better booze. No matter how great the set or how deluxe the venue, the butch is bound to drown in her own Zima Gold, while the femme lines up the Cosmos like hot chicken pies. Laughter, schmafter. In the comedy business, the crowd's appreciation is measured not in laughs, but in free cocktails!

Mary C. Matthews is a San Francisco writer, comedian, and solo performer. She is known for her unique blend of stand-up and live folk-punk comedy music. She won San Francisco's *Talent Search 2000* and was the official comedy pick of the 2001 San Francisco Lesbian/Gay Film Festival. Contact her at <mcmpress@yahoo.com>.

[Haworth co-indexing entry note]: "The Butch/Femme Tango." Matthews, Mary C. Co-published simultaneously in *Journal of Lesbian Studies* (Harrington Park Press, an imprint of The Haworth Press, Inc.) Vol. 6, No. 2, 2002, p. 59; and: *Femme/Butch: New Considerations of the Way We Want to Go* (ed: Michelle Gibson, and Deborah T. Meem) Harrington Park Press, an imprint of The Haworth Press, Inc., 2002, p. 59. Single or multiple copies of this article are available for a fee from The Haworth Document Delivery Service [1-800-HAWORTH, 9:00 a.m. - 5:00 p.m. (EST). E-mail address: getinfo@haworthpressinc.com].

Genesis of a Femme and Her Desire: Finding Mommy and Daddy in Butch/Femme

Robin Maltz

SUMMARY. This essay explores the erotically resignified roles of Mommy, Daddy, girl and boy in butch and femme. Using Freud's "Case of Homosexuality in a Woman" and personal narrative, the author focuses on the primal need for family and questions how, rather than why, butches and femmes inhabit these powerful, consensual roles in butch/femme relationships. *[Article copies available for a fee from The Haworth Document Delivery Service: 1-800-HAWORTH. E-mail address: <getinfo@haworthpressinc.com> Website: <http://www.HaworthPress.com> © 2002 by The Haworth Press, Inc. All rights reserved.]*

KEYWORDS. Femme, butch, butch/femme, Freud, "Daddy," "Mommy," "girl," queer, lesbian

In the last decade queer identifications, gender awareness, and the inner workings of same-sex relationships have been spread open for examination, and the eroticized roles of "Mommy," "Daddy," "girl," and "boy" have bub-

Robin Maltz is a doctoral candidate in Performance Studies at NYU. Her work explores intersections of queer female sex and gender roles and sexual trauma. She is currently writing her dissertation, "Recovery and Resistance: Childhood Sexual Trauma, Therapeutic Feminism, and Performance."

[Haworth co-indexing entry note]: "Genesis of a Femme and Her Desire: Finding Mommy and Daddy in Butch/Femme." Maltz, Robin. Co-published simultaneously in *Journal of Lesbian Studies* (Harrington Park Press, an imprint of The Haworth Press, Inc.) Vol. 6, No. 2, 2002, pp. 61-71; and: *Femme/Butch: New Considerations of the Way We Want to Go* (ed: Michelle Gibson, and Deborah T. Meem) Harrington Park Press, an imprint of The Haworth Press, Inc., 2002, pp. 61-71. Single or multiple copies of this article are available for a fee from The Haworth Document Delivery Service [1-800-HAWORTH, 9:00 a.m. - 5:00 p.m. (EST). E-mail address: getinfo@haworthpressinc.com].

bled to the surface as fabulously perverse sexualized performances. While the dynamic of Daddy/boy has been a mainstay in male/male sex practice, s/m, and porn for decades, more recently Mommy/girl, Mommy/boy, Daddy/girl and Daddy/boy roles have garnered attention in female butch/femme, femme/femme, butch/butch, and ftm relationships. These roles, which are considered "identities" by some queers, are discussed on e-mail lists, in bars, and at queer conferences; depicted on Web sites and in lesbian and s/m porn; and commodified on T-shirts, keychains, greeting cards. Familial role-play is portrayed as hot sex practice, but these performances are also fraught with trauma reenactment and melancholia for a family that never was.

In this essay I will explore "Daddy," "Mommy," "boy" and "girl" roles in butch/femme as relations of power, trust, love and loss. My work is inspired by butches and femmes who construct familial roles in conscious, deliberate ways with a queer feminist awareness, astute imaginations, and keen understanding of the power of gendered difference–and always between consenting adults. Gender, not status, is what informs the roles. It is not the age, social standing, or profession of either partner that is vital in constructing the dynamic, but rather the synthesis of butch or femme and Mommy, Daddy, girl, or boy–all highly-gendered roles–and a need to work out, on, or through unfinished business. For that reason, familial role enactments are often a vital part of various aspects of butch and femme lives, not simply relegated to sex practice.

Mommies and Daddies are tops; dominant figures who are experienced, trustworthy, "run the fuck," give direction, manage the everyday household. "Girl" and "boy" are bottom or submissive roles. Since butch masculinity and femme femininity are fairly strict interpretations of gender, butches are generally Daddies or boys, and femmes, Mommies or girls.

When writing about queer relationships, the terms "power," "dominance," and "submission" strongly evoke sadomasochism or leather play. While I cherish these dynamics as vital within queer communities, I am writing about acts that are less about performance and more quotidian than the self-conscious, exhibitionistic realms of S/M and leather. Pat(rick) Califia expresses a similar notion in the introduction to *Doing It for Daddy*, an anthology of queer Daddy/boy and Daddy/girl stories, when s/he writes; "A daddy is more accessible, flexible, and loving than a master or a sadist. A daddy-boy or daddy-girl scene is also more likely to include genital sex than an S/M scene" (15).

Califia also points out that the book, *Doing It for Daddy*, does not romanticize or advocate incest or "justify nonconsensual sex between adults and minors" (11). Although that position is relevant to my work as well, it is disappointing to read it as a disclaimer in the intro of a book subtitled: "Short and sexy fiction about a very forbidden fantasy." In the last two decades, therapeutic models of healing from the residual effects of incest and familial trauma have been so heavily promoted, that to even suggest a sex-positive approach to reclaiming the body and psyche from the perpetrator is met with suspicion and charges of re-victimization.

In writing about Mommy and Daddy in butch/femme, I am writing about a queer melancholia for family that does not exile its queer children–about the primal need for family. I am looking at the ways we imaginatively transform our butch/femme relationships into families through resignification, incest re-enactment, and affiliation with other self-named butch and femme Daddies and Mommies, boys and girls. My focus is not on why, but *how* butches and femmes rediscover, reenact, resignify family. At the heart of my topic is a question about the genesis of a butch or a femme. In thinking about my child-hood relationship to parental figures, my desire for a mother or father replace-ment, and the ways in which those desires shaped my adult needs, wants, gender, and desire, I can't help wondering if the desire to reconstruct family exists prior to formation of a butch or femme identity.

Maternal and paternal roles in queer relationships are grist for a psychoana-lytic discussion, but in this essay I will side-step the psychoanalytical richness of my theme, and instead focus on the performativity of Mommy and Daddy in butch/femme practices of seduction, sex, and domesticity in my own life and in a narrative that has resonated with me for years. Ironically (or not), the nar-rative in which I locate similarities to my own story of Mommy and Daddy roles and butch/femme desire is a psychoanalytic text–Freud's 1920 case study, "The Psychogenesis of a Case of Homosexuality in a Woman." Seeking similarities to my desire and identity in historical texts–especially one as sig-nificant as Freud's–is driven by my need to belong to something larger and more definitive than my self-interpretations, a need which derives from the same locus as the urge to recreate family.

I first encountered Freud's case study as an armchair lesbian trying to come out in a straight marriage with two children. Behind my stacks of conventional novels and how-to baby books, I secreted lesbian pulp fiction, transsexual tes-timonials, coming-out stories, butch/femme erotica, s/m manifestos–any queer piece of literature I came across on my journey to femme self-discovery. I outed my secret stash to a lesbian therapist who told me I *must* read Freud's case study, as if it were the latest juicy bestseller. She gleefully wrung her hands and proclaimed with certainty that the "homosexual woman" was the in-famous (lesbian) analysand, "Dora," of Freud's "Fragment of an Analysis of a Case of Hysteria ('Dora')." Her theory did not interest me as much as her de-tective's inclination to give subjectivity to an historical lesbian figure closeted in a male-scribed text, and proclaim it as "fact" based on lesbian "knowing" ("I know one when I see one").

Freud's motive in ". . . Case of Homosexuality in a Woman" was to construct a theory of female inversion. In the process he created a narrative symp-
tomatically rife with counter-transference for the female subject he could not
top, and frenetic identifications with the other players in her life. I find Freud's
femme-like sighing, crossed arms, and toe-tapping impatience endearing. I am
a fan of his efforts, his chutzpah, his hubris, and his intellect. However, with a
feminist irreverence towards the self-congratulatory patriarchal methodology
of psychoanalysis, I often read Freud's case studies as fairy tales complete
with suspense, caution, symbolism, and a moral ending. I will therefore infuse
my reading of "Case of Homosexuality in a Woman" with the fairy tale echoes
of my own history, imagination, and desire.

Upon first reading Freud's case (study) my question was not "Is she Dora?"
In the spirit of a femme-detective, I queried with a foot-tapping impatience,
"So, is she or isn't she a butch?" After deciding, for my own edification, that
the unnamed eighteen-year-old "woman" is a butch, I was then left with the
quandary of deciding whether she is a burgeoning butch top Daddy or an eter-
nal butch boy bottom. Plus, who is the "lady" in relation to the "homosexual
woman"? A femme top? A queer mother figure? With these questions in mind,
I will begin my investigation of Freud's family escapade.

Freud's narrative is a "once upon a time" story of an eighteen-year-old female (whom I will hereafter call "HW" for "homosexual woman") who has
time on her hands and a family with some wealth. Her life is unfortunately full
of males–her father, three brothers, and now a male analyst. The males fuss a
lot but are ineffectual at controlling the women, all of whom are self-pos-
sessed. HW does not bother with "girlish pleasures," and has no interest in
young men (148). She is brought to Freud because of her deep and pub-
licly-displayed attachment to a woman.

HW does not express the appropriate œdipal desire for her father or for the
increasingly restless Freud, the wannabe father-replacement who eventually
recommends a woman analyst for his charge. If HW does not desire Father,
than she must be stuck in precedipality, desiring her mother and identifying
with her father's desire for her mother. Freud writes:

> Her libido had flowed in two streams, the one on the surface being one
> that we may unhesitantly designate homosexual. The latter was probably
> a direct and unchanged continuation of an infantile mother-fixation.
> (156)

Precedipality or infantile mother-fixation is at the heart of Freud's excursion
into female homosexuality. Before he reaches this conclusion he must exhaust
all possibilities that his analysand identifies with mothering, or is looking for a

mother substitute (another identificatory, rather than desiring option) instead of what she is doing, which is seeking a love object in a female. Identification suggests an appropriate œdipal route towards adult heterosexuality (or at least bisexuality, which Freud believes is a universal human trait), but HW is a subject for whom identification is merely a short path towards understanding the subject whom she desires–an older woman with the parental-type authority and qualities of a "mother." According to Freud's theory, HW is stuck in a permanent girl-baby state of mother-fixation (157).

HW has a history of attachments to mature women from the time she was a young girl. Her first love was for a "strict and unapproachable" schoolmistress, whom Freud deems an obvious mother substitute. She next pursued a film actress at a summer resort. Like a butch lothario of the playground, she then "takes a lively interest in a number of young mothers" (168). Her own mother, who is rather young and coquettish, or as Freud snidely notes, "was evidently unwilling to give up her own claims to attractiveness," enjoys hearing about HW's naughty desires (149). On the flowing stream from daughter to mother, HW is a girl who is not going to win her mother's attention unless she is a boy like her brothers, or like the men whose attention and affection her mother greatly enjoys (158). Her male-identified behaviors must be somewhat effective since HW's mother entertains her musings, thereby encouraging HW's masculine-inscribed lust for women. The vicarious pleasure HW's mother thus receives, and the pleasure HW has in recounting her desire, is an interaction with incestuous echoes, but HW is cast in the role of son. HW is closest to getting a (her) mother when she resignifies herself as a boy.

HW did have a brief mothering episode, which Freud recounts in the breathless detail he used for matters of great significance–although the incident strikes me as much less notable than his heightened account. At thirteen HW developed an attachment to a three-year-old boy which Freud calls an "exaggeratedly strong affection." Perhaps HW took up extreme mothering as an attempt to master the mother she both lacked and desired. Maybe her mothering of the boy was a rehearsal of power relations–of topping, bottoming, dominance and submission. It is no surprise that "after a short time she grew indifferent to the boy, and began to take an interest in mature, but still youthful, women" (156). I understand the frenzy with which HW–a clever, impatient, assertive female–was acting out in order to learn who she was, ultimately in relation to the person she loves. It is a human characteristic to discover one's identity, desires, and needs through affiliation, the recognition of ourselves as reflected by others and through those who desire us–as friends, lovers, companions, parents and parent-substitutes.

Diana Fuss points out that Freud's "often incoherent writings on female homosexuality" present a dilemma by linking female homosexual identity formation to maternity (51). In fact, Freud has an 'inability to think of homosexuality outside the thematics of mothering." Fuss backs up this assertion with a detective's clue: "the first word of Freud's narrative is 'homosexual' and the final word is 'motherhood'" (52).

If HW is a burgeoning butch then perhaps it is useful to think of her desire and identity as working on and against motherness. I have never met a butch who did not at one time court her mother and compete with her father and/or brother for her mother's affections, and as an adult had a fraught relationship to her mother–vying persistently for her acceptance and attention. While it may be reductive to theorize all lesbian identity through mother-desire and father-identification, it is a theme that makes sense in the highly gendered identity of butch.

ONCE UPON A TIME

Freud's story begins with HW's hot pursuit of a *cocotte*, a "lady" ("Lady" for my purposes, since I prefer to capitalize the names of dominant players) who, according to Freud, has open affairs with men and women but lives with a female lover. Freud romanticizes and exoticizes the Lady under a thin veil of class snobbery. (It is also of note that if the Lady is having sex with males and females, she is acting on bisexuality which Freud theorizes as inherent to all humans. Therefore, the Lady might be the one psychoanalytically "whole" player in this drama.) I am eager to know more about the Lady's female lover. Freud tells us the lover is a married woman, but she lives with the Lady (and they live with the husband as well?). I find it very appealing that the Lady has found so many doting companions!

The lady humors HW but keeps her at a distance. HW, nevertheless, pursues her single-mindedly and publicly, often in places where her father might see them, since her rivalry is with him. She sends her beloved flowers, and treats her in a courtly, gentlemanly (i.e., butch) manner. She fawns over the mention of the Lady's beauty, kisses her hand, is humble in her presence. Freud claims HW has "adopted the characteristic masculine type of love" in relation to the Lady (160). He says that she has "not only chosen a feminine love-object, but has also developed a masculine attitude towards that object" (154). One day HW and the Lady do encounter her father, and after lying about the glaring man, HW admits who he is. This ruse of trotting her past his office angers the Lady, who does not want to be manipulated. She then, in true high-femme fashion, tells HW "to leave her then and there, and never again to wait for her or to address her–the affair must now come to an end!" (162). HW throws herself over a wall in plain view of her father and the Lady. After she has convalesced, or as Freud tactlessly sputters, "She paid for this undoubtedly serious attempt at suicide with a considerable time on her back in bed," the Lady understands the intensity of HW's desire, is perhaps moved by the chivalry of her act, and allows (returns?) her affections (148). HW's father responds by marching her off to Freud.

Freud presents lengthy theories about HW's need for a mother-substitute. I do not intend to address those theories in this essay. What interests me more is an answer to the question, "Just what kind of butch is HW?" Freud provides enough information about HW's sexuality and gender to extrapolate meaning but only of course from my present-day context. As I have noted throughout this essay, Freud has deemed HW's behavior and desire that of a masculine female homosexual, so I will suggest that it is a given–the girl is a butch. In the history of public lesbian identity, all visible lesbians are deemed masculine; however, Freud is analyzing HW contrary to how he wants to perceive her. Her masculinity is a reluctant analysis for Freud, a hindrance to psychoanalytic success–not a knee-jerk bias.

What we learn about HW's sexuality is that she and the Lady have exchanged a few kisses and embraces, and that HW's "genital chastity, if one may use such a phrase, is intact" (153). Earlier Freud writes that the "unfavorable features" of HW's case are not neuroses, hysteria, or illness (basically, any woman-attributed malady of the time), but "in converting one variety of genital organization of sexuality into the other." Does Freud mean that penetration relieves "genital chastity," or perhaps oral sex does? Does he mean that her genitals should stir for a male rather than female? Freud reveals in his remark, "if one may use such a phrase," that his knowledge of female homosexual sex acts is limited. In any case, would HW admit the intricacies of her sex practices (even if they had occurred) to Freud? And would a butch, especially one who is so tenacious in her pursuit of a woman, be likely to roll over and be topped by penetration or oral sex? Would she not want to please her lover first? How confusing!

Genitals aside, I locate HW's sexual expression in her rescue fantasies. Freud theorizes that HW has a tendency, like some males, to choose a woman of " 'bad repute' sexually" as a necessary condition of love so that she can rescue her from those dire circumstances (161). Although HW is of a higher socioeconomic class than her beloved, her sexualized desire is to rescue her through love, not wealth. HW is drawn to independent women such as the actress and the schoolmistress, and she respects the autonomy of the Lady. Freud explains that HW's rejection "without hesitation [of] the willing advances made by a homosexual friend of her own age" was because her chivalrous rescue fantasy is so strong (161). I suspect that HW wanted to rescue her mother from the doldrums of domesticity. A butch I know who wanted to rescue her neglectful, abusive mother from poverty and drink transformed this desire into fantasies in which schoolgirl heartthrobs were nearly hit by cars and she was the brave rescuer. This butch grew up to be a Daddy butch who has a knack for healing wounded femme girls.

I reluctantly must conclude that as a butch, HW is yet unformed. There is not enough evidence to know whether she will be a Daddy or a boy. However, like many a butch, her identity is formed on and against the representation of mother, and from there perhaps she will become a Daddy who self-sacrificingly needs to take care of a girl (a femme confident and powerful enough to submit to another female), and in return earns a girl's trust and dependence, which ultimately is what Mother gives Father. Or perhaps she will be a boy who finds satisfaction in worshipping and submitting to a powerful and demanding mother figure.

My femme identity also began with mother-desire, a yearning for a mother-replacement, an acting-out of mothering, and then real mothering (I have two children), and ultimately finding a butch Daddy father-replacement in motherly flesh; one who deeply appreciated my real mothering, and had a complex relationship to me as both a dominant mother-replacement and a submissive girl.

ONCE UPON MY TIME

When I was a child in the 1960s I watched the puppeteer Shari Lewis on television. I liked her thick swaying ponytail, her perky dresses and sweater sets, her breasts pressed into a pointy bra above a slender waist, and especially the way she manipulated, with fist and fingers, the fluffy, sleepy-eyed, wide-mouthed puppet Lamb Chop. She had other puppets, Charley Horse and Hush Puppy, but her interactions with Lamb Chop fascinated me most.

I studied Shari Lewis closely. Her strict but tender manner with the sassy Lamb Chop aroused me in a way that I now know, decades later, was the beginning of my femme desire to be topped by an authoritative parentified female, a butch Daddy with the female body of a Mommy.

Shari Lewis was the mother and love object a queer girl like me could not attain. My own mother was a very pretty, young and aloof woman, who was all mine until I was five years old, at which time she married a man whom I despised, a man with two sons around my age. Six months after the marriage, my half-sister was born.

I suspect I wanted my mother in the way this new man in our lives had her, but as a young girl my desire would be cast in the Freudian pre-œdipal sense of never progressing past an infantilized desire for Mother through an identification with Father; a nascent lesbian desire. I found my mother-replacement in Shari. Shari and my mother were about the same age and resembled one another, but Shari was a children's television star who performed with puppets and with kids lucky enough to be on her show, and my mother was a distracted suburban housewife with a new husband, new stepsons, a new baby, and an insatiable flirting streak. Shari had no men on her show, while my world was suddenly and irritatingly filled with males–a sexually abusive self-appointed "step-father," men who wanted my mother, men who played cards in our small dining room, a TV repairman who visited too often to fix our never-broken television, boy children punching each other in the back seat of our car with me stuck in the middle as a buffer. Like HW, my childhood was filled with males and babies, an aloof, attractive mother, and a woman love object of unattainable status.

Shari was my escape. She was a goddess who nuzzled puppets against her ample chest, spent her days with children, and loved make-up, dress-up and make-believe. Her penetrating puppeteer fingers encased within the folds of Lamb Chop (her fictive child) manipulated and controlled the little lamb puppet; what a good Mommy she was. Shari maintained a masterful and hypnotic possession of me (something television, not my mother, could do)–Shari as the full-breasted woman whose flesh could smother me; Shari as authoritarian; Shari as dominant manipulator of willful puppets; Shari as penetrating hand; Phallic Shari; Shari as top; Shari as Mommy; Shari as Daddy. Shari as ventriloquist whose Lamb Chop spoke her words back to her. Shari, the maternal creator of a feminine subject who resides at the end of her fist, talks back to Mommy and needs frequent light scoldings.

In my childhood games I played Mommy-puppeteer, assimilating Shari's authoritative mothering so that my puppets were transformed when I inserted my tiny hand into their inanimate, waiting cavities and clutched them to my small girl chest, at once admonishing them and forgiving them for being so naughty. I was both puppet and Mommy. I wanted to feel what it was like to be both Shari and a soft puppet beneath her fingers, against her chest.

In these early erotic performances of being Shari and wanting Shari, I was acting out the abuses of sex and power in my young life, and acting against the many obstacles that came between me and my mother. Perhaps I was enacting something similar to HW's extreme mothering of the toddler–mothering for mastery, but with the end result being submission to my love object, rather than dominance over her. Trying to understand the workings of queer desire, I performed both the dominant mother and the submissive, eager-to-please girl. My hand was a stern Mommy and my puppet, a recalcitrant pouting girl who needed discipline. I was the still body of a sexually abused child and the Daddy who manipulated it with penetrative force–although in my fantasy play, neither my characters nor I were ever male. HW might have enacted dominant mothering on a subject, a boy, whom she identified with as her submissive object. (The nascent beginnings of a butch bottom Mommy's boy?)

Those games, and my fascination with Shari Lewis, were an awakening of the Mommy and Daddy dynamics embedded in the butch/femme erotics and desire that would later mean so much to my femme identity. Those early enactments held the kernels of valuable erotic lessons for me: An imbalance of power in a female-female relationship is hot; to be a satisfied bottom one must understand the dynamics of topping; and the highly gendered roles of Mommy and Daddy, as understood in Western heterocentric cultures, inform my femme consciousness, and suffuse my butch/femme relationships in ways both examined and unwittingly enacted.

I first read Freud's ". . . Case of Homosexuality in a Woman" as I was coming out as a queer and a femme. It was one of several texts that helped me understand the power that femininity, coupled with submission, holds for a butch with a Daddy streak. Reading narratives of butch/femme and filtering them through with Mommy, Daddy, girl, boy desire gave me the hope that I no longer had to repress my gender because of its significance in heterosexist cultures and relationships. Once I found my butch, my queer Daddy, I became a high-femme girl/woman. The quandary after all this reading and pondering my identity, gender, and desire, was how to construct my femininity. I had longed to be both mother and slut–to be Shari Lewis and the Lady. I would end up modeling my femme identity after a woman who reminds me of the Lady.

I was in my early twenties, visiting New York City with a friend. We hailed a cab on a busy Saturday night in midtown on our way from one nightclub to another. A straight couple pushed in the cab after us asking if they could share a ride downtown. The woman, in her early forties, was pressed against me. I could smell the strong scent of her body mixed with her perfume. She wore a red lipstick shade that was audaciously loud, her hair pulled up hastily in a clip, and a green satin cocktail dress that showed ample flesh. It was a dress that even a younger woman with a trim figure might wear self-consciously, but as I watched this woman walk away from the cab on her mate's arm, I was struck by her confidence. The woman paid me no mind. Her interest was on the man and his pleasure in her, but at the same time she was aware of herself performing and being watched. Was her entire persona autoerotic, and the male a prop for her validation? My arousal, curiosity, fascination felt like desire, but I wanted to be consumed by the woman as an enveloping mother, taken into her scents and tacky dress. I also identified with the woman. I wanted to be her. Thinking back, I must have been aware of her vulnerability, the trust she placed in her companion. She did not carry a purse or anything that could hold money or keys; she could not possibly get anywhere fast in her heels. Her body was exposed and she did not pay attention to her surroundings. I have become a woman who wears my scented body, perfume, lipstick and dresses with confidence for my butch. I trust my companion with my vulnerability; when I go out in the evening I carry no more than a lipstick case and some coins. I am also always my butch's girl, enacting the inability to do for myself what my butch can do for me. She, in turn, needs to take care of me in a way that heightens the authority of her masculinity. And I–like the Lady of Freud's story, like her butch paramour, and like the woman in the green dress–do not have much time for people who do not interest me.

WORKS CITED

Califia, Pat, ed. *Doing It for Daddy*. Boston: Alyson, 1994.

Freud, Sigmund. "The Psychogenesis of a Case of Homosexuality in a Woman." *The Writings of Sigmund Freud: The Standard Edition*. Vol. 18. Trans. James Strachey. London: Hogarth, 1955. 145-172.

Fuss, Diana. "Freud's Fallen Women: Identification, Desire, and 'A Case of Homosexuality in a Woman.'" *Fear of a Queer Planet: Queer Politics and Social Theory*. Ed. Michael Warner. Minneapolis: U of Minnesota P, 1993.

Femme/Butch Family Romances:
A Queer Dyke Spin
on Compulsory Heterosexuality

Laura A. Harris

SUMMARY. My essay theorizes femme/butch family romances against the grain of dominant feminist and lesbian thought that desexualizes the space of mother/daughter desire. I do so through a reading/recoding of the infringing incestuous mommie-boy desires that surface in an archetypal lesbian novel, Jane Rule's *Desert of the Heart*. *[Article copies available for a fee from The Haworth Document Delivery Service: 1-800-HAWORTH. E-mail address: <getinfo@haworthpressinc.com> Website: <http://www.HaworthPress. com> © 2002 by The Haworth Press, Inc. All rights reserved.]*

KEYWORDS. Femme/butch, queer dyke desire, mother-daughter, ellipsis, sexuality, gender, feminist theory, lesbian theory, perverse, cliché, compulsory heterosexuality, literature

Love, when little boys want to marry their mothers, they have a hard enough time of it, but they manage. When little girls want to marry their mothers . . .

Jane Rule, *Desert of the Heart*, 136 (1964)

Laura A. Harris publishes in the areas of feminist and queer studies, black studies, African diasporic studies, and fiction/poetry. Harris edited *Femme: Feminists, Lesbians and Bad Girls (1997)*, a collected anthology that sought to centrally situate femme identities within queer studies and as paramount to feminist and lesbian histories.

Address correspondence to the author by e-mail: <lharris@pitzer.edu>.

[Haworth co-indexing entry note]: "Femme/Butch Family Romances: A Queer Dyke Spin on Compulsory Heterosexuality." Harris, Laura A. Co-published simultaneously in *Journal of Lesbian Studies* (Harrington Park Press, an imprint of The Haworth Press, Inc.) Vol. 6, No. 2, 2002, pp. 73-84; and: *Femme/Butch: New Considerations of the Way We Want to Go* (ed: Michelle Gibson, and Deborah T. Meem) Harrington Park Press, an imprint of The Haworth Press, Inc., 2002, pp. 73-84. Single or multiple copies of this article are available for a fee from The Haworth Document Delivery Service [1-800-HAWORTH, 9:00 a.m. - 5:00 p.m. (EST). E-mail address: getinfo@haworthpressinc.com].

That the power regimes of heterosexism and phallogocentrism seek to augment themselves through a constant repetition of their logic, their metaphysic and their naturalized ontologies, does not imply that repetition itself ought to be stopped–as if it could be. If repetition is bound to persist as the mechanism of the cultural reproduction of identities, then the crucial question emerges: What kind of subversive repetition might call into question the regulatory practice of identity itself?

Judith Butler, *Gender Trouble*, 32 (1990)

Anticipating that the psychiatrist would make a predictable link between her lesbianism and maternal desire, Irene described the ecstasy of sex with a lesbian lover whom she could treat as her "son" by day but at whose passionate mercy she would be by night. Here we see a subversive lesbian spin on the family romance:

Irene: "A girl twenty-eight years old wished herself on me. . . . For a year she wore boys' clothes and I introduced her as my son. That satisfied my maternal complex. She was powerful and aggressive as far as sex was concerned but in everything else she was completely childish . . ."

Jennifer Terry, Theorizing Deviant Historiography, 65 (1991)

I always thought I'd begin my [butch] story with my mother, the Eldorado of my desire, but . . . the fathers and their masculine principle have pushed their way forward.

Esther Newton, *A Hard Left Fist*, 111 (2001)

FAMILIAL GENDER NARRATIVES/INCESTUOUS SEXUAL PRACTICES[1]

What does the ellipsis at the end of the quandary Jane Rule presents above signal? Does it signal that for little girls who want their mothers there is no location where this desire can exist? Why don't little girls who want to sleep with their mothers have an oedipal conflict or theoretical space for their desire? The linguistic space of the ellipsis marks the containment of the mother's and daughter's gender and sexuality within the imperative of heterosexual reproduction. Little boys can indeed manage to marry their mothers; clichés about wife-mother parallels attest to that. While Rule's ellipsis marks the absence of queer dyke desire in heterosexual narratives, it also marks the limits and failure of heterosexuality. In other words, it demands an articulation of mother/daughter desire as it points to the spatial parameters of its absence. Socio-psychological analyses might conclude the sentence with the pathology of lesbian deviance. Feminism(s) might suggest that elliptical lesbian desire is best, whereas mother-daughter dyads can offer the ideal metaphor of woman-to-woman bonding. Lesbian theories, where a mother-hungry, breastfeeding butch might expect to find reprieve from such sexual repression, tend to ignore or disavow any sexual association to the mother. How might a femme/butch theory of family romance then finish Jane Rule's sentence, "When little girls want to marry their mothers . . ." or, more urgently, how might such a theory respond to queer dykes who grow up to want and do just that?

Femme/butch identifications, as a number of authors have posited, deconstruct and resist the static burdensome gender and sexual roles that sustain compulsory heterosexuality. Although writers on the topic differ somewhat in their understanding of how this femme/butch resistance occurs, they do tend to agree that much of the negative assessment of femme/butch communities, and thus their political activism, is in direct relation to the renegade and public display of sexuality represented by femme-butch coupling. Elizabeth Kennedy and Madeline Davis write, "At a time when lesbian communities were developing solidarity and consciousness, but had not yet formed political groups, butch-fem roles were the key structure for organizing against heterosexual dominance. They were the central prepolitical form of resistance" (*Boots of Leather* 6). Situated historically by dominant culture and some but not all lesbian-feminist ideology as self-oppressing heterosexual mimicry, femme-butch dyads offer not only a highly charged sexual and gender specific way of caring for each other as lovers, but these self-identifying expressions also recognize the political urgency of reclaiming gender and sexual roles.

Most writers on the topic might agree that the overtly gendered sexual display of femme/butch expression is a politicized erotic space through which heterosexuality is recoded, transformed, duped, and parodied, especially in terms of female gender, sexual pleasure, and domestic/public space. However, in the main they do not address the corresponding and core familial romance narratives that proliferate within femme/butch communities and representations. If a femme/butch erotic reproduction of much of the symbolic and ideological private and public domains of heterosexuality rends its hegemony, then how do femme/butch sexual communities engage the attendant heterosexual narratives of taboo family erotics? Though it has been largely overlooked or only alluded to in many valuations, within the erotics of the femme/butch dynamic, there are significant familial gender role identifications and erotic re-inventions of familial sexual taboo narratives. These identifications with the familial romance contribute profoundly to the construction of femme/ butch identities as well as to the eroticization of this gendered desire. A femme/butch theory of gender and sexuality must take into account that through identificatory and erotic transformation of heterosexual familial structures, these roles, desires, and taboos are at liberty to proliferate perversely, and do, in femme/butch communities as daddy-mommie, daddy-girl, mommie-boy, and further queer combinations.[2]

In a brief outline in this essay and as an antidotal queer method of developing something like a beginning, I explore the theoretical potential of femme/ butch family romances not in self-identified femme/butch representation but rather in the infringing incestuous mommie-boy desires that surface in the consummate mother-daughter dyad of an archetypal lesbian novel, Jane Rule's *Desert of the Heart*. Rule's novel is archetypal in the sense that in the mid-1960s it refutes dominant stereotypes of lesbian desire–it takes on compulsory heterosexuality–and in doing so furthers the development of white, middle-class, lesbian feminism. This philosophical subtext, coupled with its groundbreaking mother-daughter portrayal of lesbian desire, renders it a classic of white, lesbian, feminist canons. In my reading of Rule, I appropriate notions of deviant dyke desire to give further form to the queer imagining that dyke sexuality brings to vermiculated familial narratives. I do so against the grain of theories of gender and sexuality that either desexualize mother-daughter desire as feminist bonding or refute the puissant sexual reclamation of such erotics. I begin with an engagement of the works of Adrienne Rich and Judith Roof, both of whom articulate feminist/lesbian-feminist theories in relation to mother-daughter dyads. These particular writers opened an important dialogue on this queer locale of familial sexual tensions. However, a femme/butch theory pushes the envelope of the space of mother/daughter desire beyond the choices of feminist bonding and/or lesbian refutation through a sexualized gendering of these narratives. Finally, I turn to a close reading of Rule's novel to position femme/butch incestuous erotics as theoretically useful in dissembling tensions over mother-daughter desire in dominant feminist and lesbian sexual theories. In this pursuit, I pirate the stereotype of the deviant queer dyke whose œdipal/electral/maternal conflicts are confused–or better yet, are decidedly perverse–as a model for developing a femme/butch theory of gender and sexual representation in relation to "family values." Specifically, with Rule's novel, I forward this theory by reading the maternal seductress and the gender-errant, mother-desiring "girl-childs" as *the* fiendishly dynamic duo of insurrectionary familial romances.

Through the lens of incestuous femme/butch identifications and desires, the troubled question of mother/daughter desire within dominant feminist and lesbian theories of sexuality that Rule's 1964 ellipsis represents–compulsory heterosexuality–becomes remapped as defiant familial eroticism. That is to say that the troublesome ultra-taboo presence of queers within the familial narrative is recast to become felonious sexual play and political transgression. Playing with, not against, the idea of these erotic relationships allows for a theorizing of relationships of power and desire, of gender and sexuality, amongst women (and other identities), unencumbered by compulsory heterosexuality and decidedly incorrigible in relation to it. While there are certainly myriad subversive means of accomplishing the task of calling "into question the regulatory practices of identity itself," incestuous femme/butch erotics are particularly useful in terms of being part of historical butch-femme practices that have already withstood accusations of hetero imitation. This historical survival, so to speak, is sustained at least in part through methodologies of transgression that do appropriate for pleasure and power, that do politicize the world through which transgressors must move, and that account for a lived experience of these elliptical spaces.

Femme/butch family romance narratives are important to unpack as lived experience, to push the parameters of theorizing the representation of queer dyke sexualities, and to disrupt heterosexual regimes of identity and practice. Such analysis is a necessary endeavor in order to fulfill the 1980s sex war's agitation for and promise of radical sexual theories and practices to reclaim a desexualized space of queer dyke desire.[3] Further, a theoretical forwarding of queer familial desire is of pressing concern to advance a counter-discourse to a contemporary discourse of "gay" families who seek to reproduce themselves as members of a mainstream family narrative premised upon disturbing notions of biology (race), national identity, economic status, and moral values. While queers forming families is indeed a politically salient issue, this privileged discourse seeks to frame a middle-class liberal strategy of inclusivity as *the* progressive identity cause, when it arises from an economic elite who posit their familial concerns as parallel to those of middle America, whatever, wherever, and whoever they imagine that may be.[4]

FEMINIST AND LESBIAN THEORIES/QUEER SEX?

Adrienne Rich and Judith Roof both explicitly address the space of mother-daughter desire in U.S. and French feminist thought and have decidedly influenced discussions of mother/daughter sexuality in a lesbian context. In her now renowned essay "Compulsory Heterosexuality and Lesbian Existence" (1980) Rich posed a radical theoretical question: If the first erotic bond is to the mother, then are not both men and women sexually oriented towards women? This essay sparked the understanding of lesbian desire on what is widely known as the "lesbian continuum," a model for understanding "lesbian" as a wide range of exchanges between women rather than solely in relation to sexual orientation. Coming at a time when the radical stances of seventies feminist communities were encountering burgeoning liberal feminist positions in relation to sexuality, patriarchy and legal social systems, the intellectual reception of Rich's question and its consequent answer provided feminist and lesbian theories with first a subversive disruption of heterosexual norms, but finally with a containment of lesbian desire that became acceptable to the continued dominance of those norms.

Rich's question challenged the norms of heterosexuality, particularly as defined by psychoanalytical and other cultural institutions. Additionally, Rich's model of a lesbian continuum engendered an especially intense and productive feminist debate surrounding the essential definition of lesbian identity. However, her theoretical query simultaneously became a means of abstracting lesbian desire and moving away from recognizing lesbian identities as part of diverse sexual communities. Rich writes:

> Any theory or cultural/political creation that treats lesbian existence as a marginal or less "natural" phenomenon, as mere "sexual preference," or as the mirror image of either heterosexual or male homosexual relations is profoundly weakened thereby, whatever its other contributions. Feminist theory can no longer afford merely to voice a toleration of "lesbianism" as an "alternative lifestyle," or make token allusion to lesbians. (4)

Clearly Rich's emphasis on a radical revision of the term lesbian as a cultural signifier of sexual otherness played a crucial role in locating it as core to feminist analyses concerned with relationships between women and between women and social systems. It is the distancing of the term lesbian from "mere" sexual preference that now needs reconsideration.

Rich's downplaying of lesbian as a sexual orientation is integral to her argument for understanding a history of lesbian existence and a wide range of lesbian interaction socially and emotionally. However, sexuality, sexual practice, can no longer (if it ever could) be said to be merely a facet of lesbian and certainly not of queer dyke identities. Indeed, it is precisely for their "deviant" sexual practice that queers of all sorts have been marginalized in dominant culture or redefined in feminist, lesbian, and leftist political communities. Radical theories of feminism and the more recent queer theories of sexuality instruct us that gender, sexuality, and sexual acts are and always have been central locations for a convergence of knowledge, oppression, representation, and resistance. Rule's ellipsis in the epigram of this essay signifies this aptly.

Judith Roof presents us with a more recent examination of lesbian desire, mothering, and mother-daughter dyads. Roof's essay "This Is Not for You:

The Sexuality of Mothering" (1991) examines the heterosexual bias of psychoanalytic feminist theory while claiming the absence of mothers as a model of how lesbian desire works in lesbian narrative. Roof writes of her own essay:

> "This is not for you": the daughter's paradox of the sexual mother, the punch line of her narrative of identity and differentiation . . . But "This is not for you" also begets a lesbian story: the tale of desire for desire. Here "this" is, but you cannot have it . . . the wish for an unfulfilled desire–the desire for desire–is sustained . . . I am perplexed by what I see as a paradoxical relation between mothering theory . . . and the absence of the mother in lesbian novels. (91-92)

Roof's line of argument seeks to revise lesbian desire and mothering in relation to heterosexuality, much as Rich did, by challenging the heterosexual bias and originary moments of identity in psychoanalytic/feminist models. In order to do so, Roof argues for a reading of lesbian narrative desire which does not make an identification with the mother and, in which, in fact, the mother is consistently absent as any type of object or subject of lesbian desire–"desire for desire" exists in her place. While Roof's project to disrupt psychoanalysis is significant, Roof's final conclusion about reading textual lesbian desire as persistently organized around an absence of mothering and mother-daughter dyads is too limiting. Roof's theoretical move is to remove lesbian desire from a pathologized position in relation to heterosexual desire by reading lesbian narrative as a refutation of psychoanalytic heterosexual accounts of mother-daughter desire. While constituting a strong contestation to heterosexual norms, Roof's argument resembles that of feminists who felt compelled to present lesbianism as a political rather than sexual choice. By ignoring maternal sexuality or gendered daughter desire as a potential aspect of lesbian desire, Roof allows lesbians to be restricted by heterosexual models in how and whom they can desire. Lesbian desire may or may not be linked to mothering, or mother-daughter dyads, but, by solely dismissing rather than marking the reconstitution of the model, the hierarchies of nature and normativity remain.

Further, Roof contends, in a list she makes of lesbian texts, that the biological mother is either absent or a troubled relation in a number of lesbian novels. I question Roof's assumption that this means mother/daughter eroticism is absent as this conclusion relies heavily on a feminist/lesbian notion of mother-daughter desire as ideal woman-to-woman bonding. The absence of biological mothers in lesbian novels instructs us that it is not solely a desire organized around locating a real mother or retrieving bad relations with lost mothers. It is often about a desire for the complexity and difference between women represented or incurred by that relationship. To read (what Roof is misreading) is to see the excess of desire in lesbian novels that arises out of differences–class, gender, age, sexual practice differences. This "excess," when viewed through the critical model offered by femme/butch family romances, invites a lesbian desire that is neither prescribed nor described by a simple refutation of heterosexuality. Instead, a femme/butch theory allows such desires self-identification, diversity, complexity, and a present and history of a queer dyke space of mother/daughter desire. It also urgently forwards a crticial dialogue about race and class divides; it locates in the work of Rich and Roof the always impinging white, middle-class family mores that sometimes permeate white, lesbian feminist thought and too often ignore or refute cross-cultural, raced and classed understandings of sexuality that femme/butch desire can encompass.

CLICHÉS OF THE HEART/A MOMMIE-BOY DYNAMIC DUO

In keeping with the motif of the ellipsis as a signifier of queer dyke desire for mother/daughter family romances, my discussion of *Desert of the Heart* begins with the geographically elliptic location in which the narrative unfolds: the desert. In nature, deserts are vast barren spaces which extreme changes of weather and lack of water render uninhabitable geographic sites. Mother/daughter desire occupies a similar barren and uninhabitable theoretical site, and "nature" has rendered it so. This desert landscape calls attention to the ellipsis surrounding mother/daughter desire by calling attention to and playing with the boundary of natural/unnatural constructions. Rule's narrative works to denaturalize "nature" by juxtaposing deserts and lesbians with the themes of sterility and fertility, by locating her narrative in the Nevada economy of a constitutive commodity–gambling (desire). While deserts and queers seem unnatural, they are only so if nature is equated with reproductive capabilities. By positing the sterile desert, which displaces the assumption of fecundity in nature, as a backdrop, Rule disentangles nature from reproduction. Queer desire appears sterile, but like the desert its fertility resides in a different production, one that complicates and diversifies "nature" by troubling the specious logic of reproduction. By setting her narrative of queer mother-daughter desire in the desert, where the reproductive logic of nature is interrogated, Rule interrogates natural versus unnatural representational divides.

Rule's narrative indeed explores the "unnatural" possibility of mother-daughter desire between an older divorcee and a rebellious young dyke (though the movie miserably failed to portray this facet) whom everyone else perceives as looking uncannily like mother and daughter. A femme/butch family romance reading/recoding locates an infringing incestuous eroticism in the lesbian mother-daughter desire of the narrative, an eroticism that revises the œdipal scene through a taboo pirating of a gendered heterosexual romance narrative. For example, contrary to the perception of others that they share an uncanny family resemblance, Evelyn Hall and Ann "Childs" experience difference as their resemblance. At their initial meeting Evelyn quotes Cummings, "Hello is what a mirror says" and quickly muses to herself, "There was no shared family resemblance. . . . It was rather an impression . . . a memory . . . not a likeness" (Rule 10). The idea of an impression or memory of a familial connection as opposed to a clear resemblance disengages the roles of mother and daughter from their expected conduct; it reproduces a space of desire that resonates with the familial but is remapped. This familial remapping begins the task of dismantling heterosexuality in the novel, especially gender roles, in relation to queer desire. This reproduced space of desire as that of Evelyn and Ann's mother-daughter dyad can also refigure the presence of taboo sexual familial codes. Immediately following this initial meeting, Evelyn's reactions as Ann stands over her, questioning her, are revealing:

> Evelyn felt a not altogether unpleasant lightheadedness. She found it difficult to follow and answer Ann's questions. . . . she thought how extraordinary the girl's clothes were. . . . she [Ann] wore black wool frontier pants, black boots, and a brilliant blue-green long-sleeved shirt. Evelyn had not been in the real West before . . . (Rule 10)

Though Ann's attire is revealed as a work uniform, the adventure Evelyn anticipates as she arrives west for the first time foreshadows her coming romance with Ann. Though this novel is not femme/butch identified and much of the rest of the narrative dresses Ann in feminine attire, moments such as these throughout the text invite a femme/butch reading that enriches and politicizes the possibilities of the mother-daughter desire Rule is proposing. In this passage, Evelyn is quite affected by Ann's cowboy attire, and, as an image of Ann as a young boy, it couples neatly with Evelyn's sense of familial impression/memory. This moment of first impression, as well as that of the familial sort, functions significantly as a frame for a mommie-boy recognition of desire, one not evident on the bodies of two women who supposedly share a mother-daughter resemblance in the eyes of a particularly heterosexual terrain (Nevada = marriage/divorce).

Yet again, shortly after meeting Ann, Evelyn muses:

> This resemblance was, she knew, not a trick need had played on her; neither was it a miracle. Ann Childs was an accident; that was all. An accident, an il-

legitimate child, sprung full grown and female out of our All Father's racked brain. And I shall feel tender towards her if I like. (Rule 57)

In this passage, as well as others, Rule confronts the lesbian stereotype of an unfulfilled and predatory maternal figure by portraying maternal need/boy desire as a sexy rebellious adult exchange between Ann and Evelyn. Rule often parallels the notion of an illegitimate child, Ann, a child not sanctioned by heterosexual norms, with the illegitimacy of mother- daughter desire.

Rule's lesbian narrative is complicated by gender differences that inscribe the mother-daughter romance she deploys with a femme/butch mommy-boy dynamic. After their initial meeting Ann's gender identification is further made ambivalent through a series of interactions she has with her stepbrother which are far more fraternal than sisterly. Ann's gender identity is displaced by the lack of a traditional gender role (the biological mother) and by the identification of Ann with her deceased father, and her rivalry with her stepbrother for Evelyn's affections. The queer dyke twist that occurs in this lesbian romance is that mommy's boy is really, as Ann is marked in the text lest there occur a mistaken reading of her gender, a "girl-childs." Evelyn's maternal desires and Ann's gender disruptions work against desexualizing lesbian desire as nurturing mother-daughter bonding by situating the differences as sexually stimulating.

Apart from differentiating gender identifications, Rule's mother-daughter desire incorporates class differences, cross-generational desire, and sexual practice differentials. Romantically, Ann is political cartoonist, casino laborer, and rebel boy to Eve's womanliness, fragility, and passionate intellect. Materially, Ann is young enough to be Evelyn's child or, as it occurs to Evelyn, one of her male students, orphaned yet financially stable. Evelyn is a college professor, economically burdened and novice student to Ann in matters of sexual practice. Rule writes, "And it was Ann then who dominated and controlled their bodies. . . . the physical intimacies she demanded aroused every vague, animal desire in Evelyn" (169). As Ann's sexual arousal of Evelyn indicates, these differentials are not only wildly exciting, but they endlessly complicate traditional power dynamics, especially those of heterosexual hierarchies, as a crucial aspect of femme/butch mommie-boy coupling.

Rule's narrative sets out to trouble heterosexual conventions and clichés; we can understand this from the first two lines of the novel, "Conventions like clichés have a way of outliving their own usefulness. They are then excused or defended as the idioms of living." Rule rewrites clichéd heterosexuality by exposing it to a mother-daughter space of lesbian desire; a femme/butch reading begins the project of theorizing a queer dyke reclamation of this space as it further rewrites this narrative lesbian desire by pirating, by remapping, mommie-boy dynamics. Forwarding a theory of femme/butch family romance evidences that when little girls desire their mothers, and vice-versa, the space of Rule's ellipsis marks the expansion, not containment, of mothers' *and* little girls' sexuality and gender. Reading incestuous familial desire in lesbian narrative in the context of a lived queer dyke expression foregrounds this elided space of practice and theory; it rewrites the many ellipses of dominant, feminist, and lesbian discourses of gender and sexuality.

NOTES

1. In my references to incest as a sexual practice or erotic play I am fully aware of the ramifications of this trauma upon those who are survivors. This essay does not mean to make light of actual incest but rather to unravel the politicized sexual practices of familial gender and sexual roles.

2. In experientially based accounts femme/butch identification with a familial gender role and desire for taboo familial relations are often central in the articulation of the femme/butch sexual and gender identity. Though it is beyond the scope of this essay, there is need for specific analyses of femme/butch erotic modes which queer the heterosexual family romance, especially class-conscious and ethnic/racial femme/butch identities. For example, in large part, Jewish and Black expressions substantiate this essay's premise. For a few examples in which direct identification with and/or desire for familial roles are strongly in evidence, see Joan Nestle, *A Restricted Country*, Barbara Smith, "Dance of Masks," Peggy Shaw, "You Are Just Like My Father," and Esther Newton, "A Hard Left Fist." In femme/butch fictive representation this desire often permeates the narrative. See Jewelle Gomez, *The Gilda Stories*, Cherry Muhanji, *Her*, Leslie Feinberg, *Stone Butch Blues*, Chea Villanueva, *Bulletproof Butches*, Sharon Bridgforth, *The Bull Jean Stories*, or even Sheila Dabney's character Agatha in the film *She Must Be Seeing Things*. For contemporary femme/butch sexual communities that overtly play with the family romance, please see personal ads at: *www.butch-femme.com*.

3. For an informed overview of some of the political tensions that occurred within feminist and lesbian-feminist communities over what is now often historically reclaimed as queer gender and sexual practice, see Alice Echols, "The Taming of the Id: Feminist Sexual Politics 1968-1983," and B. Ruby Rich, "Feminism and Sexuality in the 1980s."

4. In the recent HBO movie *If These Walls Could Talk 2*, lesbian reproductive issues are posited as *the* contemporary political issue on a par with historical antecedents such as pre-liberation economic disenfranchisement of elderly lesbians and formative clashes between middle-class lesbian-feminist and working-class butch identities.

WORKS CITED

Bridgforth, Sharon. *The Bull Jean Stories*. Austin, TX: Red Bond Press, 1998.

Butler, Judith. *Gender Trouble: Feminism and the Subversion of Identity*. New York: Routledge, 1990.

Echols, Alice. "The Taming of the Id: Feminist Sexual Politics 1968-1983," *Pleasure and Danger: Exploring Female Sexuality*. Editor Carol Vance. New York: Routledge & Kegan Paul, 1984. 50-72.

Feinberg, Leslie. *Stone Butch Blues*. Ithaca, NY: Firebrand Books, 1993.

Gomez, Jewelle. *The Gilda Stories*. Ithaca, NY: Firebrand Books, 1991.

If These Walls Could Talk 2. Director Ann Heche. Performance Ellen Degeneres and Sharon Stone. HBO Films, 2000.

Kennedy, Elizabeth Lapovsky and Madeline Davis. *Boots of Leather, Slippers of Gold: The History of a Lesbian Community*. New York: Penguin, 1994.

She Must Be Seeing Things. Director Sheila McLaughlin. Performance Sheila Dabney and Lois Weaver. First Run Features, 1987.

Muhanji, Cherry. *Her*. San Francisco: Aunt Lute Books, 1990.

Nestle, Joan. *A Restricted Country*. Ithaca, NY: Firebrand, 1987.

_____. (Ed.). *The Persistent Desire: A Femme-Butch Reader*. Boston: Alyson, 1992.

Newton, Esther. "A Hard Left Fist." *GLQ: A Journal of Lesbian and Gay Studies* 7.1. Duke UP, 2001. 111-130.

Rich, Adrienne. "Compulsory Heterosexuality and Lesbian Existence." *Signs: Journal of Women in Culture and Society vol. 5, no. 4*. U of Chicago P, 1980. 3-32.

Rich, Ruby B. Review Essay "Feminism and Sexuality in the 1980s." *Feminist Studies 12, no. 3*. Fall 1986. 525-561.

Roof, Judith. "'This Is Not For You': The Sexuality of Mothering." *A Lure of Knowledge: Lesbian Sexuality and Theory*. New York: Columbia UP, 1991. 90-118.

Rule, Jane. *Desert of the Heart*. (1964) Tallahassee, FL: Naiad, 1983.

Shaw, Peggy. from "You're Just Like My Father." *His Hands, His Tools, His Sex, His Dress: Lesbian Writers on Their Fathers*. Editors Catherine Reid and Holly K. Iglesias. Binghamton, NY: Harrington Park P, 2001. 27-36.

Smith, Barbara. "The Dance of Masks." *The Persistent Desire: A Femme-Butch Reader*. Boston: Alyson, 1992. 426-430.

Terry, Jennifer. "Theorizing Deviant Historiography." *differences: A Journal of Feminist Cultural Studies vol. 3. no. 2.* 1991. 55-74.

Villaneueva, Chea. *Bulletproof Butches*. New York: Masquerade Books, Inc., 1997.

White, Patricia. "Films for Girls: Lesbian Sentiment and the Maternal Melodrama." *Uninvited: Classical Hollywood Cinema and Lesbian Representability*. Bloomington and Indianapolis: Indiana UP, 1999. 98-131.

There Once Was a Butch

Lesléa Newman

There once was a Butch from Toledo
Who had an enormous libido
When no one would date her
She used a vibrator
That buzzed like a giant mosquito

There once was a Butch who debated
That sex was just too highly rated
Until a Femme said,
"Honey, let's go to bed."
The next morning her views were outdated

There once was a Butch from Kentucky
Who just couldn't seem to get lucky
Until she studied Elvis
And mimicked his pelvis
And then everything was just ducky

Lesléa Newman has published 35 books, including *She Loves Me, She Loves Me Not* (short stories); *Out of the Closet and Nothing to Wear* (humor); and *Heather Has Two Mommies* (children's book). She is the editor of *The Femme Mystique, Pillow Talk: Lesbian Stories Between the Covers,* and *Bedroom Eyes: Stories of Lesbians in the Boudoir.* "There Once Was a Butch" is reprinted from her poetry collection, *The Little Butch Book.* Visit her Web site at <www.lesleanewman.com>.

"There Once Was a Butch," 1998, Lesléa Newman, from *The Little Butch Book* ©1998 Lesléa Newman, published by New Victoria Publishers, PO Box 27, Norwich, VT 05055 (www.newvictoria.com). Reprinted by permission of author and publisher.

[Haworth co-indexing entry note]: "There Once Was a Butch." Newman, Lesléa. Co-published simultaneously in *Journal of Lesbian Studies* (Harrington Park Press, an imprint of The Haworth Press, Inc.) Vol. 6, No. 2, 2002, pp. 85-86; and: *Femme/Butch: New Considerations of the Way We Want to Go* (ed: Michelle Gibson, and Deborah T. Meem) Harrington Park Press, an imprint of The Haworth Press, Inc., 2002, pp. 85-86.

There once was a Butch who required
To have all her muscles admired
Once they were all counted
She loved being mounted
But by then her poor Femme was too tired

There once was a Butch from Milwaukee
Who was so incredibly talky
'Til she took her mouth
And placed it down south
Then it was her Femme who got squawky

There once was a Butch so damn pretty
All the Femmes lusted after her clitty
She gave it away
At least ten times a day
And that is the end of my ditty.

Illustration

Yohah Ralph

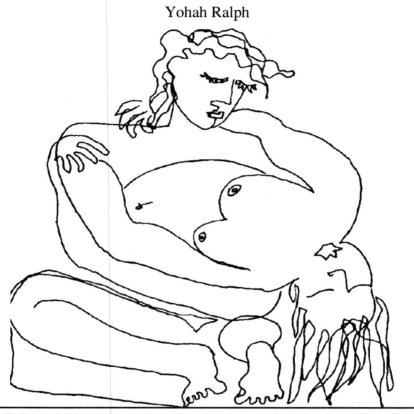

Yohah Ralph is a painter and graphic artist whose work has been exhibited in galleries and museums in New England and New York. From a studio in Easthampton, MA, she runs a fine-art business, producing paintings, prints of her artwork, silk-screened tee shirts, ceramics, and sculpture. Along with numerous awards, she has received commissions for posters, book jackets, and illustrations for publication.

©1998 Yohah Ralph, from *The Little Butch Book* ©1998 Lesléa Newman, published by New Victoria Publishers, PO Box 27, Norwich, VT 05055 (www.newvictoria.com). Reprinted by permission of artist and publisher.

[Haworth co-indexing entry note]: "Illustration." Ralph, Yohah. Co-published simultaneously in *Journal of Lesbian Studies* (Harrington Park Press, an imprint of The Haworth Press, Inc.) Vol. 6, No. 2, 2002, p. 87; and: *Femme/Butch: New Considerations of the Way We Want to Go* (ed: Michelle Gibson, and Deborah T. Meem) Harrington Park Press, an imprint of The Haworth Press, Inc., 2002, p. 87.

Female Fem(me)ininities:
New Articulations
in Queer Gender Identities and Subversion

Melanie Maltry
Kristin Tucker

SUMMARY. This article critiques the historical authentication and political legitimization of exclusively masculinized dyke identities within lesbian subcultures. Seeking to create a new analysis of performative femininity, it explores the specificity of historical and contemporary femme gender transgression and offers positionalities from which to perceive femme practices and identities as politically subversive. *[Article copies available for a fee from The Haworth Document Delivery Service: 1-800-HAWORTH. E-mail address: <getinfo@haworthpressinc.com> Website: <http://www.HaworthPress.com> © 2002 by The Haworth Press, Inc. All rights reserved.]*

KEYWORDS. Gender identities, femme, queer

The February 2001 issue of the popular lesbian magazine *Girlfriends* featured an essay entitled "The Look of Love: I Couldn't Get Laid by a Les-

Melanie Maltry received her BA from the Honors Tutorial College of Ohio University in English and Women's Studies. Kristin Tucker received her BA from Ohio University in Political Science and Women's Studies. Their research and writing focuses on historical and contemporary productions of femme gender.

[Haworth co-indexing entry note]: "Female Fem(me)ininities: New Articulations in Queer Gender Identities and Subversion." Maltry, Melanie, and Kristin Tucker. Co-published simultaneously in *Journal of Lesbian Studies* (Harrington Park Press, an imprint of The Haworth Press, Inc.) Vol. 6, No. 2, 2002, pp. 89-102; and: *Femme/Butch: New Considerations of the Way We Want to Go* (ed: Michelle Gibson, and Deborah T. Meem) Harrington Park Press, an imprint of The Haworth Press, Inc., 2002, pp. 89-102. Single or multiple copies of this article are available for a fee from The Haworth Document Delivery Service [1-800-HAWORTH, 9:00 a.m. - 5:00 p.m. (EST). E-mail address: getinfo@haworthpressinc.com].

bian–Until I Shaved My Head." The article details a young dyke's journey from long-haired datelessness into shaved-headed bliss. While mildly tongue-in-cheek in her exposition of her inability to acquire a date with her "purse, girl-jeans, and long hair," author Erin Oh ultimately affirms that, as a lesbian, these feminine signifiers need to be cast off. Taking the advice of her friend Maggie, who explains that "long hair isn't considered beautiful within the lesbian aesthetic," Oh shaves her head. Her acquisition of a girlfriend "within two weeks" of having done so confirms her success in acquiring the desired lesbian visibility needed to find a partner (48). While the story masquerades as a silly insight into lesbian culture, it also articulates a contemporary existence of a heavily policed authentic lesbian identity based on various versions of masculinity.

Although the privileging of masculinity in the development of dyke identities has a long history, it fails to accurately reflect the contemporary plurality of lesbian identities, practices, and modes of existence. Granting authenticity solely to masculinized dyke identity invalidates the identities of those who deviate from such a model and ultimately renders the existence of some invisible. Lesbians bearing the feminine signifiers so willingly cast off by Erin Oh, "long hair, girl jeans, and purses," remain invisible in the lesbian discourse, or are converted to the androgynous or masculine aesthetic privileged in young dyke culture through implicit threats of undesirability and political invalidity. Oh's article perfectly illustrates a trend in younger dyke culture to privilege masculinity, which is evidenced through the major body of work that exists analyzing various manifestations of female masculinity, including butch identification, drag king performances, and FTM transgender bodies. Not only is there a larger and more contemporary body of work on female masculinity independent of the butch-femme dyad, but as Elizabeth Kennedy asserts, in most scholarship "fems are not only less visible than butches, but also issues and problems of lesbian history are defined from a butch perspective" (16).

This article seeks to create a new analysis of performative femininity that is politically comparable to the diverse body of work on female masculinity. First, the article critiques the limitations of contemporary representations of primarily white lesbian identification through a historical analysis of the authentication and political legitimization of the "masculine lesbian" and the development of the queer social phenomenon of butch privilege. Second, it provides an analysis of various expressions of femininity within lesbian subcultures. And finally, it offers positionalities that allow for subversive femme practices and identities utilizing the theories of Judith Butler, Linda Alcoff, and Shane Phelan.

While feminine inverts participating in homogenital contact in the early 1900s and femmes in 1950s-60s bar culture were seen within their own cul-

tures as socially disruptive, as well as subversive from a contemporary perspective, little analysis has been undertaken to explore the specificity of their
transgressions. Neither has a significant amount of effort been exerted to analyze the ways in which these transgressions have historically been invalidated
as secondary to the subversion undertaken by the butch. The privileging of
masculine lesbian identities within dyke cultures can be traced from the early
1900s, reflected in Krafft-Ebing's early studies of sexual deviance. While it is
difficult to discuss the period of lesbian representation prior to bar culture in
that few lesbians were actually providing their own representations, and there
is arguably no self-identification as the cultural category "lesbian," it is still in-
structive to examine the images and analyses provided. According to Jan Zita
Grover, pulp fiction novels from the 1950s represent a perfect illustration of
sexological interpretations of "female inversion."

> Frequently, the covers of such novels depict a short, dark-haired mascu-
> line woman fully clothed, manipulating or threatening a long-haired,
> blonde, scantily clad feminine woman who is the "duped feminine in-
> vert." (172)

This dichotomy of the dark, dominant masculine invert controlling the de-
fenseless feminine woman perfectly illustrates (mis)conceptions regarding
both the gender expressions and sexualities of the characters involved. In this
representation, the feminine invert is either threatened or manipulated into the
same-sex sexual dynamic by the masculine invert. She does not then choose
her sexual expression, but is coerced into it. Another perception was that the
feminine invert expressed inversion because she had been rejected by men and
had no other option. In his work "Sexual Inversion in Women," Havelock Ellis
notes that feminine inverts "are the pick of the women whom the average man
would pass by" (qtd. in Halberstam 76). Within both of these configurations,
the feminine invert is not consciously resisting her given gender and sexuality,
but either acquiring it by default or simply misunderstanding it.

The cultural inability to read the feminine invert as an active partner in a lesbian relationship is an inability to see the feminine-looking "woman" as truly
"homosexual." In her book *Getting Specific*, Shane Phelan cites Barbara
Ponse's "principle of consistency" which "links sex assignment, gender identity, gender role, sexual object choice, and sexual identity":

> Through this linkage, "female" comes to be equated with "woman,"
> which in turn is linked to "heterosexual." Thus, a lesbian is not really a
> woman. Her gender identity conflicts with her sexual identity and this

conflict is resolved through the stereotype of the "masculine" lesbian. (61)

Thus, while the feminine invert cannot be read as "homosexual," the masculine invert cannot be read as anything *but* "homosexual." Her apparent masculinity confirms her as the innate and authentic lesbian.

The conception of the feminine invert as accidentally deviant extended into the lesbian bar culture of the mid-twentieth century in the United States, primarily in working class communities of European- and African-Americans in the urban Northeast. Bar cultures were primary centers of resistance to heteronormative culture. Yet even within this setting, fem(me)s' defined role in the lesbian communities of this time period solidified their secondary position to butches. Fem(me)s maintained an "ambivalent position in lesbian communities . . . in the sense that many butches and fems questioned whether fems were 'real lesbians'" (Kennedy 16). Fem(me)s were differentiated from butches, as the fem(me)'s perceived sexuality

> was not based on strongly internalized feelings of difference, bur rather in the commitment to a different way of life–socializing in the gay world, and having a relationship with a woman. Whereas butches had two indicators of identity–attraction to women and desire to appropriate masculine characteristics–fems had only one; logically, femininity did not set them apart from other women. Fems had to have contact with a lesbian community or a lesbian relationship to develop awareness of their difference. (Kennedy 29)

Although some fem(me) writers, such as Joan Nestle, expressed an understanding of their queer sexuality from an early age, their fem(me)inine gender expression still left their queerness open for scrutiny.

Additionally, the authentication of the butch was strengthened as she took on the primary role as public representative and actor. Although the sexual and social dynamics of butch-fem(me) were more complex than a simple queer replication of the heterosexual binary, definitive aspects of these relationships embodied the notion of separate spheres for masculinity and femininity. In their essay *"They Was No One to Mess With:* The Construction of the Butch Role in the Lesbian Community of the 1940s and 1950s," Elizabeth Lapovsky Kennedy and Madeline Davis note that

> the social pressure for clearly defined roles also grew from the increased defiance of the community, which relied particularly on the butch role. This exaggerated the difference between butch and fem and demanded

that butches perform well in defending their own and their fem's right to be a part of the world. The tough butch who could take care of business became idealized. (*Persistent* 74)

Not only were certain acts of violence directed specifically at butches (through laws regulating clothing restrictions and specific forms of violence during police raids), but an investment in masculinity propelled them towards being the public representatives of the communities. The contributions of fem(me)s, who were "responsible for making the home a comfortable refuge," became secondary largely because they took place partially, but by no means exclusively, in the private realm (Kennedy 26). This is reflected in most scholarship on butch-fem(me) history, where the accounts of assaults on fem(me)s are afforded much less attention than those describing the degradation of butch women. While most fem(me)s did not have to worry about being harassed due to the cultural acceptance of their visible gender expression, many fem(me)s' occupations as sex workers placed them in dangerous positions with the law, facing rape, harassment, and physical violence. These attacks, however, were perceived as attributable to their improper and "immoral" use of femininity, rather than to their sexuality.

Butch-fem(me) existence was harshly criticized with the advent of lesbian-feminism. However, ultimately in the post-lesbian-feminist 1990s, the butch strongly maintained her position in the lesbian discourse. Considering butch-fem(me) merely a replication of the heterosexual paradigm, lesbian-feminism sought to obliterate the confining butch-fem(me) roles. Androgyny, the new aesthetic of lesbian-feminism, sought to capture the positive qualities of both genders and embody them within the individual woman. The prescription of androgyny in lesbian-feminist attempts to politicize butch-fem(me) impacted the two lesbian genders quite differently. Lesbian-feminism frequently misread butches as men in disguise or women seeking to be men. Masculinity was perceived as being both inextricably linked to the male body as well as the very source of women's oppression. Accordingly, butches were encouraged to eliminate their masculine signifiers and resume their rightful positions as women. Because of the fem(me)'s proud display of fem(me)ininity, lesbian-feminists perceived her as a woman who did not understand her full potential as a capable and strong individual. The signifiers that she had once found powerful tools of attraction and identification became defined by lesbian-feminism as "tools of the patriarchy." Lesbian-feminists taught that high heels bound women's feet. Lipstick was a sign that women did not consider themselves beautiful and must change themselves, and it simultaneously bound women to the market as excessive capitalist consumers. Skirts and tight clothing not only made women sex objects for men, but also were a source of sexual vulnerability to men. Thus, the femme was stripped not only of her identity, but of any understanding of her identity as subversive.

Lesbian-feminism was quite effective in its obliteration of both butch and fem(me) gender expressions until their resurgence in the 1990s. While many have celebrated the re-appropriation of both roles, it has more accurately been a butch renaissance. In their article, "Bad Girls," Laura Harris and Liz Crocker cite femme Lyndall MacCowan who recognizes feminism's double-standard in the attempted erasure of gendered expressions of sexuality. She writes: "Feminism erases femme, but not butch," and asks: "How was it that butch remained named, but femme became invisible?" (94). It is precisely the lesbian-feminist demonization of femininity that permitted the butch to emerge relatively unscathed but that obliterated the femme. In her article "A Lesbian Feminist Fucks with Gender," Jennie Ruby writes that because of her feminism, femininity is "entirely associated with dishes, frailty, and weakness." In another book, *Lesbians, Levis, and Lipstick*, one interviewee writes that when she came out as a lesbian, she changed her appearance to reflect her newly recognized sexuality:

> After I came out, I started to question the clothing I wore, the style of my hair, jewelry, make-up, the playing dumb thing. I cut off all my hair, I stopped shaving my legs and armpits, I stopped wearing make-up and I literally burned my bra. I exchanged my sandals for an attractive pair of construction boots. I felt stronger, even more powerful than I had before. I wasn't playing dumb, I was playing tough. (20)

Both accounts from a feminist perspective align the signifiers of femininity (dishes, make-up, shaving, long hair, fashion) with both weakness and stupidity. Simultaneously, feminine signifiers are not merely cast off, but instead are replaced by boots, unshaven legs, and toughness. Within this construct, femininity cannot be seen as powerful because it is not androgyny that has become the ideal, but instead masculinity. As femininity and masculinity are configured within feminism, female-appropriated masculinity can at least be seen as active resistance to one's imposed feminine gender. Femininity, however, cannot be seen as resistant in any capacity.

This intellectual gulf between seeing performative masculinity as inherently subversive and performative fem(me)ininity as apolitical was widened through misinterpretations of Judith Butler's 1990 book *Gender Trouble*. In *Gender Trouble,* Butler describes gender as a "copy with no original." For Butler, gender is constructed through constant repetition both normalizing and naturalizing gender in and through the body. Butler asserts then that gender can be subverted through rupture caused by inconsistencies in the replication.

One method she identifies is drag performance. Many misinterpreted her offering of drag as *one* potential option for subversion as *the* avenue for subversion. In such a scenario, only visibly crossing the gender binary in one's drag performance (whether considered an extension of one's "real" gender or understood entirely as a performance) allows for the rupture that causes true subversion, leaving no potential for subversion for femmes.

While many read cross-gender performance as the primary means for subversion, Butler's acuteness in describing the "sexual regulation of gender" requires a focus not merely on visual signification, but on the entire discursive situation of a given subject. And this allows for far more subversive interpretations of the femme gender.

> The idea that sexual practice has the power to destabilize gender emerged from my reading of Gayle Rubin's *The Traffic in Women* . . . it sought to establish that normative sexuality fortifies normative gender. . . . Briefly, one is a woman, according to this framework, to the extent that one functions as one within a heterosexual frame and to call the frame into question is perhaps to lose something of one's place in gender . . . I belabor this point because some queer theorists have drawn an analytic distinction between gender and sexuality, refusing causal or structural link between them. But, there is a sexual regulation of gender. (xi)

When Butler cites a "causal and structural link" between sex, gender, and sexuality, she allows for theorizing methods of gender for the femme. Her assertion that "sexual practice has the power to destabilize gender" through the way in which gender and sexuality produce one another, locates the femme outside of the heterosexual construct. The femme, though sometimes appearing as a heterosexual woman, is really no "woman" at all. She is, instead, a body signifying queer acts from a queer space. Therefore the context for her sexuality and thus her gender expression is shifted entirely. Simple politics of visibility are insufficient in determining or establishing subversion. A shift from the politics of visibility to a focus on queer acts is fundamental in exploring a femme position of subversion in that such a shift gives specific attention to the position where the femme is discursively situated.

A photo spread in the lesbian pornography magazine *On Our Backs* illustrates the significance of the "causal and structural link" in one's location as well as the establishment of queer context as a site for subversion. In the photograph, the "woman" coded femme invites the "woman" coded butch to fellate her dildo (Serchuk 27). The phallic dildo, theoretically belonging to the male and historically most frequently possessed by the masculine lesbian, is in this case possessed by the femme. Additionally, the implied fellatio given to the fem(me)inine lesbian by the masculine lesbian is a violent disruption to the traditional heterosexual image of a woman sucking a man's cock. The context of the photograph in a queer location (a lesbian pornography magazine and a lesbian sex scene) causes a rupture not only of heterosexuality but also of gender. Neither the femme's possession of the phallus nor her domination of the butch are proper positions of power for a "woman" expressing fem(me)ininity.

While the significance placed on context in Butler's configuration of sex, gender, sexuality, and subversion does offer much potential for the recognition of the femme as a political actor, at least two things can be problematized. First, it could be argued that the alternate location does not necessarily cause subversion. In this case, making an important distinction between different practices of femininity within queer cultures is integral. Practices of femininity, even in explicitly queer contexts, are not all inherently politically subversive.

Femme, as a historical and political lesbian identity, is not to be confused with the contemporary configuration of the lipstick lesbian. Though both of these identities appropriate certain tenets of traditional femininity, and while both are in lesbian contexts, neither explicitly queers the femininity, and, therefore, neither disrupts femininity's normative cultural performance. In her article "How Does She Look?" Rebecca Rugg contends that

> analyses of the circulation of femme as a sign in the 1990s lesbian culture reveals femme functioning most commonly as the poster child of Lesbian Chic, promoting the vile assimilationist politics of what I mark as lipstick-lesbian culture, in which being seen as "straight acting" is taken as a high compliment. Announcing oneself as a proud femme dyke is especially complicated . . . [when] the largely white lipstick-lesbian culture is assimilationist and butch-hating. (175)

Thus, despite the fact that both the lipstick lesbian and the femme are feminine-looking "women" and both exist in "lesbian" contexts, the lipstick lesbian revels in being "straight acting." Straight acting in no way seeks to disrupt femininity or normative heterosexual practices. A non-heterosexual context does not necessarily mean that transgressive feminine acts *will be* performed; however, the queer context establishes a location where they *can be* enacted.

A second criticism of the utilization of queer context as a location for subversion is that it is still the sexual presence of another woman that marks the femme as queer and subversive. In this case, the reliance of the apparently heterosexual woman on the femme for her fem(me)ininity is equally involved in the construction as the 1950s bar femme who required a butch for her identification. Thus, a focus not only on queer femme acts must be articulated, but also a focus on the femme's individual ability to politicize herself as femme.

Since the 1950s, femmes have established themselves as possessing a distinctly different gender from that of heterosexual women. While frequently (though certainly not always), "femmes" have a similar appearance to "women," they have viewed their gender as politically transgressive, as opposed to oppressive. Many femmes have located this agency precisely in their *choice* of femininity:

> I own my femininity. I have claimed it. I choose my femininity, it does not choose me. I wear [makeup] strategically to widen the space others' perceptions of me have constructed. (Sandoval 172)

The choice of one's femininity must play a fundamental role in the future politicization of femme, and the use of Linda Alcoff's conception of intentionality helps to articulate this. In her article "Cultural Feminism versus Post-Structuralism: The Identity Crisis in Feminist Theory," Alcoff explores ways in which women can escape the patriarchal construction of femininity without merely crossing the gender binary. Alcoff critiques poststructuralism, arguing that it denies "not only the efficacy but also the ontological autonomy and even the existence of intentionality." She instead posits a positionality that focuses on "intention" as exactly the point at which oppressive and prescriptive social structures can be undermined. Subjectivity then "is produced not by external ideas, values and material causes, but by one's subjective engagement in the practices, discourses, and institutions that lend significance to the events of the world" (108). Thus, a femme's particular awareness of the ways in which femininity has been utilized to oppress women is the point at which she is no longer exclusively subject to those oppressions. While it is certainly impossible in this culture to produce a gender that is entirely outside patriarchal influence, Alcoff's conception of intentionality allows us to see that the conscious and strategic performance of gender can offer a political position from which to be subversively feminine. In her essay "Femme Dyke Slut," Tara Hardy articulates her desire to create a fem(me)ininity operating as independently as possible of patriarchally constructed femininity:

> I want to liberate femininity from its history–in my mind, in my body, and in my communities. I want to liberate it from the hands of the privileged who withhold access to it, and use it as an excuse to oppress others. I want to demolish its reputation as a cause for violation. And I want to take it from under the pestle of the dyke community and celebrate it as a radical expression of queerness. (181)

This allows for reconfigurations of the power relations between items formerly considered "tools of the patriarchy." High heels can never be simply foot-binding, and skirts do not merely accentuate the female body and place the woman in an exclusively object position.

The conception of intentionality theorized by Alcoff reflects practices that femmes have long utilized in disrupting normative practices of feminine gender. Despite the fact that femmes have for a long time articulated an awareness of their performance of themselves as "girly-girls," many have assumed their gender expressions to be emanations of an innate femininity. In a short narrative in *Femme*, Barbara Cruikshank describes an interaction with her butch partner whereby she recreates her partner sexually, yet her partner cannot do the same for her. Cruikshank tells her partner: "I can feel it when you get big. I love your big cock in me" (107). She then asks her partner to do the same for her saying: "Now what do I have? Let's say that I'm the girl." Her partner responds: "You are the girl; you're all girl. . . . You don't have to do anything different" (107). Her partner, though demanding a reinscription of her own body as masculine, refuses to reinscribe the body of her fem(me)inine partner. She assumes her partner to be inherently "girl" and thus needing no rewriting. The femme's awareness of the performativity of gender and the possibilities for its strategic employment and reinscription are what make her subversive.

Both Butler and Alcoff have articulated how gender and its subversive potential are created through acts and conscious performances. It is imperative to address how these performances function in a larger social and political context of lesbian communities. In her text *Getting Specific: Postmodern Lesbian Politics*, Shane Phelan critiques the tendency of lesbian communities to create "grand-narratives" of lesbian identity and experience which are regulated largely through a politics of visibility: "Visibility should not be the visibility of 'the lesbian,' the archetypal lesbian, but must be the visibility of lesbians in our irreducible plurality. Thus, our visibility needs to be strongly detached from the temptation to present icons of lesbianism" (96). Instead of promoting a singular image of "lesbian," one that obliterates the existence of others, Phelan emphasizes the need for "specificity" in disrupting the grand-narratives. Specificity finds politicization in the particular as opposed to the essentialized and it does so through specific attention to the location of the subject:

> [E]ach one of us is located at, and indeed *is*, the intersection of various specific discourses and structures, and . . . we each possess knowledges produced in that location. It enables us to evaluate our position in relation to those systems and to make claims based on that position without the need for hyperintellectualized epistemological claims to justify our voices and experiences. (10-11)

Phelan articulates the need to autonomously define oneself and one's communities, a move that makes the articulation of transgressive fem(me)ininities a political imperative in representing the "irreducible plurality" in our communities.

While the three theories discussed provide a very clear framework for re-articulating fem(me)ininity as subversive, creating and recognizing practices presents a greater challenge. A primary reason for the difficulty is the paucity of scholarship on and popular practice of fem(me)ininity. A far larger body of scholarship and popular practice exists on the many variations of female masculinity: butch identification, drag king performances, and FTM transgender bodies. This spans not only critical works such as Halberstam's *Female Masculinity,* but also creative work such as the photography of Catherine Opie, Del la Grace, and Loren Cameron and even popular work such as Diane DiMassa's comic *Hothead Paisan.* Additionally, the current craze of drag kinging among younger dykes creates a social culture that focuses exclusively on female masculinity. Most attention paid to the femme half of the dyad lay in an older body of literature (comprised of works by authors such as Joan Nestle, Madeline Davis, Amber Hollibaugh, and Minnie Bruce Pratt) that no longer accurately reflects the position of younger femmes on fem(me)ininity. Many of the previous generation of femmes define their sexuality in terms of their desire for and their intention to be found desirable by specifically masculine counterparts. Some younger femmes seek to liberate themselves from this dyadic history in the same way as those expressing female masculinity independent of fem(me)ininity. The remainder of this paper seeks to identify some of those transgressive femme performances which serve not as regulating icons, but as options for subversive expressions of fem(me)ininity.

Many younger femmes focus their subversion on different kinds of queer acts. Among the most popular, but probably least frequently discussed, is femmes who "strap it on." While many older femmes' sexuality focused on being the receiver of penetration, many younger femmes are comfortable with both giving and receiving, or exclusively giving. Shar Rednour, a self-defined femme, has produced a series of videos called *Hard Love and How to Fuck in High Heels.* Clad in high heels and a strap on, Rednour demonstrates fucking partners of varying genders. Femmes "strappin' it on," is closely related to the way in which b/d/s/m (bondage and domination and sadomasochism) has been a place where femmes can truly articulate themselves as powerful. B/d/s/m has been integral in allowing femmes to rewrite their sexual role as dominant and giving as opposed to submissive and receiving (though this has never been a clear cut distinction in butch-femme). B/d/s/m settings create alternate power structures in three ways. First, power in the b/d/s/m setting is always consciously negotiated and intentionally constructed. Thus, the roles are clearly understood as exclusively performative; this helps in some ways to eliminate traditional oppressive gender power structures. Second, because "top" (the partner who is dominant) and "bottom" (the partner who is submissive) are not related to one's gender expression, b/d/s/m allows for a place where one can easily choose her position in the power dynamic. Third, the two positions of b/d/s/m, though seemingly simple, really confuse traditional configurations of power. For example, while many think that the "top" is truly the one in control, many disagree, suggesting that the "bottom's" ability to stop the sex play at any point verifies her as the true holder of power. Through their redefinition of power, then, these two positions provide femmes with an easy place to defy their gender.

Another manifestation of femme subversion is through "loudness." Femmes' intentional creation of noise stands contrary to women's position in society and even femmes' position in lesbian cultures, as silent (or at least quieter). Loudness means literally making oneself heard through physical noise. It also means being vocal in the expression of one's politics, articulating oneself powerfully. Rebecca Rugg cites "loudness" as a way of uniting femmes:

> [B]y running in loudmouthed packs, we will give each other strength to put forth politics that work against assimilation and for a vision of a future that includes us and those (stereo)types we love. (188)

A good example of such political loudness is found in the performances of riot grrrl Kathleen Hanna. Although Hanna does not identify herself as femme, her performed femininity is useful in an analysis. Hanna, frequently clad in girly clothes, wails in her intentionally "little girl voice," "suck my left one."

While we previously discussed shifting the focus of subversion away from exclusively visual politics, many femme practices visually disrupt normative femininity. One potential for this kind of subversion is body modifications. An image of performance artist and author Michelle Tea provides a good example. While stereotypically feminine in many ways (Tea has glasses with sparkles, long hair in a pony tail, lipstick, and feminine looking clothing), she tweaks femininity to her liking. Her long ponytail is dyed blue, and her scant clothing reveals a number of tattoos. Both of these expressions are discordant with the idealized feminine. Many of the riot grrrls in the punk scene of the late eighties and early nineties also undertook such subversion. Frequently clad in short skirts and tight shirts, they wrote words such as "slut," "bitch," and "dyke," in large black marker either on their clothing or their bodies. This dichotomy of performed "girlyness" and disruptive, traditionally anti-feminist words literally inscribed on their bodies provides a new image for fem(me)ninity.

Recent scholarship on femme gender subversion has focused on women of size. Challenging heterosexual conceptions of an attractive female body, women of size have begun to establish a new context for dyke desirability. A conscious performance of femininity on a "super-size" body disrupts the "cult of slenderness" so historically pervasive in middle-class, white American perceptions of attractiveness. Not only do women of size work to broaden the ideas of desirability, but they also work to literally transgress the idea that feminine persons cannot take up space. Magazines like *On Our Backs* frequently feature women of size in sexual contexts that while fetishizing, do not exploit their size.

Much work remains to be done in order to bring femme into the contemporary political and theoretical discourse on gender. Viewing femme as both a legitimate lesbian identity as well as a politically and socially transgressive one, means liberating it from a long history of relegation to secondary status in favor of female masculinities. The three theories provided, a focus on queer context and acts, an understanding of intention as a viable position from which to articulate subversive fem(me)ininity, and a refusal to identify one image as authentically lesbian, create a solid foundation from which to proceed. Indeed, observing the diversity of images of younger subversive femmes, however few those images may be, is nothing if not hopeful. Lesbian communities and the broader discourse on gender must open up, must allow for "the irreducible plurality" that is us.

WORKS CITED

Alcoff, Linda. "Cultural Feminism versus Post-structuralism: The Identity Crisis in Feminist Theory." *Culture/Power/History*. Eds. Nicholas B. Dirks, Geoff Eley, Sherry B. Ortner. Princeton: Princeton UP, 1994.

Butler, Judith. *Gender Trouble: Feminism and the Subversion of Identity*. NY: Routledge, 1999.

Cruikshank, Barbara and Joan Nestle. "I'll be the Girl: Generations of Fem," *Femme: Feminists, Lesbians, and Bad Girls*. Eds. Laura Harris and Elizabeth Crocker, London: Routledge, 1997.

Davis, Madeline, Amber Hollibaugh, and Joan Nestle. "The Femme Tapes." *The Persistent Desire: A Femme-Butch Reader*. Boston: Alyson, 1992.

Grover, Jan Zita. "Dykes in Context: Some Problems in Minority Representation." *The Contest of Meaning: Critical Histories of Photography*. Ed. Richard Bolton. Cambridge: MIT P, 1989.

Halberstam, Judith. *Female Masculinity*. Durham: Duke UP, 1998.

Hardy, Tara. "Femme Dyke Slut." *Sex and Single Girls: Straight and Queer Women on Sexualities*. Ed. Lee Damsky. Seattle: Seal, 2000.

Harris, Laura and Liz Crocker. "Bad Girls: Sex, Class, and Feminist Agency." *Femme: Feminists, Lesbians, and Bad Girls*. Eds. Laura Harris and Elizabeth Crocker. NY: Routledge, 1997.

Kennedy, Elizabeth Lapovsky. "The Hidden Voice: Fems in the 1940s and 1950s." *Femme: Feminists, Lesbians, and Bad Girls*. Eds. Laura Harris and Elizabeth Crocker. NY: Routledge, 1997.

Kennedy, Elizabeth Lapovsky and Madeline Davis. *"They Was No One to Mess With*: The Construction of the Butch Role in the Lesbian Community of the 1940s and 1950s." *The Persistent Desire*. Ed. Joan Nestle. Boston: Alyson, 1992.

_____. *Boots of Leather, Slippers of Gold: A History of a Lesbian Community*. NY: Penguin, 1994.

Myers, Anna, Jennifer Taub, Jessica Morris, and Esther Rothblum. "Beauty Mandates and the Appearance Obsession: Are Lesbian and Bisexual Women Better Off?" *Lesbians, Levis and Lipstick: The Meaning of Beauty in Our Lives*. Eds. Jeanine C. Cogan and Joanie M. Erickson. NY: Hayward, 1999.

Nestle, Joan. "Flamboyance and Fortitude: An Introduction." *The Persistent Desire*. Ed. Joan Nestle. Boston: Alyson, 1992.

Nestle, Joan and Barbara Cruikshank. "I'll be the Girl: Generations of Fem." *Femme: Feminists, Lesbians, and Bad Girls*. Eds. Laura Harris and Elizabeth Crocker. NY: Routledge, 1997.

Oh, Erin. "The Look of Love: I Couldn't Get Laid by a Lesbian–Until I Shaved My Head." *Girlfriends*. February, 2001.

Phelan, Shane. *Getting Specific: Postmodern Lesbian Politics*. Minneapolis: U of Minnesota P, 1994.

Rednour, Shar and Jackie Strano. "Hard Love and How to Fuck in High Heels," S.I.R. Video, San Francisco 2000. (video).

Ruby, Jennie. "A Lesbian Feminist Fucks with Gender." *Off Our Backs*. September, 1993. 4+.

Rugg, Rebecca Ann. "How Does She Look?" *Femme: Feminists, Lesbians, and Bad Girls*. Eds. Laura Harris and Elizabeth Crocker. NY: Routledge, 1997.

Sandoval, Gaby. "Passing Loqueria." *Femme: Feminists, Lesbians, and Bad Girls*. Eds. Laura Harris and Elizabeth Crocker. NY: Routledge, 1997.

Serchuk, Michele. "The Bride Wore Latex." *On Our Backs*. August, 2000: 22-27.

Emotional Butch

Vickie Shaw

Vickie Shaw

Let's just take a moment to talk about this butch femme thing. Now, I don't want anyone getting all huffy about this. I always get women coming up to me after shows and saying crap like "I'm not butch or femme . . . I don't like to be labeled!" Oh, please!!! Look around the room! All I am saying is there are some of us that like tools a little more than the rest of us. Butches get all weird about their tools, too. My girlfriend asked me to get her a screwdriver the other day, so I got her my screwdriver . . . a butterknife! Boy, was she pissed! Why, you would have thought I had told her I wanted to be on top! I love butches, though. I dated a femme once. That was wrong on so many levels. It's against God's law! You don't have two queen bees in a hive! My girlfriend came up with a new one the other day, though. She told me I was the "Emotional Butch." And I guess I am; I'm not romantic. She is always saying stuff like, "Do you love me? Do you love me the most?" I just look at her . . . "Honey, I told you I loved you once, if I change my mind I'll let you know!"

Vickie Shaw was performing to rave reviews in the straight community club circuit for a long time before coming out. Now she is the newest gay comic sensation. Vickie is to lesbian comedy what Mary Kay is to cosmetics: cheap, but looks good in the dark (E-mail: txcom521@aol.com).

[Haworth co-indexing entry note]: "Emotional Butch." Shaw, Vickie. Co-published simultaneously in *Journal of Lesbian Studies* (Harrington Park Press, an imprint of The Haworth Press, Inc.) Vol. 6, No. 2, 2002, p. 103; and: *Femme/Butch: New Considerations of the Way We Want to Go* (ed: Michelle Gibson, and Deborah T. Meem) Harrington Park Press, an imprint of The Haworth Press, Inc., 2002, p. 103. Single or multiple copies of this article are available for a fee from The Haworth Document Delivery Service [1-800-HAWORTH, 9:00 a.m. - 5:00 p.m. (EST). E-mail address: getinfo@haworthpressinc.com].

Listening to the "Wives" of the "Female Husbands": A Project of Femme Historiography in Eighteenth-Century Britain

Liberty Smith

Liberty Smith is a doctoral candidate in Literature-Cultural Studies at the University of California, San Diego. She specializes in twentieth-century "American" literature (including literature of Anglo U.S., U.S. Latino literature, and their relationships to literatures of the Americas more broadly), and critical theory, especially queer and feminist theories. Her dissertation, "Relations of Power: Femme/Butch Articulations with the Political," addresses the collaborative political interventions of "American" femmes and butches in and through writing and intimate relations in the twentieth century. Smith is especially interested in theorizing femme along the lines of the present project and in considering the intersections of this and other queer identities with disability, race/ethnicity, and class. She is a committed teacher and activist, working consistently with students on the difficult topic of difference, and has participated in queer and women's activist projects for the past decade.

Author note: Just as I see the challenges to the heteronormativity of eighteenth-century England to be the product of collaboration and co-conspiracy, so the writing of this article has felt very collaborative. I'd like to thank my many co-conspirators in this project: First, at the University of California, San Diego, Professors Shelley Streeby and Judith Halberstam with whom the project was first developed, Professor Kathryn Shevelow (in whose excellent seminar on Charlotte Charke the project began to take shape), and Professors Michael Davidson and Nicole Tonkovich, as well as the many other friendly colleagues and collegial friends who have responded to drafts of this paper. I'd like to give special thanks to my writing group partners, Mary Gray, Omayra Cruz, Sangeeta Mediratta, and Clarissa Clò; my co-panelists, respondents, and very generous audience members at the 2000 University of Chicago Futures of the Queer Past Conference, and the 2000 UCLA QGRAD Conference; as well as the editors of this volume: Michelle Gibson and Deb Meem.

[Haworth co-indexing entry note]: "Listening to the 'Wives' of the 'Female Husbands': A Project of Femme Historiography in Eighteenth-Century Britain." Smith, Liberty. Co-published simultaneously in *Journal of Lesbian Studies* (Harrington Park Press, an imprint of The Haworth Press, Inc.) Vol. 6, No. 2, 2002, pp. 105-120; and: *Femme/Butch: New Considerations of the Way We Want to Go* (ed: Michelle Gibson, and Deborah T. Meem) Harrington Park Press, an imprint of The Haworth Press, Inc., 2002, pp. 105-120. Single or multiple copies of this article are available for a fee from The Haworth Document Delivery Service [1-800-HAWORTH, 9:00 a.m. - 5:00 p.m. (EST). E-mail address: getinfo@haworthpressinc.com].

105

SUMMARY. This article treats two of the central queer texts of eighteenth-century Britain, the autobiographical narrative of Charlotte Charke, a well-known cross-dressing actress who spent a portion of her life as a husband to another woman, and Henry Fielding's pamphlet, *The Female Husband.* Focusing on these texts, this study moves away from the traditional subject of such work–the female husbands themselves–and instead centers on the wives and lovers of these figures. In this way, the author offers a model of what she calls a project of imaginary coalition-building across time between contemporary femmes and the differently–but still queerly–desiring feminine women in Charke's and Fielding's texts. Tracing two models of queer but gender-normative feminine subjectivity in these texts, the "wife" in a same-sex companionate marriage, and the "duped woman," this article challenges assumptions by mainstream as well as queer scholars about just who should be our subjects of study and why, ultimately calling into question definitions of both "heterosexuality" and "queer." *[Article copies available for a fee from The Haworth Document Delivery Service: 1-800-HAWORTH. E-mail address: <getinfo@haworthpressinc.com> Website: <http://www.HaworthPress.com> © 2002 by The Haworth Press, Inc. All rights reserved.]*

KEYWORDS. Femme, femininity, female husband, cross-dressing, eighteenth-century Britain, Charlotte Charke, Henry Fielding

This article treats two of the central queer texts of eighteenth-century Britain, where "queer" is understood quite loosely to signify any of a number of positions (whether apparently intentional or unacknowledged) that were, in gender, desire, or another aspect of identity, non-heteronormative for this moment and this location. Specifically, I focus on the autobiographical narrative of Charlotte Charke, a well-known cross-dressing actress who spent a portion of her life as a husband to another woman, and Henry Fielding's pamphlet, *The Female Husband.* While scholars including Lillian Faderman, Terry Castle, and Judith Halberstam have already made significant strides in eighteenth- and nineteenth-century queer studies by addressing these and other texts of the female husbands, these narratives still represent an important source for new scholarship. Textual information on the *wives* of the female husbands is an especially rich but largely untapped resource in this genre; in fact, my own review of criticism on Charke's and Fielding's texts suggests that none of the ten or more articles focusing on sexuality in these works addresses the wives at any length (Faderman, Castle, Halberstam, Baruth, Campbell, Chaney,

DeRitter, Friedli, Mackie, Nussbaum, Rehder, Smith, Straub, and Trumbach). While I will not be arguing that the wives, lovers, and admirers of female husbands were either femmes or even proto-femmes, I would be disingenuous not to acknowledge that a part of the stakes of this project is to begin to construct a history in which today's femmes can participate in an imaginary coalition with such earlier figures. Like today's political coalitions that bridge a range of identity differences for the sake of particular political ends, I imagine coalitions spanning temporal difference to be another useful tool–this time not for constructing, but rather for helping us think about our political projects. I hope the present project acts as an initial location for forming such imagined coalitions.

I would further recommend a study of the wives for the ways it could expand the queer canon. For example, such work would usefully add to studies like Faderman's *Surpassing the Love of Men: Romantic Friendship and Love Between Women from the Renaissance to the Present,* in which she begins to construct a canon for a recovered "lesbian" past. Here, despite her far-reaching intentions and even her attention to cross-dressing and passing women, we find very little mention of the women who loved these figures. In addition to thus expanding the archive for some studies, I would argue that attending to the partners of female husbands could also challenge and thereby enrich other studies of female husbands. For instance, an analysis of the wives would likely usefully trouble Castle's theories on the "apparitional" or "phantasmagoric" lesbian, where figures I would call quite visible are read as apparitional and the women I argue are largely invisible (i.e., feminine "lesbians" like the partners of female husbands) are not registered at all. Further, work on the wives might have the most direct relationship to that of scholars like Halberstam who have opened up such important conversations about the relationship (or lack thereof) between sex and gender. Here, attending to the wives as well as to the husbands would enable us to broaden our understanding beyond an image of the female husbands as acting alone as they construct and experience their oppositional subjectivities, and instead allow a reading of the wives and their husbands as collaborators in their projects of challenging heteronormativity.

I would additionally suggest that an exploration of possible reasons for the differences of focus in these scholars' works and my own could be fruitful, seeming to reflect, as they do, not simply a matter of taste, but also something of the deeper theoretical interests and even assumptions on which our studies are based. In particular, I think our divergent notions of whether gender or desire (or some other aspect of subjectivity altogether) should be a primary marker of queerness might be an important starting point for understanding these differences. While for me, it makes sense that both gender and desire could mark the queerness of different kinds of queers, many other scholars, including most of those who have considered the Charke and Fielding texts, seem to focus on gender. Further, it seems that for most of these scholars, the subjects they consider as queer must possess at least a degree of self-awareness about their non-normativity. As I hope to suggest, though, what we understand as this self-knowledge—as well as what we understand as the relationship between such self-awareness and subjectivity—is likely quite a bit more complicated than we have believed. As I hope will become clear in the following pages, whatever our theoretical underpinnings, though, attention to the wives stands to open up important questions about what each understanding of sexuality allows us to see and keeps us from seeing about desire and identity generally, as well as about sexuality in the eighteenth century specifically.

To begin, as Deborah Laycock argues, the development of a marketplace centered on credit and "the associated fashion economy stimulated by credit" (128) in the seventeenth and eighteenth centuries in England, along with an expanding British empire, did much to promote popular anxiety regarding the mutability of identity and the related difficulty of maintaining class, gender, and national boundaries. While Laycock focuses on the ways these economic changes translate into cultural narratives of metamorphosis and masquerade generally, Jill Campbell and Terry Castle use Fielding as a case study to argue in part that cross-gender identification and male effeminacy are especially important locations for expressing such concerns. In their readings, the increasing popularity of the cross-dressing actress on stage and of narratives of the lives of female husbands are special cases of this phenomenon, especially as they represent a response not only to these cultural anxieties, but also to the changing material conditions of women at this time. Specifically, the growing likelihood that the needs of empire would call husbands away from their homes created the possibility that women might cross-dress in order to follow their husbands into battle (Castle in "Matters . . . ," 70-71, and Friedli). In addition, it certainly demanded that more women find their own means for economic survival. As Carolyn Woodward argues and as we might imagine, this need for women to work represented a significant difficulty in eighteenth-century Britain, for at this time "women were generally under the physical and economic control of their fathers (and sometimes their brothers) and, later, their husbands (and sometimes their sons). Few paid occupations were open to middle- and upper-class women, most of whom needed the economic protection of marriage" (843). We can easily imagine that in a situation in which the financial opportunities available to single women were so few, female-to-male cross-dressing would have offered some women an important set of economic opportunities, allowing them to work with relative freedom in the market as men, and providing them otherwise unavailable safety while traveling for work. In addition, the possibility of partnerships forming between a female husband and a normatively gendered woman would have offered even further opportunities for subverting the patriarchal nature of this economy, offering benefits to the cross-dresser as well as to her wife.

At the same time as these material shifts were occurring around the subject of the female husband herself, cultural texts were increasingly reflecting anxiety about the observer's ability to decipher the "truth" of on- and off-stage cross-dressing (and of identity generally). In her article, "The Guilty Pleasures of Female Theatrical Cross-Dressing and the Autobiography of Charlotte Charke," Kristina Straub finds, for instance, that the use of the female in drag "calls into question the naturalness of an economy of spectatorial pleasure that works on the premise of rigid boundaries between categories of gender and sexuality" (127). For her, as her title suggests, cross-dressing actresses provided their audiences an opportunity to enjoy the "guilty pleasures" of a spectacle without rigid demarcations of gender or sexuality. In her study of eighteenth-century texts of metamorphosis, Deborah Laycock also attends to the implications of a new attention to ambiguity, though she focuses less on the pleasures and more on the anxieties produced by increasingly complex and even illegible identities. She argues, "The destabilizing forces of transformation . . . were put into play. The natural body was thought to disappear, and with it, the means by which identity could be read" (136). In such an environment in which both enjoyment and anxiety circulated around an increasingly heightened degree of illegibility in identity, it makes sense to see the proliferation of novels like Daniel Defoe's 1724 *Roxana* and Fanny Burney's 1778 *Evelina*, or Jonathan Swift's 1734 poem, "A Beautiful Young Nymph Going to Bed." In each of these texts and others from throughout the century, changing material circumstances for the heroine necessitate radical changes in her public self-presentation, and in each, the authors attend meticulously both to the transformations themselves as well as to their implications for their spectators. Texts on the female husbands operate similarly; here, the wives in particular are offered as sites for commentary on the spectacle and its impact on desire and knowledge at this time of radical cultural flux.

Turning to these works, we find that along with court records and newspaper articles, two detailed accounts of the female husbands remain. Fielding's 1746 pamphlet, *The Female Husband: or the Surprising History of Mrs. Mary, alias Mr. George Hamilton,* fictionalizes the case of George (born Mary) Hamilton, who was tried for impersonating a man in a marriage to another woman. As in the case of the actual Hamilton, in Fielding's text, this court case emerged out of a clause in the vagrancy act which prohibited the use of "any subtil craft to deceive and impose on any of his Majesty's subjects" (quoted in Baker, 223). However, while the court was apparently not concerned with the gendered or sexual nature of the transgression, but rather with the fact of fraud in general, both the viciousness of the court's response (sentencing Hamilton to six months jail time and four public whippings) as well as the sensationalism of Fielding's discussion of the case, and the focus on romance in the manner of that sensationalizing, suggest the special concerns raised by the specifically queer nature of the transgression. In addition to thus meeting the demand for sensational sexual material, Fielding's text also fit well into the genre of criminal biographies so important at this moment. In this way, in addition to providing a picture of Hamilton, though as we can well imagine, a quite distorted one, Fielding's text also gives us information about the interests and anxieties of the time.

The second important text on female husbands in the eighteenth century, *A Narrative of the Life of Mrs. Charlotte Charke* by Charlotte Charke, has much in common with Fielding's text, including significant attention to the cross-dressing protagonist's intimate relationships with women. Further, it seems likely that Fielding himself made a connection between Hamilton and Charke, and, given his work with Charke in the theatrical world in the years before his publication of *The Female Husband*, used this well-known cross-dressing actress (Campbell 80 and Castle, "Matters," 79) as well as Hamilton, as models for his pamphlet. In 1755, nine years after the publication of his work, Charke published her own serialized autobiography in which she recounts her experiences as the impoverished daughter of the famous, or infamous, poet laureate, playwright and actor, Colley Cibber, from whom she was estranged. Despite its source in the author's real life, this text, like any other autobiography, is certainly shaped by authorial intention, the writing and publishing process, as well as concern for audience reception. In the case of this text, the combined effect of these forces results in a narrative in some ways quite similar to Fielding's, especially in the sensationalizing of romantic and adventurous elements of Charke's life presumably to fit literary trends. In addition, Charke also—and, given the lack of a reconciliation, apparently unsuccessfully—attempts to frame elements to fit a prodigal daughter theme, hoping thus to renew her relationship with her father. Further, she uses a tone of penitence and self-deprecating humor to influence her father in her favor via the pressures of public opinion. Charke also seems to use the picaresque as a model for her text, emphasizing as well the adventurous aspects of her experiences as an actress who was well-known in her own right, both for her on-stage success, especially in breeches parts, and for her off-stage exploits in female garb and as Mr. Brown. Also, as in Fielding's text, she stresses her struggle for economic survival. More than merely another literary tool for capturing the public's sympathies or heightening the tone of adventure in her text, this choice seems to represent a response to the realities of acting under The Licensing Act of 1737. This act, regulating and censoring all theatrical material and closing all but the two official patent theaters, along with Charke's own history of professional bridge-burning, essentially forced her out of what was a fairly promising theatrical career in established theaters and into a life as a strolling player and at times as a passing man in a series of primarily male occupations. Before continuing, I should briefly explain my use of pronouns here. While Fielding describes Hamilton as presenting himself only as male (at least after he first cross-dressed), so, despite Fielding's own slippage between male and female pronouns, I will only refer to Hamilton in the masculine. On the other hand, because throughout her text Charke identifies herself as alternatingly performing female and male genders, my discussions of her will similarly shift between references to a female Charke, the author of and sometimes figure within the narrative, and a male Mr. Brown.

While not its focus, this text, like Fielding's, also recounts Mr. Brown's romantic encounters with women, often, much as we will see when we turn to *The Female Husband,* relying on the image of the admirer/lover of the female husband as a duped innocent. However, in the case of Charke's relationship with Mrs. Brown, the woman with whom Charke lived and traveled for many years, we see another, very different representation of the counterpart of a female husband. Here, Mrs. Brown not only knows of Charke's cross-dressing, but also actively takes part in it, sometimes in her travels with Charke herself masquerading in the role of Mrs. Brown to Charke's Mr. Brown, while at other times sharing in a long-term, affectionate, and domestic partnership with a female Charke. Despite the clear importance of Mrs. Brown both as Charke's source of emotional support and as her fellow adventurer, though, as Philip Baruth notes in his introduction to a recent collection of essays on Charke, never in the text do we know her true name. Similarly, when the figure it seems likely is Mrs. Brown first enters the text, Charke does not even refer to her by the false name of "Mrs. Brown," instead referring only to "a young lady, whose tender compassion was easily moved to be the obliging messenger" (*Narrative,* Ashley edition 120). Further, and not surprisingly, even when Mrs. Brown is named, the references are subtle and center on notions of friendship and companionship rather than romantic love. For instance, Mrs. Brown is repeatedly referred to as Charke's "friend" as well as by such ambiguous descriptions as "the gentlewoman . . . that traveled with me" (224), and "my fellow sufferer" (232). Certainly, a modern reader might hope to see the level of commitment and affection between Charke and Mrs. Brown more fully fleshed out in these moments, especially given Charke's apparent willingness to portray herself in a relatively scandalous light in other ways. However, I would argue that keeping in mind Charke's fairly deep investment in using the narrative to construct a "positive" public image, it is her willingness to take the risk of being as revealing about her relationship as she is that is most telling.

That said, however, it becomes easier to understand how, without the use of some kind of intentionally perverse reading strategy like the ones I use to read the wives, some of Charke's strategies for discussing Mrs. Brown might have helped set the stage for later misreadings or complete erasures of her. For instance, we might consider the way a visit to Charke by the printer, Mr. Whyte, is described both by Whyte himself and by Fidelis Morgan in her extensive 1988 commentary on Charke's narrative. Here, not only does Whyte misrecognize a woman who it seems logical to assume is Mrs. Brown as merely a "squalid hand-maiden" (quoted in Morgan, 182). Also, though, perhaps by virtue of Whyte's description of the figure as "what otherwise was doubtful, that it was a female before us" (quoted in Morgan, 181), Morgan apparently conflates the gen-der-ambiguous older Mrs. Brown with the gender-ambiguous Charke. Ulti-mately, in this conflation Morgan erases Mrs. Brown's presence in this scene altogether, thus further contributing to the erasure of this important figure.

As is clear, Mrs. Brown certainly poses some special problems for a queer study, not only because of her somewhat marginal position in the text and her erasure in recent scholarship on Charke, but also because, as I have suggested, rather than expressing an overtly amorous relationship like that between Ham-ilton and his wives, the relationship between Charke and Mrs. Brown is repre-sented as one of "real friendship and a tender regard" (239). For some, such a discussion of friendship, along with the lack of textual or archival evidence of sex-ual desire between Mrs. Brown and Charke, combined with Mrs. Brown's gener-ally normative gender, would neutralize any possibility of reading her as queer. For others, the only possibility for imaging her as challenging heteronormativity would be via the romantic friendship model Faderman uses to describe rela-tionships between two women usually of similar (normative) genders. I find both of these models fairly limiting for discussing Mrs. Brown's queerness. In-stead, I would suggest that given her role in the narrative as Charke's advisor and judge as well as constant companion and friend, their relationship more closely matches the "companionate marriage" ideal that many scholars argue was beginning to displace traditional notions of marriage as primarily an ar-rangement for the exchange of power and resources. Lawrence Stone, who popularized this term in his crucial text on the subject, argues that the shift to the companionate model, in addition to marking a change in the emotional tenor of relationships, also "demanded a reassessment of power relations be-tween the sexes since it depended on a greater sense of equality and sharing" (225). Throughout the narrative, Charke and Mrs. Brown certainly seem to dis-play such an egalitarian notion of power, sharing equally in their few financial successes and many economic hardships, and in the plans that lead to both. While Stone expresses great optimism about the effects of the companionate relationship between a man and a woman for challenging heteropatriarchal relations and for improving the quality of life for women generally, in their own studies of eighteenth-century marriages, on the other hand, William C. Horne, Lynne Friedli, and Susan Moller Okin all argue that this model actually functioned to solidify the woman's role as mother, as well as ensuring her place in the home. In essence, they argue the companionate model was an important factor in introducing the "angel in the house" image of women that would become so oppressive in the Victorian period.

Although generally I follow these authors in challenging a reading of this model as liberatory, I would argue that when two women take up a companionate relationship, as I suggest Charke and Mrs. Brown do, its functions can be very different from those of heterosexual companionate marriages, often including elements fairly subversive to the patriarchal order. For instance, when Mrs. Brown is named in an inheritance, both she and Charke decide together how best to gain access to these funds. Charke writes: "I consulted my pillow what was best to be done, and communicated my thoughts to my friend. Upon which we concluded, without speaking a word to anybody, both to set out and fetch the money, according to order from her relation" (232). This scene is important as an example of the collaborative, egalitarian nature of this relationship. Also, though, given that Charke can deliberate about the matter on her pillow and immediately communicate those thoughts to Mrs. Brown, it suggests the two are bed-partners. Further, this scene has been extremely important for the rather telling problems it has represented for recent critics, myself included. First, Morgan performs yet another homophobic mistranscription of the text she herself edited, stating, "In her own, unwitting defence, Charlotte gives one tiny indication that when she was traveling with Mrs. Brown, the two women slept separately, for she 'consulted my pillow what was best to be done. And communicated my thoughts to my friend'" (205). Here, by breaking what was one sentence into two, mistakenly inserting a period between the words "done" and "and," Morgan stresses a supposed time lag between Charke's deliberations and her discussion with Mrs. Brown, thereby attempting to prove the two did not share a bed, a misreading according to my understanding of the text. Philip Baruth provides another tellingly troubled reading of this scene, this time suggesting that by taking an active role in claiming the legacy Charke "simply assumes the traditional male role here. . . . It is a role Charke plays to the hilt" (47). While this interpretation does some important work for drawing out Charke's own agency in this moment, it also leaves Baruth little option but to conclude as he does that "Mrs. Brown becomes an absolutely passive partner" (48). Certainly, such a conclusion is at odds with the present study, and later in his argument Baruth himself apparently recognizes the unnecessary disempowerment of such a reading of Mrs. Brown, arguing the two are merely performatively critiquing the traditional patriarchal imbalance of power with their extreme displays of misogyny on Charke's part and utter submission on Mrs. Brown's. While this notion of performativity does much to reposition Mrs. Brown as a complex figure with some agency, I would suggest this scene offers even more in this regard. Specifically, in my own early readings of this scene, I made the mistaken assumption that inheritance laws at this time would have necessitated that a male relation collect the funds for Mrs. Brown, thus explaining Charke's role in the affair. That not being the case, however, the reasons for Mrs. Brown's decision to allow Charke to be involved in this project are quite ambiguous, involving the operation of a *preference* to work with Charke as opposed to a clear material incentive, something that again underscores both Mrs. Brown's choiceful position in the text as well as her investment in the kind of sharing of resources that would be expected in the companionate relational model. Further, in the at least partial transition in the eighteenth century from traditional intimate relationships of extremely hetero*geneous* interests, backgrounds, education, and temperament to companionate relationships based in part on homo*geneity* and nominally on equality, we find a more profound transition from something like a hetero*sexual* to a homo*sexual* logic, suggesting that even relationships between a biological man and woman had increasingly more in common with those between a woman and her female husband.

Of course, whatever work the companionate nature of Mrs. Brown and Charke's relationship does to question the primacy of the heteronormative and to subvert patriarchal exchanges of power, in order to discuss an overtly non-normative *desire* in these texts we must turn to the figure of the duped woman. This figure occurs (primarily in Fielding's text) apparently in part as a facet of the sensationalizing of the Hamilton and Charke events. In particular, while Fielding emphasizes the sexual desires and pleasures of Hamilton's partners, when addressing Hamilton's concerns and desires, he expresses them as primarily economic rather than sexual. In this way, Fielding marks the wives as duped innocents, taken advantage of economically, as well as sexually, by the female husbands. Though this specific formulation of the duped woman is potentially anachronistic for this moment, the notion of "heterosexual" women unknowingly falling in love with female husbands in the eighteenth century certainly has much in common with nineteenth- and twentieth-century sexological and popular discussions of feminine lesbians as duped, confused, or misguided straight women. For example, we might recall the depictions of the feminine woman with non-normative desires in the sexological text, "Studies in Feminine Inversion" by F. W. Stella Browne, or in Radclyffe Hall's novel, *The Well of Loneliness*. Although, as I have suggested, other scholars do not attend to the duped woman as queer at all, instead either ignoring her completely or operating on the notion that her duped position means she is devoid of anything that could be useful for a queer reading, I argue ultimately that this figure represents an especially rich location for considering queerness in these works. Specifically, in Charke's and Fielding's texts, the duped woman is multiply queered by the openness and strength of her desire, the non-normativity of her object of desire, as well as her odd relationship to knowledge about that desire.

While the wives and lovers of female husbands themselves are generally described as "normal" women, the very strength of their apparently normative desire gives us some reason to question this construction. For instance, in Charke's narrative, the young "orphan heiress" (107) and her pursuit of Charke through her servant are depicted as unquestionably unusual both for the strength of feeling they suggest and for the ends to which their strength drives the heiress. If this attraction to and pursuit of the female husband is strong here, it is even stronger in Fielding's text where women like the sixty-eight-year-old widow Rushford sometimes very actively pursue Hamilton. About the widow's seduction, Fielding writes, "taking her [Hamilton] for a beautiful lad of eighteen, she [Rushford] cast the eyes of affection on her, and having pretty well outlived the bashfulness of youth, made little scruple of giving hints of her passion of her own accord" (9). As Sheridan Baker and others have noted, the similarities between the widow Rushford (or Widow "Rush-for-it") and the common eighteenth-century figure of the older lustful woman—like William Congreve's Lady Wishfort in *The Way of the World*—are unmistakable and only further underscore the inappropriate desire of this figure. This does not suggest, however, that as something of a stock character the widow's desire is normal or to be expected; on the contrary, it is the very laughable impropriety or queerness of this character's desire (given her age, adamance, and her reversal of traditional roles of the woman as pursued and the man as pursuer), that functions to mark her as a stock character in the first place. In addition, in Fielding's text the extremity of the wives' level of contentment in their romantic choice is also a marker of sexual transgression. In fact, in the cases of both of Hamilton's wives, it is the wives' bragging about their luck in finding such an "accomplished" partner that leads to Hamilton's discovery. Here, the wives' extraordinary claims inspire great jealousy on the part of their friends and families, who respond by suggesting that their friends' claims must be untrue. Mary Price's mother, for instance, upon hearing her daughter talk about how satisfied she is, declares "O child, there is no such thing in human nature" (20). In addition to expressing such jealousy, this exclamation serves to reveal just the kind of anxiety around the destruction of or indifference to "natural" categories the female husbands and their partners create, thus ironically anticipating just the kind of anti-essentialist argument about gender that queer scholars would make hundreds of years later.

Of course, the fact of the gender transgression of the husbands also adds an important element to the transgressive desire of the wives. Whether or not the wives recognize their partner's sex (and I will show that this question is much more difficult to answer than we might imagine), both texts repeatedly–if unconsciously–demonstrate that the wives desire the "something odd" (Fielding, 14) of their husbands' non-normative masculinity. In Charke's text, this is only suggested. For instance, we find that one of Mr. Brown's admirers had found no man attractive before meeting him; thus we might wonder what attributes Mr. Brown might have (or not have) to merit this rare attention. In Fielding's text, the genderedness of the female husband's oddness is clearer still. At times this is marked by Hamilton's hyper-masculinity and special prowess bragged about by his wives and provided with the much referred to "wherewithal" (11), or dildo, Hamilton uses. Importantly for our purposes, though, Hamilton's oddness is as often marked by suggestions of an underlying femininity, as when it is noted that Hamilton is beardless (10), a bit effeminate (10), or even when the widow Rushford, upon discovering Hamilton's sex, says, "I always thought indeed your shape was something odd, and have often wondered that you had not the least bit of beard" (14). Certainly this attraction despite (or more often, *to*) the "something odd" in Charke's and Hamilton's genders suggests that their admirers desire a specifically non-normative masculinity, even when they seem to believe that non-normativity belongs to a biological male.

In addition to the role of the non-normativity of their objects of desire, the wives' complicated position of knowing and unknowing, acceptance and disavowal, similarly functions to mark their queerness. While both texts provide examples of these conflicts between epistemology and ontology, in the interests of time, I will only consider one such moment from Charke's narrative. Here, the unnamed kinswoman of Charke's employer, Mrs. Dorr, is the duped woman. When Charke reveals her sex to the kinswoman, she replies, "No, truly, I believe I should hardly be enamoured with one of my own sect" (163-164). In addition to marking her as of limited intellectual or at least verbal resources generally, and thus suggesting she might be predisposed to being duped, this passage also gives us a clue to the kind of desire this figure exhibits. In this moment of conflict between what she knows and what is "real," the kinswoman performs a strange twist of logic, simultaneously affirming her desire for Mr. Brown–she admits she is enamored–while also disavowing it as a Sapphic desire–because she does not acknowledge she is enamored "with one of her own sect." Of course, this only occurs by denying what we know to be "really true," that Mr. Brown is in fact one of this woman's own "sect." Whatever her protestations, and regardless of whether she even believes them or not, then, in the very possibility that Mr. Brown could be female lies a crucial questioning of his masculinity, a questioning that ultimately marks not only Charke's gender–but also the kinswoman's desire–as queer. Further, her willingness and ability to perform this gesture of disavowal suggests something important about the nature of both knowledge and identity for the duped woman. First, if such an elaborate maneuver as this concentrated suspension of disbelief is needed to maintain heterosexuality in this instance, we might be led to wonder about the "virility" of the construction of heterosexuality generally. Further, these conflicts between knowledge and willful unknowledge raise questions about just how duped the duped woman is, and about how crucial this fiction is for her or any lover in constructing a desiring self (and even an other to desire); and, again, such questioning also leads to reflection about the role of knowledge and unknowledge for desire and being generally.

While the two texts are rich with further examples of the queerness of the wives and lovers of female husbands, in the interests of space, rather than continuing to enumerate them, I will close by returning to the queries and concerns with which I began this article, drawing some provisional conclusions. First, in the shift in focus from the female husbands to their wives this study represents, I believe we are especially well positioned to "queer" heterosexuality. As I have shown, this occurs in Mr. and Mrs. Brown's queering of the heterosexual (if not yet heteronormative) paradigm of the companionate marriage. Further, though, we are led to ask how straight heterosexuality can be if what is actually being desired in heterosexual *form* is truly homosexual *content,* and even if such a distinction between form and content or heterosexual and homosexual makes sense any more at all. In other words, if arguably heterosexual figures like Molly Price or Mrs. Dorr's kinswoman can so clearly express love and desire for their cross-dressing partners, and if, as I have argued, this love is marked by an attraction to the "something odd" of femaleness within their lover's masculinity, and if it is that very attraction to masculinity (whatever else it contains) that defines the wives as heterosexual in the first place, we must ask what on earth heterosexuality can mean. In addition to thus calling attention to the tenuous and constructed nature of heterosexuality, the wives of the female husbands also question central assumptions about the meaning(s) of queerness. First, the gender (but not desirous) normativity of the wives forces us to decouple gender and sexuality, instead understanding these women relationally; their attractions, their choices of partners, and thus their relationships are all that mark their queerness. Further, since the wives in these texts assume such varied and complicated positions *vis-à-vis* these relationships–some claim to believe they are simply in love with a man; some notice they may love a non-normative man, but a man nevertheless; and some, like Mrs. Brown seem content in a queer companionate marriage with a (sometimes) female husband–we are also precluded from using these desires to define the wives in a reductionist way as unequivocally Sapphic, lesbian, or even queer. Further, along the lines of Madeline Davis's description of present-day feminine lesbians as "women who look and act like girls and who desire girls. We're just the queerest of the queers" (270), the epistemologically tricky and "queerest of queer" desires of the duped women in these texts necessitate that we rethink some of our basic assumptions about not only what constitutes desire, but also what constitutes knowledge, and most interestingly, about what the relationship is between knowledge and desire. Finally, in addition to thus opening up such new lines of questioning, the preceding pages have been a place for me to explore my own curiosity about the wives of female husbands. I believe this in itself is important, for, as femme theorist and historian Joan Nestle explains, "Curiosity builds bridges between women and between the present and the past. . . . Curiosity is not trivial; it is the respect one life pays to another" (140).

WORKS CITED

Ashley, Leonard R. N. Introduction. *A Narrative of the Life of Mrs. Charlotte Charke (Youngest Daughter of Colley Cibber, Esq.) Written by Herself.* Charlotte Charke. Ed. Leonard Ashley. Gainesville: Scholars' Facsimiles & Reprints, 1969. vii–xxiv.

Baker, Sheridan. "Henry Fielding's *The Female Husband*: Fact and Fiction." *PMLA* 74.3 (1959): 161-224.

Baruth, Philip E. Introduction. *Introducing Charlotte Charke: Actress, Author, Enigma.* Ed. Philip E. Baruth. Urbana: U of Chicago P, 1998. 9-62.

Browne, F.W. Stella. "Studies in Feminine Inversion." *Sexology Uncensored: The Documents of Sexual Science.* Eds. Lucy Bland and Laura Doan. Chicago: U of Chicago P, 1998. 61-66.

Burney, Frances. *Evelina.* London: Penguin, 1994.

Campbell, Jill. " 'When Men Women Turn': Gender Reversals in Fielding's Plays." *The New Eighteenth Century.* Eds. Felicity Nussbaum and Laura Brown. NY: Methuen, 1987. 62-83.

Castle, Terry. *The Apparitional Lesbian: Female Homosexuality and Modern Culture.* NY: Columbia UP, 1993.

_____. " 'Matters Not Fit To be Mentioned': Fielding's The Female Husband." Terry Castle. *The Female Thermometer: Eighteenth Century Culture and the Invention of the Uncanny.* NY: Oxford UP, 1995. 68-81.

Chaney, Joseph. "Turning to Men: Genres of Cross-Dressing in Charke's *Narrative* and Shakespeare's *The Merchant of Venice.*" *Introducing Charlotte Charke: Actress, Author, Enigma.* Ed. Philip E. Baruth. Urbana: U of Chicago P, 1998. 200-226.

Charke, Charlotte. *A Narrative of the Life of Mrs. Charlotte Charke (Youngest Daughter of Colley Cibber, Esq.) Written by Herself.* Ed. Leonard Ashley. Gainesville: Scholars' Facsimiles & Reprints, 1969.

Congreve, William. *The Way of the World.* Ed. Trevor R. Griffiths. London: Nick Hern, 1995.

Davis, Madeline. "Epilogue, Nine Years Later." *The Persistent Desire: A Femme-Butch Reader.* Ed. Joan Nestle. Boston: Alyson, 1992. 270-271.

Defoe, Daniel. *Roxana.* London: Penguin, 1987.

DeRitter, Jones. " 'Not the Person She Conceived Me': The Public Identities of Charlotte Charke." *Sexual Artifice: Persons, Images, Politics.* Eds. Ann Kibbey, Kayann Short, and Abouali Farmanfarmaian. NY: NYU Press, 1994. 3-25.

Faderman, Lillian. *Surpassing the Love of Men: Romantic Friendship and Love Between Women from the Renaissance to the Present.* NY: William Morrow, 1981.

Fielding, Henry. *The Historical Register of the Year 1736.* Lincoln: U of Nebraska P, 1967.

_____. *The Female Husband* (1746). Ed. Claude E. Jones. Liverpool: Liverpool UP, 1960.

Friedli, Lynne. " 'Passing Women': A Study of Gender Boundaries in the Eighteenth Century." *Sexual Underworlds of the Enlightenment.* Eds. G.S. Rousseau and Roy Porter. Chapel Hill: U of North Carolina P, 1988. 234-60.

Halberstam, Judith. *Female Masculinity.* Durham and London: Duke UP, 1998.

Hall, Radclyffe. *The Well of Loneliness.* NY: Doubleday, 1990.

Hitchcock, Tim. *English Sexualities, 1700-1800.* NY: St. Martin's, 1997.

Horne, William C. *Making a Heaven of Hell: The Problem of the Companionate Ideal in English Marriage Poetry, 1650-1800.* Athens: U of Georgia P, 1993.

Laycock, Deborah. "Shape-Shifting: Fashion, Gender, and Metamorphosis in Eighteenth-Century England." *Textual Bodies: Changing Boundaries of Literary Representation.* Ed. Lori Hope Lefkovitz. NY: SUNY Press, 1997. 127-160.

Mackie, Erin. "Desperate Measures: The Narratives of the Life of Mrs. Charlotte Charke." *ELH* 58 (1991). 841-865.

Morgan, Fidelis. *The Well-Known Troublemaker.* Ed. Fidelis Morgan. London: Faber and Faber, 1988.

Nestle, Joan. "The Femme Question." *The Persistent Desire: A Femme-Butch Reader.* Ed. Joan Nestle. Boston: Alyson, 1992. 138-146.

Nussbaum, Felicity. Afterword. *Introducing Charlotte Charke: Actress, Author, Enigma.* Ed. Philip E. Baruth. Urbana: U of Chicago P, 1998. 227-243.

_____. *Torrid Zones: Maternity, Sexuality, and Empire in Eighteenth-Century English Narratives.* Baltimore and London: The Johns Hopkins UP, 1995.

Okin, Susan Moller. "Women and the Making of the Sentimental Family." *Philosophy and Public Affairs* 2.1 (1981): 65-88.

Rehder, Robert. Introduction. *A Narrative of the Life of Mrs. Charlotte Charke.* Charlotte Charke. Ed. Robert Rehder. London: Pickering & Chatto, 1999. ix-liii.

Smith, Sidonie. "A Narrative of the Life of Charlotte Charke: The Transgressive Daughter and the Masquerade of Self-Representation." *A Poetics of Women's Autobiography: Marginality and the Fictions of Self-Representation.* Bloomington: Indiana UP, 1987. 102-122.

Stone, Lawrence. *The Family, Sex and Marriage in England 1500-1800.* Abridged ed. NY: Harper Colophon, 1979.

Straub, Kristina. "The Guilty Pleasures of Female Theatrical Cross-Dressing." *Sexual Suspects: Eighteenth-Century Players and Sexual Ideology*. Princeton: Princeton UP, 1992. 127-150.

Swift, Jonathan. "A Beautiful Young Nymph Going to Bed Written for the Honour of the Fair Sex." *British Literature: 1640-1789, An Anthology*. Ed. DeMaria, Robert, Jr., Cambridge: Blackwell Publishers, Inc. 652-654.

Trumbach, Randolph. "London Sapphists." *Body Guards: The Cultural Politics of Gender Ambiguity*. Eds. Julia Epstein and Kristina Straub. London: Routledge, 1991. 112-41.

Woodward, Carolyn. " 'My Heart So Wrapt': Lesbian Disruptions in Eighteenth-Century British Fiction." *Signs* 18.4 (1993): 838-865.

I'll Set You Straight!

Suzanne Westenhoefer

Are you butch or femme? If you don't know by now, ask me and I'll set you straight!

Suzanne Westenhoefer has played to sell-out crowds all over North America. She both hosted and performed at the International Montreal Comedy Festival. Suzanne recently headlined with Eric McCormack (*Will & Grace*) at the famous Improv Club in Hollywood. She is currently shooting a major role in the feature film *A Family Affair*. Suzanne's the girl next door and the brazen hussy. A quick-witted personality, her material keeps changing–sometimes on the spot. She loves her audience even as she ribs them. Suzanne makes her home in Los Angeles, and she is currently developing her new special for HBO entitled *TOUR DE FEMME!* Suzanne's official Web site is <http://www.westenhoefer.com/pages/homepage.html>.

[Haworth co-indexing entry note]: "I'll Set You Straight!" Westenhoefer, Suzanne. Co-published simultaneously in *Journal of Lesbian Studies* (Harrington Park Press, an imprint of The Haworth Press, Inc.) Vol. 6, No. 2, 2002, p. 121; and: *Femme/Butch: New Considerations of the Way We Want to Go* (ed: Michelle Gibson, and Deborah T. Meem) Harrington Park Press, an imprint of The Haworth Press, Inc., 2002, p. 121. Single or multiple copies of this article are available for a fee from The Haworth Document Delivery Service [1-800-HAWORTH, 9:00 a.m. - 5:00 p.m. (EST). E-mail address: getinfo@haworthpressinc.com].

Thoughts on Lesbian Genders
in Contemporary Chinese Cultures

Helen Hok-Sze Leung

SUMMARY. This article introduces readers to the debates on lesbian genders in Chinese cultures. Through an analysis of the dynamics of the *tongzhi* movement, as well as ethnographic and literary works not currently available in English translation, the article hopes to instigate dialogues between lesbian studies in diverse cultural contexts. *[Article copies available for a fee from The Haworth Document Delivery Service: 1-800-HAWORTH. E-mail address: <getinfo@haworthpressinc.com> Website: <http://www.HaworthPress.com> © 2002 by The Haworth Press, Inc. All rights reserved.]*

KEYWORDS. Lesbian, gender, China, culture

TONGZHI POLITICS AND THE BUTCH/FEMME QUESTION

I used to believe that an "originary" image of a woman inhabits the heart of every man's life, and he would end up loving a woman who comes closest to this image. Even though I am a woman, the "originary" image deep inside me is also that of a woman. Like a beautiful fantasy arising at the moment of cold death, it permeates and then disappears

Helen Hok-Sze Leung received her PhD in Comparative Literature from the University of Wisconsin-Madison. She is Assistant Professor in the Department of Women's Studies at Simon Fraser University in Canada.

[Haworth co-indexing entry note]: "Thoughts on Lesbian Genders in Contemporary Chinese Cultures." Leung, Helen Hok-Sze. Co-published simultaneously in *Journal of Lesbian Studies* (Harrington Park Press, an imprint of The Haworth Press, Inc.) Vol. 6, No. 2, 2002, pp. 123-133; and: *Femme/Butch: New Considerations of the Way We Want to Go* (ed: Michelle Gibson, and Deborah T. Meem) Harrington Park Press, an imprint of The Haworth Press, Inc., 2002, pp. 123-133. Single or multiple copies of this article are available for a fee from The Haworth Document Delivery Service [1-800-HAWORTH, 9:00 a.m. - 5:00 p.m. (EST). E-mail address: getinfo@haworthpressinc.com].

123

from my reality. I believed that this image is life's utmost perfection. I be-
lieved in it for four years. I spent all of my university years, all of my hon-
esty and courage towards life, believing in this image.

Thus begins *Crocodile's Journal*, the first novel by the late Taiwanese author
Chiu Miao-chin that was instrumental in launching a distinctly new lesbian
culture and community in Taiwan during the 1990s. Chiu's tragic suicide in
1995 further reinforced the legendary status of her works and practically
crowned Chiu as the martyr-saint of Taiwan's fledgling lesbian community
(*Babylon* 141-2). Not only are these famous opening lines already evocative of
Chiu's signature aesthetic, but their implicit comparison of the desiring lesbian
subject to a heterosexual male lover also foreshadows some of the most con-
tentious debates around lesbian genders in the *tongzhi* movement today.
Tongzhi, literally "comrade," is now the most common identity label around
which sexual minorities in Taiwan, Hong Kong, Mainland China, as well as
some overseas Chinese communities in Southeast Asia and North America,
are organized. The term is not without its critics and detractors, many of
whom, like Taiwan's Lin Xianshou and Hong Kong's Anson Mak, have made
compelling arguments against its usage (Lin 38-42; Mak 21-33). The very
strength of *tongzhi*–its ability to instill a sense of *esprit du corps* amongst a diverse constituency–often also becomes an obstacle, as the (some will argue,
false) sense of unity threatens to erase differences which are not easily recon-
cilable. One of the most divisive of these differences is the issue of queer gender identification. The recent publication of the proceedings of the 1998
Tongzhi Conference–an annual or biannual gathering of sexual minorities
from Chinese communities–documents a deep tension that has always been
felt, even when it may not have found explicit articulation, in the *tongzhi* community. The 1998 conference, organized around the theme of "unity," was be-
set with disagreements between different groups, most notably–though not
exclusively–between gay men on the one hand, and lesbian and bisexual
women on the other. While many of the gay male organizers felt that they went
out of their way to accommodate panels on women's issues, their presumably
good intentions completely misfired and were perceived by many queer
women as acts of tokenism or even ghettoization. One panel in particular, entitled "The Gender Roles of *Tongzhi* Women," which addressed the issues of
butch/femme roles and their local inflections in Taiwan, Hong Kong, and
Mainland China (Loo 153-162), drew severe criticism from some prominent
lesbian activists who argued that the organizers favored a panel that perpetu-
ates received stereotypes about lesbian role-playing while the question of 1/0
roles (roughly equivalent to top/bottom distinction) amongst gay men was
"exempt" from such limelight (Loo 371). Others, however, felt that the panel

was worthwhile precisely because it provided an opportunity to examine the complex relationship between queer gender identification and dominant ideologies as well as the nuanced local variations of queer gender categories (Loo 254-258).

Some of the differences that erupted at the 1998 conference had led to productive self-reflection in the *tongzhi* movement. The 1999 conference, for instance, focused on "diversity" in an attempt to critically reexamine the romanticized politics of "unity." The contention over the butch-femme panel, however, points to a more complicated set of dynamics. First of all, as most of the *tongzhi* movement organizers and participants are very well-versed in debates on queer issues in North America, their arguments are informed, willy-nilly and simultaneously, by almost half a century's debates on butch/femme, from the 70s feminists' critique, to Joan Nestle's famous reclaiming of butch/femme relationships in the 50s as a historically important and sexually courageous practice, to more recent works such as that of Judith Halberstam on female masculinity and Lesléa Newman on femme subjectivity that seek to theorize gender diversity amongst queer subjects. Furthermore, while these debates often take place within lesbian and/or feminist circles in North America, they are complicated here by the context of a movement which purportedly represents all sexual minorities. At the same time that it is deeply influenced by these debates, the *tongzhi* movement also retains a certain distance from them as it seeks to define itself in culturally specific terms. One of the most productive interventions by *tongzhi* politics into butch/femme debates is the exploration of local categories of lesbian gender identification that are not reducible to the category of butch-femme. Finally, since there has been very little systematic and comparative documentation of same-sex relations between women in historical or contemporary Chinese communities, many of the disagreements within the movement arise out of different lived experiences that are unanchored in their specific social and historical contexts.

Given these complex dynamics, it would indeed be an enormous and difficult task—one which would demand sustained and collaborative efforts—to explore the question of lesbian genders in Chinese cultures and communities. In this article, I would like to attempt a very modest beginning to such efforts by identifying a range of relevant material and pointing to various possible entries into the question.

SCATTERED ETHNOGRAPHIES

One important entry into the question of lesbian genders in Chinese communities is an investigation into the process of subject formation. Much of the contention surrounding the discussion of butch/femme roles, as evidenced by the incident at the 1998 *Tongzhi* Conference, arises out of different interpretations of the relation between queer subject formation and the dominant ideology of heterosexual genders. Petula Sik-Ying Ho's nuanced study of gay male subject formation in Hong Kong since the 1980s provides a valuable theoretical model of queer subject formation. Ho traces a genealogy of multiple and intersecting discourses on homosexuality in Hong Kong and shows that gay male subjectivity is continually being constituted by discursive practices that are constantly in negotiation with each other. According to this logic, it would be missing the point to argue whether lesbian gender identification such as that of butch/femme is a "mystified" (in ideological terms) reproduction of heterosexual gender roles or a matter of autonomous lesbian agency. A much more productive model of inquiry would explore how different discursive processes, including that of the dominant gender system as well as that of queer appropriations, are in negotiation with each other in specific contexts. Unfortunately, as is the case in so many other cultural contexts such as those documented by Evelyn Blackwood and Saskia E. Wieringa (39-66), the study of female same-sex relations in Chinese communities are far overshadowed by, if not made completely subservient to, the study of male homosexuality. While a number of theoretically engaged studies have recently emerged in Taiwan (Cheng; Tsang; Zhang; Zhao), there have only been sporadic and scattered ethnographic efforts to study lesbian communities in Hong Kong (Chou; Lam) and Mainland China (Li). The data from these studies provide some interesting points of departure for further studies.

In a brief and schematic discussion, Wang Qingning compares the dynamics of gender identification in three different Chinese lesbian cultures:

> The gender role-playing amongst *tongzhi* women refers to the roles of T [tomboy] or *po* [wife] (or butch and femme). In Hong Kong, the T/*po* roles are very prominent. In Taiwan, some make such distinctions, some don't. In Mainland China, one rarely hears of such role-playing. The Hong Kong scene resembles the T-bar scene in Taiwan during the 1980s . . . In Taiwan, *tongzhi* women who went through their university years during the 90s, and who were influenced by feminism, either don't engage in gender role-playing at all or they make minute distinctions in gender categories (such as little T, more prone to T, more prone to *po,* etc.). In Mainland China, due to the influence of the Cultural Revolution, women are already under pressure to look androgynous. In addition, they live in a social context where most people are ignorant of homosexuality, so they tend to relate to each other without specific gender role-playing. (Loo 256)

Wang's characterization generally corresponds to the conclusions of the few ethnographic studies available. However, there is also an interesting contradiction between the ethnographers' professed beliefs and the ethnographic material they present. Wang's characterization of the Hong Kong scene–where gender role-playing is most salient–as a mirror of Taiwan's past implicitly constructs a narrative of progress according to which butch/femme role-playing is perceived to be old-fashioned or even pre-feminist. Such a sentiment is also echoed in Chou Wah-Shan's work on *tongzhi* women in Hong Kong:

> Mainstream (heterosexual) media always interpret homosexual love from a heterosexual perspective. Whenever they encounter a *tongzhi* woman, they never forget to ask if she plays the male role (Tomboy/TB) or female role (Tomboy girl/TBG), as though *tongzhi* women must fit into one or the other. Amongst local lesbian couples, a very high percentage distinguishes between TB and TBG. I interviewed five *tongzhi* women from different walks of life and they all claim that over 70% of the lesbians they know clearly distinguish between TB and TBG (*Hong Kong Tongzhi* 106).

For Chou, the distinction between TB and TBG is both a stereotype (a "heterosexual perspective") and a salient self-identification amongst *tongzhi* women in Hong Kong. Yet, Chou does not theorize the relation between the two. Is such lesbian self-identification a reproduction of the "heterosexual perspective"? Why is TB/TBG role-playing a "stereotype" if over 70% of lesbian couples actually practice such role-playing? Even more suggestively, out of the case studies presented by Chou, only *one* affirms her TB identity, though more as a sexual (i.e., an indication of what one enjoys in bed) rather than gender identity (113). All the others are extremely critical of TB/TBG roles. One claims that she is "misidentified" as a TB because she enjoys wearing her hair short. She claims that many *tongzhi* women "lack confidence and play the masculine role to reject their femininity" (109). One dismisses her TB identification as a sign of her past "immaturity" which she finds "horrifying, absurd, and a little tragic" (111). One simply attributes TB/TBG roles to Hong Kong's "backwardness" in comparison to the lesbian scene in the U.S. (115). This attitude is documented again in Chou's subsequent study of interracial relationships amongst *tongzhi* women where one interviewee suggests that TB/TBG distinction is only popular amongst the younger crowd and is almost entirely absent amongst those who are more Westernized and educated (*Postcolonial Tongzhi* 151). In another book project where *tongzhi* women are invited to write their own stories, the words TB/TBG are not even mentioned once in the five narratives that are eventually published (Lee 2-53)!

I am not disputing the validity of these ethnographic data, but it is interesting to note that in a community that has been characterized by the researchers themselves as heavily invested in gender role-playing, over 90% of the data collected reflect critical or dismissive attitudes towards the putative "reality." Where are the 70% who purportedly identify unproblematically as TB/TBG? Why is the discrepancy between this majority and the interviewed minority not explained or theorized? In a response to C. Jacob Hale's work on gender in the leather-dyke community, Eve Sedgwick notes a striking departure in Hale's account from most other theoretical accounts of cross-gender embodiment. By the latter accounts, "the critique and exposure of dominant ideologies, which are the sole yardsticks by which gender practices are nowadays thought to be measured," are also ascribed to be the motives of the subjects under study (237). Hale's account is valuable to Sedgwick because it pays attention to the affective and the relational, where subjects' motives behind gender identification involve "spiritual exercise and self-development, excitement and fun . . . self-construction, self-legibility, and self-recognition" (237). Indeed, these affective and relational motives are often overshadowed to the point of invisibility by a zealous impulse to critique and expose dominant ideology, as is the case with the ethnographic work on Hong Kong lesbians' gender identification. Researchers like Chou seem much more interested in proving his own point about the conservative nature of TB/TBG roles than in analyzing the complicated motives behind his subjects' identification. Paying attention to such motives does not necessarily lead to an endorsement of the gender practices in question. It would, however, result in a far more nuanced account of subject formation and the relation between dominant ideology and queer gender identification.

Comparative study of cross-cultural data can also enrich our interpretive methodology. One of the most interesting theoretical resonances to come out of ethnographies on Taiwan's *tongzhi* women is the proliferation of local gender categories that are irreducible to binary categories like butch/femme, T/*po*, or TB/TBG. Wang gives a wonderful description of some of these playful and inventive categories:

> Now one speaks of little T, and camp T–that is to say a very gentle and soft-spoken kind of T. There are also different kinds of *po* and they don't necessarily wear long hair. For example, a tragic *po* [*ku po*] is a very strong, able woman who is so devoted to her girlfriend that she gives off a tragic air. Most brilliant of all are those who become "*po* when encountering a T, and T when encountering a *po*." They can switch between the two roles depending on whom they are with. (Loo 153)

These categories reflect both a sense of humor and an active attempt to negotiate between the limits of available gender categories and lived experience. Is such negotiation simply absent in Hong Kong, or is it invisible to researchers like Chou because it does not support a critique of TB/TBG as dominant ideology? The theoretical implications of data collected on Taiwan could benefit and enrich the methodology of research on other Chinese communities.

Research on lesbian lives in Mainland China (PRC) is very scant (Li; Evans), partly due to the extremely difficult research environment. Yet there is a very rich body of work on women and feminism in the PRC that barely mentions lesbian practices. Wang's speculation on the "androgynising" influence of the Cultural Revolution has actually been discussed in some detail in these (predominantly heterosexual) feminist contexts. For instance, Lydia Liu argues that the construction of an "official feminism" in the PRC depends on a process of gendering:

> The category of women, like that of class, has long been exploited by the hegemonic discourse of the state of China, one that posits the equality between men and women by depriving the latter of *their* difference (and not the other way around!) . . . The image of the liberated daughter and the figure of strong female party leader celebrated, among others, in the literature of socialist realism are invented for the purpose of abolishing the patriarchal discriminatory construction of gender, but they end up denying difference to women . . . Post-Mao Chinese women are therefore dealing with an order of reality vastly different from that which feminists in the West face within their own patriarchal society, where the female gender is exploited more on the grounds of her difference than the lack thereof. (24)

Liu goes on to suggest that the resurgence of a "female tradition" in Chinese literature, which insists on constructing the "difference" of femininity, can be explained as acts of defiance against such a revolutionary tradition (31-40). Liu's observation that gender equality in the PRC is achieved by depriving women, rather than men, of their difference (in other words, women are encouraged to become more like men but not vice versa) can have immense significance for the study of lesbian gender identification. What Wang identifies as PRC women's "androgyny" is more appropriately a version of masculinity. Thus, while the butch or T or TB in Hong Kong and Taiwan most visibly marks lesbian presence because of their *difference* from the heterosexual gender of straight femininity, she would be relatively invisible in the PRC because she resembles the masculine gender of the revolutionary image of women. How does such a context inflect lesbian gender identification? How might versions of femme gender be constructed against the masculinity of the straight woman? How might the "difference" of femme gender generate erotic appeal? Furthermore, as the PRC becomes more entrenched in the movement of global capital and as the younger generation of women becomes more distant to the revolutionary tradition of gendering, is there a generational gap between older and younger lesbians, especially in their gender identification? The very established tradition of feminist work on gender in the PRC is actually very poised to answer such questions if it starts paying attention to its heterocentric blind spot.

LITERARY MODULATIONS

In a discussion of the genealogy of contemporary lesbian fiction in Taiwan, Hung Ling postulates a narrative of progress that situates the desexualized and melodramatic representation of lesbian relations in Ling Yan's and Cao Lijun's fiction at one end of the spectrum, and Chen Xue's and Hung's own consciously queer, avant-garde fiction at the other. Poised uneasily in the middle is Chiu Miao-chin's *Crocodile's Journal*, which Hung recognizes as the "first time Taiwan's lesbian voice asserts its power in the arena of fiction" (99). Despite its importance as a watershed work, Hung identifies the limits of the novel's subversive power in this way:

> We suddenly discover that in *Crocodile's Journal*, the central question for Lazi [the lesbian protagonist] is whether or not she could successfully transform herself into a masculine "man" who can legitimately love women. . . . Thus, the subversive potential of *Crocodile* has been considerably weakened by this construction of a subject/object relation. . . . To put it simply, the danger lies in the recuperation of the heterosexual institution and the formation of T/*po* (butch/femme) roles. (101)

Once again, butch/femme identification–here characterized as the possible corollary of a literary expression of desire–is unproblematically equated to heterosexual gendering. Hung's critical strategy is characteristic of Taiwan's new generation of queer theorists and authors who identify as *ku'er*. *Ku'er*, literally "cool child," was first used by Chi Ta-wei, Hung Ling, and Tan Tang-mo as a transliteration of "queer" in a special issue of the avant-garde literary journal *Island's Edge* in 1994. Even though *kuer* was originally inspired by *queer,* the term has since, as Chi suggests, cross-bred with local meanings (*Carnival* 11). It has also spawned several variations. For instance, Hung Ling sometimes rewrites *kuer* as *kuyi*, which reinscribes an element of queerness (*yi* means "strange") in the term. In a similar spirit, the critic Chang Hsiao-hung prefers the term *guai' tai* (literally "weirdo") in her queer rereadings of canonical works. Despite these variations, writers and critics who are associated with the *kuer* movement share a contempt for fixed categories and a preference for works that celebrate fluidity and ambivalence. Such a critical environment has produced many important challenges to received notions of homosexual identity. It also offers much-needed theoretical resources to rethink many of the assumptions inherent in the *tongzhi* movement. However, the too-ready dismissal of any kind of stable categories sometimes also runs the risk of erasing difference. Hung's reading of *Crocodile Journal*, for instance, only interprets Lazi's gender identification as an approximation of heterosexual masculinity. However, as Judith Halberstam's genealogy of female masculinity embodied in and by (representations of) queer women has shown, the apparent "naturalness" of male masculinity is absolutely dependent on a rejection or marginalization of alternative forms of masculinity. By exposing and challenging the "complex social structures that wed masculinity to maleness and to power and domination," Halberstam is calling for a more nuanced understanding of gender variance, especially in queer lives and queer representations (2). Similarly, the figure of Lazi does not have to be linked exclusively to heterosexual figures of the male lover. How might she be situated within the Chinese literary tradition of female same-sex eroticism? Is it possible to trace a genealogy of alternative forms of gender such as female masculinity or lesbian femininity?

Much like the imbalance found in ethnographic studies, the study of same-sex eroticism in Chinese literature has also disproportionately focused on male homoerotic desire (Xiaomingxiong; Hinsch). The scattered references discussed by Xiaomingxiong (306-320), however, show ample instances of gender role-playing. Whether it is the two Beijing opera singers Qiang Guan and Wei Guan who live as "husband and wife" in Cao Xueqin's (1715-1763) *Dream of the Red Chamber* (Xiaomingxiong 310-312); or Chen Yun who cross-dresses as a man to seduce a courtesan for her husband but ends up falling in love herself in Shen Fu's (1763-?) *Six Chapters in a Floating Life* (Xiaomingxiong 309-310); or Cui Jianyun who becomes so mesmerized by a fifteen-year-old girl at a temple that she cross-dresses as a man and vows to become the girl's husband in the next life in Li Yu's (1611-app. 1680) *Intimate Companions* (Xiaomingxiong 307-308), erotic gender role-playing is being practiced, though its significance needs to be analyzed in their proper social, historical, and literary contexts. There are also literary and artistic icons whose lives and aesthetics certainly contribute to a tradition of "female masculinity" that is not reducible to heterosexual imitation: the late Qing patriotic poet-martyr Qiu Jin, who likes to dress in men's clothes and writes in a distinctly masculine style; or "Brother Xia," the filmmaker Wu Jinxia who made the first all-female cast film in Hong Kong during the late 30s; or Yam Kim-Fai, the Cantonese opera diva who specializes in roles of handsome, literary heroes and was wildly popular amongst both straight and lesbian women in Hong Kong throughout the 1950s and 1960s (Xiaomingxiong 316-8; 305-6; 303). How might these scattered data be rethought in the study of queer genders? How might we use this material to construct a queer genealogy that would shed new light to the masculine identification found in lesbian works such as *Crocodile's Journal*?

The questions raised in this article are meant to instigate projects that trace a queer past as well as explore current queer expressions *not* in order to "prove" that categories like butch/femme also exist in Chinese cultures. Rather, they are meant to provoke efforts to explore ways in which we can productively bring categories that arguably originate from the West into crisis. Such efforts are of paramount importance to the *tongzhi* movement in its continuous quest to define, on its own terms, the histories, theories, aesthetics, and politics of sexual minorities in Chinese communities.

WORKS CITED

Blackwood, Evelyn and Saskia E. Wieringa. "Sapphic Shadows: Challenging the Silence in the Study of Sexuality." Evelyn Blackwood and Saskia E. Wieringa, ed. *Female Desires: Same Sex Relations and Transgender Practices Across Cultures.* New York: Columbia UP, 1999. 39-66.

Chang, Hsiao-hung. *Queer Family Romance* [*Guai'tai jiating luoman shi*]. Taipei: Shibao, 2000.

Cheng, Mei-li. *There's a Women's Community in Taiwan: Taiwan Lesbians' Gender, Family, and Community Life* [*Taiwan youge nuer juan: Taiwan nu tongzhi de xingbie, jiating yu juan nei shenghuo*]. Taipei: Nushu, 1997.

Chi, Ta-wei. *Goodbye Babylon: Desire, Dissidence, and the Politics of Reading in the Internet Generation* [*Wan'an babilun: wanglushidai de xingyu, yiyi, yu zhengzhi yuedu*]. Taipei: Tanshuo wenhua, 1998.

Chi, Ta-wei, Hung Ling and Tan Tang-mo, ed. *Island's Edge* [*Daoyu bianyuan*] 10 (1994).

Chiu, Miao-chin. *Crocodile's Journal* [*Eyu shouji*]. Taipei: Shibao wenhua, 1997.

Chou, Wah-Shan, *Hong Kong Tongzhi Stories* [*Xianggang tongzhi gushi*]. Hong Kong: Tongzhi yanjiu she, 1996.

_____. *Postcolonial Tongzhi* [*Hou zhimin tongzhi*]. Hong Kong: Tongzhi yanjiu she, 1997.

_____. "On *Ku'er*: Thoughts on Contemporary Taiwan's *Ku'er* and *Ku'er* Literature" [*Ku'er lun: sikao dangdai Taiwan ku'er yu ku'er wenxue*]. Chi Ta-wei, ed. *Queer Carnival: A Reader of Contemporary Queer Literature in Taiwan* [*Kuer kuanghuanjie: Taiwan dangdai kuer wenxue dupin*]. Taipei: Yuanzuhuangn, 1997. 9-16.

Evans, Harriet. *Women and Sexuality in China: Dominant Discourses of Female Sexuality and Gender Since 1949.* Cambridge, U.K.: Polity Press, 1997.

Halberstam, Judith. *Female Masculinity*. Durham: Duke UP, 1998.

Hale, C. Jacob. "Leatherdyke Boys and Their Daddies: How To Have Sex Without Women Or Men." *Social Text* 52-3 (1996). 223-236.

Hinsch, Bret. *Passion of the Cut Sleeve: The Male Homosexual Tradition in China*. Berkeley: California UP, 1990.

Ho, Petula Sik-Ying. "Politicizing Identity: Decriminalization of Homosexuality and the Emergence of Gay Identity in Hong Kong." Ph.D. Dissertation, University of Essex, 1997.

Hung, Ling. "Between the Lace and the Whip: The Flow of Lesbian Desire in Contemporary Taiwanese Fiction" [*Leisi yu bianzi de jiaohuan: cong dangdai taiwan xiaoshuo zhuxi nu tongxinglian de yuwang liudong*]. *Queer Journal: Sodom the Holy City* [*Kuyi zhaji: suoduoma shengcheng*]. Taipei: Wanxiang, 1996. 95-120.

Lam, Chuen-Ping. "Sexuality in Formation of Lesbian Identity: An Exploratory Study in Hong Kong." M.S.S. Dissertation. Hong Kong University, 1998.

Lee, Men-Chao et al. *Stories of Tongzhi Desire in Hong Kong* [*Xianggang tongzhi qingyu wuyu*.] Hong Kong: Ming Chuang, 1998.

Li, Yinhe. *Love and Sexuality of Chinese Women* [*Zhongguo nuxing de gangqing yu xing*]. Beijing: Jinri, 1998.

Lin Xianshou, *Seeing Homosexuality?* [*Kangjian tongxing lian?*]. Taipei: Kaixin Yangkuang, 1997.

Liu, Lydia. "The Female Tradition in Modern Chinese Literature: Negotiating Feminisms Across East/West Boundaries." *Genders* 12 (1991). 22-44.

Loo, John. (Ed.) *New Reader For Chinese Tongzhi* [*Huaren tongzhi xin dupin*]. Hong Kong: Worldson, 1999.

Mak, Anson et al. *Bisexual Desire* [*Shuangxing qingyu*]. Hong Kong, Christian Women's Association, 2000.

Nestle, Joan. *A Restricted Country*. Ithaca: Firebrand, 1987.

Newman, Lesléa. (Ed.) *The Femme Mystique*. Boston: Alyson, 1995.

Sedgwick, Eve. "A Response to C. Jacob Hale." *Social Text* 52-3 (1996). 237-240.

Tsang, Deborah Tze-lan. "Feminism's Double: Lesbian Activism in the Mediated Public Sphere of Taiwan." Mayfair Mei-hui Yang, ed. *Spaces of Their Own: Women's Public Sphere in Transnational China*. Minneapolis: Minnesota UP, 1999. 132-161.

Xiaomingxiong. *History of Homosexuality in China* [*Zhongguo tongxinglian shilu*]. Revised edition. Hong Kong: Rosa Winkel Press, 1997.

Zhang Qiaoting. "From Bodily Desire to Identity Consciousness: *Tongzhi* Women's Structure of Being in High School Space" [*Cong shenti yuwang dao shenfen rengtong–jiaoyuan kongjian zhong nu tongzhi de cunhai jizhi*]. Proceedings of Second International Conference on Sex Education, Sexuality Studies, Research on Gender and Homosexuality. Zhongli: Zhongyang Daxue Sex/Gender Research Centre, 1997. 1-24.

Zhao Yanning. "Chest-Binding, Sex, and Sexuality: The Body Politics and Aesthetics of Taiwanese Lesbians" [*Shuxiong, xing, yu xingai: Taiwan nu tongxinglian de shenti meixue*]. Proceedings of First International Conference on Sex Education, Sexuality Studies, Research on Gender and Homosexuality. Zhongli: Zhongyang Daxue Sex/Gender Research Centre, 1996. 47-60.

Reflections on Butch-Femme and the Emerging Lesbian Community in Bulgaria

Monika Pisankaneva

SUMMARY. This article features several women who are part of the present-day Bulgarian lesbian scene and discusses the significance of butch/femme identities in the absence of a tradition of lesbian community life. *[Article copies available for a fee from The Haworth Document Delivery Service: 1-800-HAWORTH. E-mail address: <getinfo@haworthpressinc. com> Website: <http://www.HaworthPress.com> © 2002 by The Haworth Press, Inc. All rights reserved.]*

KEYWORDS. Self-identified subculture, identity, Bulgaria, lesbian

Researching the present-day Bulgarian lesbian scene creates an opportunity to explore whether butch/femme identities can be constructed in the absence of a self-identified lesbian subculture. By "self-identified" I mean a subculture that is conscious of its own existence, that has created some public spaces for

Monika Pisankaneva founded a lesbian group at the Bulgarian Gay Organization "Gemini" (1998). She earned her MA in Philosophy from Sofia University, Bulgaria (1992), and Certificate in Comparative European Social Studies from Amsterdam University, The Netherlands (1998). She currently manages a social development program of an American NGO in Bulgaria, works as a freelance lecturer at the department of Anthropology, New Bulgarian University, Sofia, and actively participates in the lesbian and gay rights movement in Bulgaria.

[Haworth co-indexing entry note]: "Reflections on Butch-Femme and the Emerging Lesbian Community in Bulgaria." Pisankaneva, Monika. Co-published simultaneously in *Journal of Lesbian Studies* (Harrington Park Press, an imprint of The Haworth Press, Inc.) Vol. 6, No. 2, 2002, pp. 135-144; and: *Femme/Butch: New Considerations of the Way We Want to Go* (ed: Michelle Gibson, and Deborah T. Meem) Harrington Park Press, an imprint of The Haworth Press, Inc., 2002, pp. 135-144. Single or multiple copies of this article are available for a fee from The Haworth Document Delivery Service [1-800-HAWORTH, 9:00 a.m. - 5:00 p.m. (EST). E-mail address: getinfo@haworthpressinc.com].

135

socializing of its members, and which has elaborated (and/or adopted) recognizable appearance and behavior patterns that are reinforced in the places where lesbians go to meet other lesbians. None of the aforementioned elements characterized the Bulgarian lesbian subculture until the late 1990s when a small lesbian presence became a permanent component of the gay bar scene. The first gay bars were opened in Bulgaria around 1995, but initially they did not welcome lesbians, unless the latter were personal friends of the owners or arrived in the company of gay men who could persuade the owner to let them in. The situation changed in 1997 when the first gay disco was started in Sofia, and became a market rival for the bars. Economic stagnation was another factor that contributed to diminishing the number of clients frequenting the gay bars and thus to changing the owners' policy that was restrictive of women and heterosexual men in order to protect the privacy of the gay clientele. Even after 1997 the number of lesbians in the gay bar scene was so small that it would be difficult to detect a pattern in the appearance and behavior of women who went there. This number was growing as the gay bars and discos became more open to the youth popular culture and abolished entrance restrictions based on gender or sexual orientation. New restrictions were developed based on appearance and one was required to be trendy and chic in order to enter into *Spartakus* (the former gay disco in Sofia that was later converted into a mixed club). Lesbian existence became visible in that particular context of the club scene in which notions of "chic" were appropriated from either youth unisex fashion, or the eccentric style of drag queens. The drag queens' fashion did not have a particular appeal to lesbians, most of whom preferred to dress androgynously. Consequently, manifestations of traditional butch/femme identities where some lesbians look "masculine" and others "feminine" (no matter how elusive these terms are) were and still are rare in the club scene. Nonetheless, notions of active/passive, intermingled with notions of male/female roles within the couples, are sometimes to be found in lesbian small talk. This article features several cases that show how butch/femme identities are constructed in the absence of a lesbian community that enforces its own norms through discussion and action. The names are changed at the request of the women who were interviewed.

Understanding the present-day Bulgarian lesbian scene requires a quick look into the communist past. During the communist regime (1944-1990) the homosexual subculture existed completely underground and was accessible only to a small number of people living in the big cities. The communist repressions against homosexual intellectuals who were sent to corrective labor camps during the 1960s did not affect women. Lesbians were much more closeted than homosexual men, and this saved them from the tortures, but at the same time hindered the development of a self-identified lesbian subculture in the sense described above. Lesbian women lived in great isolation and only few of them succeeded in finding partners. A common way to avoid suspicion was heterosexual mimicry: getting married to a man. During communism, lesbian relationships developed mostly as extramarital affairs. The importance of butch/femme in such relationships is difficult to estimate, since both partners felt obliged to adhere to traditional images of femininity in order to prevent disclosure of the nature of their relationship.

Katya is one of the few women who never married and who self-identified as a lesbian during communism (though until 1990 she never shared that with anyone except for very close gay friends). She says that many of the women she slept with at that time identified as heterosexual. She always played the active part in her short-term relationships with heterosexual women, but she admits that she was "the wife" in her longest, ten-year relationship with a partner who played "the husband." Her partner was the breadwinner of the family, while Katya worked part-time and took care of the housework. Katya says there was a visible difference in their appearance, way of dressing and manners, so that everyone could recognize who played the man's role. A butch/femme dynamic is obviously present in the relationship that Katya describes, though she does not use the same terms. In fact, there are no exact equivalents to "butch" and "femme" in the Bulgarian language. In the absence of a lesbian subculture during communism, such terms were not coined, and they have not been adopted until the present moment. Today most lesbians use active/passive or masculine/feminine when they want to illustrate the difference between partners in a relationship. At the same time "my wife" and "my woman" are commonly used both ways (sometimes jokingly) when partners refer to each other.

The lesbians who started frequenting the gay bars in the late 1990s were mostly in their twenties or early thirties. Lesbians like Katya who are in their forties or older do not feel comfortable going out and socializing in the bars. Consequently, lesbian identities have emerged primarily as part of the youth popular culture. These women enjoy the youth unisex fashion and commonly both partners in a couple have androgynous looks. Many young lesbians share that it is usually the one having more experience who plays the active role at the beginning of a relationship. They hesitate to identify as either masculine or feminine in the traditional sense of the words. Many would say that there are no roles within the couples, or that there is a constant exchange of roles. Most of them are not familiar with the butch/femme tradition and its development in lesbian subcultures in the West. Learning about lesbian life abroad happens mostly through the Internet (lesbian chat rooms usually preferred), or through the stories of women who have been to other countries, and not from lesbian history books (no such books have yet been translated into Bulgarian). Lesbian chat rooms created at local servers have become virtual meeting points for women from around the country. Today it is somewhat easier to meet a lesbian partner with the help of the Internet, as well as to have a lesbian relationship and lead a male-independent life, though strong pressure is still exercised on women by their closest relatives to get heterosexually married and have a "respectable" life. Traditional notions of femininity (as well as masculinity) are still widely reinforced by older generations, by the education system, and by the media, and lesbians who have passed their twenties may experience problems with relatives and with employers if they do not adhere to them. Being an adult woman still means to dress in skirts and wear make-up, though short hair is acceptable, and was even recommended during the communist past. At the same time the androgynous youth culture is gaining recognition and it is quite safe for a young woman to wear unisex clothes without being stigmatized for her looks. Consequently, lesbians who frequent the clubs and are most visible have chosen unisex style as the safest way to express sexual non-conformity to traditional norms.

However, the bar scene in Sofia, Varna and Plovdiv–the three Bulgarian cities in which there are publicly known mixed clubs–does not represent all lesbians. There are stories of lesbian couples living in smaller towns in Bulgaria who have managed to hide the nature of their relationship for years due to the boyish appearance and behavior of one of the partners. One such couple contacted me after an interview that I gave for a women's magazine. They live in a town in which there is no gay-and-lesbian-friendly public place. They have been together for seven years now, and none of their friends know about the nature of their relationship. Jina is 27 and looks very feminine in the mainstream sense: she has long hair and always goes out with make-up and high heels. Dana is 25 and looks like a boy in her black leather jacket, chain-link black leather boots and blue denim jeans. In fact Jina's parents still think that Dana is a boy. She was never introduced to them personally; they have only seen her in the dark in front of their house taking Jina home after a date. Both Jina and Dana are college graduates and it is common for a woman who goes to college to get married around 25. Women are perceived to achieve self-realization mainly through partnering a man, and even career-oriented women are subjected to intense social pressure to engage in a heterosexual relationship that will lead to having a child.

Consequently, parents start pushing their daughters to begin looking for the "right man" after they graduate college or university (or after high school for those who are not planning to continue their education). More pressure was exercised on Jina who has had some male suitors, while Dana's parents have somehow put up with the boyish appearance of their daughter and with the fact that no man may wish to get married to her. Besides, Jina is an only child and her parents desperately want grandchildren, while Dana has an older sister who is already married and her parents are quite busy with the sister's children. The two women shared with me that they want to be in contact with other couples like them, but have been unable to meet any in their own town. They had had much more freedom while studying in Plovdiv, and are currently planning to move there for good. I encouraged them to escape from their parents' pressure for the sake of saving their relationship, while at the same time I realized that this is a hard choice that may cost them lots of suffering. Many young women in Bulgaria continue living with their parents until they get married to a man, no matter how late in life this happens. This is due to economic reasons: women encounter more difficulties than men in starting a career; they are driven to low-rank professions like teachers, secretaries, nurses or shop-assistants; these "female" professions are so poorly paid that no one could live independently earning so little.

Parents tolerate the heterosexual relationships of their daughters and pre-marital sex if it is going to lead to marriage (although this is less true in small towns and among Bulgarian Muslims), but very few parents would accept a child's homosexual relationship. That is why young lesbians are more motivated than heterosexual women to leave their homes and start independent lives, but they may experience more difficulties in finding jobs if they do not look feminine in the mainstream sense of the word. In long-term lesbian relationships it is usually the more feminine partner who becomes the breadwinner, since she has more opportunities to find a job that matches her education level. Masculine-looking women usually find low-paid jobs such as shop assistants, construction or service workers and the like, regardless of their qualifications. Lesbians who frequent the bars are usually more willing to talk about their sexuality and their relationships. Here are four stories of women whom I met at the bars.

Meg is 30 years old. She realized that she was attracted to women at the age of 25. Before that she had dated many men, and was married to a man for about a year due to getting pregnant by him when she was 18. After their divorce, the father was given full custody of the child (because of Meg's own decision), and she moved from her home town to Varna, the so-called "summer capital" of Bulgaria. Among lesbians Varna is also known as the "lesbian capital" of the country. Its seaside location attracts many lesbians during the summer months and some of them do not go back once they experience the benefits of living in a big city with a lot of job opportunities during the high season, and two gay discos where the lesbians are quite visible and very open to newcomers. The gay and lesbian scene has developed rapidly in Varna since 1997, the year of the opening of the first gay disco there. That was the year when Meg started her first long-term lesbian relationship with Niki. Meg and Niki are both very masculine in appearance. They wear only unisex clothes, and never use any make-up. Meg loves sports and trains her body regularly. Niki has played football on a women's team for some years. Meg likes to tell stories of how she was once asked to pay the men-only entrance fee at a night club in Varna, and how she and Niki have often been addressed with "Hey, guys!" by teenagers asking them for a cigarette when they were walking together in the park. They lived together for almost three years. Niki used to call Meg "my wife" and pretended to be the head of the family. At the same time she was the one who did most of the housework. "I cannot fully understand this," says Meg. "When we are together with friends, Niki always says that she is the man in the house; however, when we are at home she does the cleaning, the cooking and the washing." In Meg's opinion Niki's behavior was inconsistent with playing the man's role. At the same time she does not want to replicate traditional gender roles in her relationships. She believes that the two partners within a lesbian couple should be equal. She says she is only attracted to women who are like her (sporty, somewhat masculine in appearance, independent, non-submissive). After breaking up with Niki, she fell in love with Sia, who is a former national champion in kayaking. They have lived together for about a year now, and are very happy that there is no division of roles in their family. Meg says she has finally found someone who is exactly like her, neither trying to be submissive when they are at home, nor attempting to play dominant when they are out. Meg is clearly dissatisfied with traditional gender roles and the power division (dominant-submissive) associated with them. She strives for equality in the couple, which she understands as both a behavioral and an appearance characteristic. Meg admits that she has had sex with some very feminine women, but she feels more comfortable when she is with someone who is more like her–athletic and tough. She looks for reciprocity in the sexual act and believes in the absence of roles, or in their constant shifting from one partner to the other.

Lia is 22, a university student and a striptease dancer in an erotic bar in Sofia. She has never dated a man in her life. From a very early age she knew that she was attracted to women. Her first lesbian relationship began when she was 18, and lasted two years. Then she accidentally fell in love with Ivon and they have been together ever since. Lia is very feminine, with long hair and a sexy body. She loves to dance and strip in the clubs, and earns money in that way to cover at least partially her college tuition. At the same time she is deaf and blind to the comments and offers of the men in the bar. Her partner always watches her from a table close to the dancing floor and takes her home at the end of the show. Ivon has androgynous looks. She likes to shave her head or to keep very short hair, and always dresses in a sporty style. She used to play tennis professionally a few years ago. Lia and Ivon are always together and do not hesitate to hold hands, exchange tender glances, or even kiss in public. Their behavior is quite brave considering the dominating negative stereotypes of same-sex couples in Bulgaria. When asked whether there is a division of roles in their couple, Lia replies: "Yes, there is. I am the man." Her statement confuses everybody. When asked to explain why she thinks that she is the man, Lia says that she has always played the active role in seducing her partners, and she is usually the one that "leads" in the couple. She adds that playing the man's role has nothing to do with one's looks. For Lia, "man" means active and "woman" means passive. She admits she has never self-identified as a woman, and if she could afford it, she would rather go for a FTM sex change, and would still date women. Lia's statement that being a man has nothing to do with appearance is like a heresy compared to the mainstream Bulgarian understanding of gender roles, which prescribes clearly defined appearance and behavior characteristics to each gender. Lia is obviously trying to separate female from feminine and male from masculine in her thinking, and yet she accepts some of the traditional understanding of gender related to behavior: masculine being active and feminine being passive. She believes that her own behavior subverts traditional gender roles because her sex is female, her appearance is feminine, but her behavior is masculine, i.e., active.

Tina is 26 and has had many short-term relationships with women. She says she wanted to be a boy when she was young, and had difficulty accepting her maturing female body. Her favorite sport is boxing and she is a professional boxer. Tina boasts about having had sex with over 100 women, most of whom were one-night stands. She says most women were attracted to her boyish looks and very few have said "no" to her courting. Until about three years ago she used to play the "stone butch" in the American sense of the word, never letting her partners touch her while making love. The term that she uses about herself is "mannish lesbian." She admits that most of her early partners have self-identified as heterosexual, and she has felt obliged to play the man. As the lesbian scene in Sofia became more visible after 1997, Tina had the opportunity to start meeting more women who self-identified as lesbians. She was pleasantly surprised that the number of women who dress and behave in a sexually ambiguous way is growing. In the last two years Tina has started dating women who are more like her—masculine looking, non-submissive and sexually active, and wanting greater reciprocity in the sexual act. She admits that now it is much more difficult for her to stop her partners from taking up the leading role in sex. Her taste for women has also changed. She used to like very feminine women with long hair, curved body and lots of makeup. "But one cannot tell what is feminine any more!" complains Tina. "Now everybody has short hair and wears the same kind of clothes." Her last partner, with whom she spent almost six months, had an appearance similar to Tina's. They went to the boxing club together. However, Tina kept assuring everybody that she was the dominant one. She always refers to partners as "my wife" or "my woman," revealing a sense of possessiveness that is often the cause for her break-ups. She cannot easily give up traditional notions of gender division in the couple according to which one partner needs to be "the man," i.e., to play tough and be sexually more active, and the other partner needs to be more submissive and wait for the sexual initiation of the first. That other women have started to take the sexual initiative often troubles her. She feels obliged to dominate in some other area, so that she does not entirely lose her sense of butch dignity.

D. is 20 and is known as Soldier. She started dating women at 14. She has had sex with a man only once in her life "to make sure that this is not what I want." Soldier has grown up with the growing up of the gay and lesbian scene in Sofia. She says her real home is *Spartakus*, the first gay disco in Bulgaria. Her appearance is androgynous. She likes camouflage outfits and crew cuts. She believes that there are no roles within couples, but at the same time asserts that she has always played the active role in her relationships. My friend Tina (described above) and I were introduced to Soldier two years ago at *Spartakus*. I will never forget the way she introduced herself to us. Turning to me, she made a quick decision that I must be the feminine partner in the couple, shook my hand strongly, and said in a deep voice, "I am Soldier. Nice to meet you." Then she turned to Tina and almost whispered, "Nice to meet you. I am D." Tina and I could hardly keep from laughing at that moment, but when I think about it now, it seems to me that Soldier made a very wise decision. Her way of approaching other lesbians was so flexible that she would even use a different name for different people. In this way she could potentially partner anybody, she could play hard with more feminine women, and at the same time play soft with more masculine ones. Other young lesbians whom I met later have the same attitude to masculine and feminine roles (the terms they use instead of butch/femme). To them these are just roles, designed to facilitate communication among lesbians, and to make the game more interesting by introducing some polarity into it. They should be used flexibly and not rigidly. Depending upon circumstances and the other's personality, one and the same woman could play butch (dominant, active) with one partner and femme (submissive, passive) with another. They do not feel a necessity to stick to the same identity (role) forever.

Butch and femme or the terms used to designate the difference of roles in a lesbian couple in Bulgarian, "masculine" and "feminine lesbian" (or active/passive and dominant/submissive), do not have high importance for the majority of lesbians who are part of the club scene. The reason for that is probably the lack of a lesbian subculture that could reinforce its own norms for appearance and behavior. The present-day visible Bulgarian lesbian scene is part of the youth popular culture which tolerates mostly androgynous identities. Consequently, lesbians who frequent the bars are usually wearing unisex clothes, and there is no obvious difference between partners in a couple. They approach the question of roles flexibly and are willing to switch from one role to another for the sake of partnering different women. Of course, there are some who find it difficult to switch. They believe it will contradict their internal sense of "who am I" to play one role with one partner, and another role with somebody else. The switch of roles is somehow more problematic for the lesbians who identify as "masculine" than for those who identify as "feminine." A femme (or what we call "feminine lesbian") might easily take up the leading role when she finds herself with a partner who is less experienced than herself. Later on, as her partner gains more confidence, she may start to play passive again. A division of roles is more common for lesbians who do not socialize in the clubs, including young lesbian couples living in smaller towns and older lesbians who have grown up during communism. They stick to a more traditional understanding of gender which does not allow for switching of roles or complete equality between the partners. One of the partners takes up the leading role and this is usually associated with doing the "man's work" at home and taking care of "her woman" in all possible ways. There is a visible difference in appearance associated with the division of roles. The partner who plays "the man" never wears make-up, and dresses in jeans, jackets and boots, while the one who plays "the woman" sticks to the current mainstream women's fashion. Some discretion is allowed with respect to sexual initiation with the feminine partner being more active in initiating sex, something that has become possible within the mainstream culture in recent years too.

Butch/femme appears to be a more or less old-fashioned way of approaching lesbian relationships in Bulgaria today. Most young lesbians who live in big cities and socialize in public places do not attach high importance to butch/femme. They regard their lesbian relationships as a game between equals who may decide to play a division of roles for the sake of variety and pleasure. Neither active/passive, nor masculine/feminine are very often used by them as terms that describe consistent identities. Each lesbian who comes out in the club scene is regarded as having both masculine and feminine qualities, and some would argue that a lesbian is neither a man nor a woman in the traditional sense of the words. The absence of a widely accepted butch/femme rhetoric, or butch/femme images can be attributed to the lack of tradition in developing a lesbian community in Bulgaria. However, with the new possibilities for meeting other lesbians that have recently emerged, some form of community life has started to appear. It is a question of time to see what kind of identities this new situation will produce, and if there will be a need for butch/femme in the post-communist Bulgarian lesbian scene.

The significance of butch/femme for lesbians in Bulgaria is hard to estimate since most lesbian relationships are completely invisible. The few visible young lesbians who live in big cities and socialize in public places do not attach high importance to butch/femme. Most lesbians who come out in the club scene approach different partners flexibly and it is difficult to say whether they stick to a particular behavior pattern. Active/passive and masculine/feminine are regarded as roles in a specific relationship, but not as lifelong identity features. The absence of a widely accepted butch/femme rhetoric or butch/femme images can be attributed to the lack of a fully developed lesbian community in Bulgaria. However, with the new possibilities for meeting other lesbians that have recently emerged, some form of community life has started to appear. Only time will tell what kinds of identities this new situation will produce, and if there will be a need for butch/femme in the post-communist Bulgarian lesbian scene.

Ruth the Butch

Karen Williams

Karen Williams

I have to have roles 'cause when I get to a closed door I want to know who's going to open it. I am standing there waiting for a butch to come along. And all those androgynous people and codependent people come along and line up right behind me. Actually, we are really waiting for the UPS or Federal Express truck to come because we know that's where all the butches work. I used to be a secretary and I had my favorite butch from UPS: Ruth the Butch. I was putting in requests. I was wrapping up huge packages with nothing in them but paper clips.

"Can Ruth come by today? I got 49 boxes just for her." And, sure enough, she'd come over there and I'd say, "Ruth, please pick up that box," and she'd pick it up with the two paper clips and say, "Oh, this is so light!" And I'd say, "That's because you're so strong!"

Karen Williams is the founder of the International Institute of Humor and Healing Arts (HaHA), which offers a series of workshops designed to build self-confidence and self-esteem. Sessions offered include: Humor and Healing; Dream Work and Goal Setting; Dealing with Difference; Exploring Cultural Heritage; Humor and Writing; Let's Laugh About Sex; and Humor and Stress Management in the Workplace. Her most recent CD is entitled *Human Beings: What A Concept.*

[Haworth co-indexing entry note]: "Ruth the Butch." Williams, Karen. Co-published simultaneously in *Journal of Lesbian Studies* (Harrington Park Press, an imprint of The Haworth Press, Inc.) Vol. 6, No. 2, 2002, p. 145; and: *Femme/Butch: New Considerations of the Way We Want to Go* (ed: Michelle Gibson, and Deborah T. Meem) Harrington Park Press, an imprint of The Haworth Press, Inc., 2002, p. 145. Single or multiple copies of this article are available for a fee from The Haworth Document Delivery Service [1-800-HAWORTH, 9:00 a.m. - 5:00 p.m. (EST). E-mail address: getinfo@haworthpressinc.com].

Clothes Make the (Wo)man:
Marlene Dietrich and "Double Drag"

Rebecca Kennison

SUMMARY. Dietrich, like Madonna, has been called *gender-bending* and *androgynous*, but Dietrich's on- and offscreen fluidity of gender identity, as reflected in her adoption of the "double drag," upsets the traditional dichotomy encoded more generally as that of male or female and more particularly as that of the butch or femme. *[Article copies available for a fee from The Haworth Document Delivery Service: 1-800-HAWORTH. E-mail address: <getinfo@haworthpressinc.com> Website: <http://www.HaworthPress.com> © 2002 by The Haworth Press, Inc. All rights reserved.]*

KEYWORDS. Dietrich, drag, gender roles, performance, subversion

She steps out on stage to sing, dressed in a man's suit, short blond hair brushed back from her face, legs apart, one hand on her hip, the other holding a monocle to her eye–for all the male garb, very much a woman. She looks into the camera–provocatively, seductively, erotically. Madonna on her 1990 Blond Ambition tour? Or Marlene Dietrich, who defined blond ambition 60 years earlier? Although it is Madonna who has been called "the virtual embodiment of Judith Butler's arguments in *Gender Trouble*" (Mistry) on the fluidity of gender roles and the subversiveness of drag, Dietrich performed that role well before *Gender Trouble* was ever written–or Madonna even born. In

Rebecca Kennison, an independent scholar who lives in Berkeley, California, has contributed articles, reviews, and photographs to several academic publications.

[Haworth co-indexing entry note]: "Clothes Make the (Wo)man: Marlene Dietrich and 'Double Drag.' " Kennison, Rebecca. Co-published simultaneously in *Journal of Lesbian Studies* (Harrington Park Press, an imprint of The Haworth Press, Inc.) Vol. 6, No. 2, 2002, pp. 147-156; and: *Femme/Butch: New Considerations of the Way We Want to Go* (ed: Michelle Gibson, and Deborah T. Meem) Harrington Park Press, an imprint of The Haworth Press, Inc., 2002, pp. 147-156. Single or multiple copies of this article are available for a fee from The Haworth Document Delivery Service [1-800-HAWORTH, 9:00 a.m. - 5:00 p.m. (EST). E-mail address: getinfo@haworthpressinc.com].

fact, through Dietrich's appropriation of gay male and lesbian fashion, combined with a femme sensibility, her on- and offscreen fluidity of gender identity upsets the dichotomy and tautology of the roles encoded by traditional gender identification as either male or female, as well as that of the traditional lesbian terminology of butch or femme.

Gender theorists–most famously Judith Butler–have argued that, rather than being imitations of heterosexual identities, butch and femme are parodies that expose the fictionality of heterosexual norms. At first glance it would seem that butch and femme simply reinscribe heterosexual notions of gender roles–something that Lillian Faderman takes as an historical given (167-174, 263-265). Instead, Butler argues, these performances expose as constructed an apparent heterosexual "original" that is in fact only a copy, there being no "original" gender roles at all: "The replication of heterosexual constructs in nonheterosexual frames brings into relief the utterly constructed status of the so-called heterosexual original. Thus, gay is to straight not as copy is to original, but, rather, as copy is to copy. The parodic repetition of 'the original'. . . reveals the original to be nothing other than a parody of the idea of the natural and the original" (Butler, *Gender Trouble* 41). Annika Thiem describes this as a "double mimesis," explaining that "the 'original' is rendered original in a process . . . where the second mimetic duplication functions to disavow precisely the mimetic character. . . . The so-called copy, therefore, could not be [a] copy without the so-called original and the so-called original could not be [an] original without the copy." This double mimesis underscores the instability of the very terms *butch* and *femme*, rendering both parodic.

But even as a parody of heterosexual norms, whether intentional or not, appearance plays a large part in a lesbian's perceived role as butch or femme–or as something else. In Kristin Esterberg's discussion of the importance of a distinctive look as crucial to a performance of lesbian identity in general and of butch-femme roles in particular, she quotes one woman who draws this connection between her sexual and emotional self-identity and her appearance:

> The times I really tune in to being a lesbian *per se* are the times that I get caught up in the role. You know, when I see a woman in a shirt and tie and a leather jacket. And I go wild. Or the times that I put certain clothes on, and I am struck by the effect, you know, whether it makes me feel really butch or whether it makes me feel really fem[me]. I'm often struck by *feeling* a certain way, you know–a certain swagger when I walk, checking myself in the windows in my sunglasses and, you know, really cool . . . I'd say, "Yeah!" (qtd. in Esterberg 265; italics in original)

Clearly this woman would agree with Alisa Solomon's observation that "[b]utch and femme are not just the costume, but they're nothing without the costume" (273). In this (in)vested performance, most lesbians establish their own sense of social norms, whether or not they think of them as parody of heterosexual ones and hence as some sort of drag performance. In establishing her own norms, as neither solely butch nor only femme but constantly both, Dietrich was, in a sense, always in drag. She was known both on- and offscreen for her "mannish clothes," although she soon discovered that what was acceptable onstage or on-screen was not so readily accepted off it; she regularly scandalized the American and European press in the 1930s by wearing pants in public (Bach 167, 174; Faderman 125; Riva 187, 206-207). While Dietrich preferred to wear a "man's outfit of sports jacket, slouch hat, and tie" with trousers or (on rare occasions) a skirt (Riva 122) when offstage or offscreen, she was equally well known for her onstage gowns, so much so that years later the flamboyant Liberace compared his outfits to Dietrich's by commenting, "For me to wear a simple tuxedo onstage would be like asking Marlene Dietrich to wear a housedress" (Thomas 243; qtd. in Garber 357).

Both forms of attire, then, were a kind of drag performance, for the public when she wore men's clothing, for herself when she did not. Even more gender-bending, especially on-screen and onstage, was Dietrich's sly mix of "male" and "female" styles and her subversion of gender roles to create what she often called an "interesting" effect. For all of Butler's insistence on drag as a subversion of gender roles through its parodic imitation of those roles (*Gender Trouble* 174-175), she goes on to admit, "Parody by itself is not subversive, and there must be a way to understand what makes certain kinds of parodic repetitions effectively disruptive, truly troubling, and which repetitions become domesticated and recirculated as instruments of cultural hegemony" (*Gender Trouble* 176-177). For drag in particular to continue to be disruptive and subversive, there must be something to disrupt and subvert in place first; without gender roles that are somehow already codified and understood, no drag—and no subversive parody—can occur.

That just such a theatrical and performative parody of gender roles is the very purpose of drag lies at the heart of Marjorie Garber's argument. Garber sees drag as a "discourse of clothing and body parts" that critiques from within gay performance the whole stricture of structured roles as symbolized by clothing and accessories: "[S]ex-role referents within the sartorial system may be deliberately mixed or self-contradictory: an earring, lipstick, high heels, and so on, worn with traditionally 'masculine' clothing. Onstage, this method is called, significantly, 'working with (feminine) pieces'—so that the artifactuality of the 'feminine' (or the 'feminine piece') is overtly acknowledged and brought to consciousness" (152). In some ways, this is precisely what Madonna attempts to communicate about the "masculine" in her videos and stage shows, and what Dietrich before her did by her adoption of both lesbian butch and gay men's "pieces" while affecting a femme stance.

Like Madonna, Dietrich has been called "sexually ambiguous, androgynous" (Weiss 42), "genderless" (Riva 78), "a divinely campy androgyne" (McLellan 113). Dietrich, however, rejected any view of herself as androgynous. She complained to Eryk Hanut that her gay fans "have turned me into an androgynous Madonna. . . . Rubbish!" (44), and in the 1984 documentary *Marlene*, she went on a rant about those she considered to be masculinized women: "Don't talk to me about women's lib! I hate it. . . . If they were like men, they would have been born like men. So then they are women, so stay women . . . It's very nice to be a woman!" Despite this insistence on her own implied contentedness with being a woman, Dietrich, nevertheless, consistently engaged in what can only be called "double drag": not androgynously devoid of masculinity and femininity, but constantly playing with those concepts, always fully feminine and fully masculine, and thus appealing to all audiences, gay and straight, female and male. "[S]he has sex but no particular gender," Kenneth Tynan once described her. "Marlene lives in a sexual no man's land– and no woman's, either. She dedicates herself to looking, rather than to being, sexy. The art is in the seeming. The semblance is the image, and the image is the message. She is every man's mistress and mother, every woman's lover and aunt" (qtd. in Dietrich 255). And an image, a message, needs an audience. Donna Haraway (among others) has argued that, because the audience's gaze is unidirectional, turning subjects into objects, the gaze is thus a masculinist form of knowledge. Mikkel Borch-Jacobsen, however, insists that it is only through a "mimetic identification" with the object that "the desiring subject [is brought] into being" at all (47). Similarly, Butler comments that gender and sexuality positions are always formed and assumed as "identifications" and that as such they are "phantasmatic" (*Bodies That Matter* 265). For Butler, fantasy provides the setting for desire, so the subject emerges as the locus of desire, where "the 'subject' [is installed] in the position of both desire and its object" (*Bodies That Matter* 268). By "recall[ing] the heterosexual scene"–something Dietrich did in all her performances by way of her costumes, whether tuxedos or gowns, top hats or boas–"[i]n both butch and femme identities, the very notion of an original or natural identity is put into question; indeed, it is precisely that question as it is embodied in these identities that becomes one source of their erotic significance" (Butler, *Gender Trouble* 157).

Long before Madonna, Dietrich embodied this "erotic significance" by incorporating classic elements of lesbian butch dress along with traditional elements of gay drag. Because Dietrich insisted on designing her own costumes, often drawing from what she had in her closet at home, she proudly took responsibility for her look in all her movies. Much of this look had its origins in the gay and lesbian "underworld" of 1920s Berlin, Paris, and New York. The tuxedos and top hats that became her trademark had long been the "uniform" for lesbians (or for those who wanted to imitate them) in the bars, ballrooms, and salons in those cities (Faderman 59, 66, 83; see also Benstock 180-181), and Dietrich frequently attended drag balls in Berlin dressed in a tuxedo made especially for her by her husband's tailor (Riva 46; Martin 37-39, 41-42, 46). Other affectations of 1920s lesbian chic also made their way into Dietrich's costumes, although for her they often had very personal connections, not only to the lesbian subculture she knew so well, but also to men she admired. For her audition for Joe May's 1922 silent film *Tragödie der Liebe* (*Tragedy of Love*), she showed up sporting a monocle. This was to become her signature in her theater and film performances throughout the 1920s; a cast photograph from the play *Duell am Lido* (*Duel on the Lido*), performed in 1926, for example, shows her dressed in a silk vest and harem pants, monocle in her eye. The monocle began as an affectational accessory of the upper-class male dandy (Garber 153). By the 1920s, lesbians in Paris and Berlin had adopted it as part of their standard dress, along with the tuxedo (Garber 153; Martin 40; see also Benstock 307), and Dietrich was hardly the first to use it as a costume accessory in German film; Lil Dagover's cabaret singer in Fritz Lang's *Doktor Mabuse* (1922) also wore a monocle. For Dietrich, however, this particular monocle was not merely an emblem of masculine appropriation, although it was surely that as well, but a very personal symbol: the monocle she wore was her father's, and she donned it not only because she wanted to look "provocative" (Dietrich 43), but also because it symbolized for her the role she wanted to play in her family, that of taking over "my father's place–against my mother's will" (Dietrich 37).

Having thus started to create an "image" that incorporated a certain style of dress–that of feminine attire with masculine accessories–Dietrich then firmly established that image in her breakthrough movie, the first German "talkie," Josef von Sternberg's *Der blaue Engel* (*The Blue Angel*) (1930). Here the enduring visual image of the cabaret singer Lola Lola–designed by Dietrich herself, who thought Sternberg's initial costumes were "stupid–uninteresting, boring–nothing to catch the eye" (qtd. in Riva 65)–is that of the garter belt and white satin top hat (see *http://www.bombshells.com/gallery/dietrich/marlene_gallery. shtml*). This combination was to become, as Dietrich herself acknowledged, "a symbol . . . for my personality" (Dietrich 57). Dietrich's incorporation of the garter belt came not from standard feminine dress of the time nor even from that of the prostitutes she was supposedly mimicking, but directly from her experiences in Berlin with gay men in drag, for whom the garter was "obligatory" (Riva 46, 66). At the same time, the top hat was not only typical attire for a gentleman of that time, but also part of the lesbian haute couture subculture. To-gether, like the combination of monocle and harem pants, these two items were central to Dietrich's double-drag act.

She built on this image for her next film, her first made in Hollywood, in which the top hat was joined by a tuxedo, both items coming straight out of Dietrich's own closet (Riva 85, 101). Although on the surface *Morocco* (1930) seems to tell the stock story of a woman who gives up everything to follow her man–in this case tossing off her shoes and walking across the hot sands of the Sahara after him–that is not what the audience tends to remember from this movie. What sticks in the memory, and what has long appealed to lesbian audi-ences in particular (White 44-45), is the famous scene in which Dietrich, as nightclub singer Amy Jolly, comes onstage in a black tuxedo and top hat, that mark of a cross-dressing lesbian, a cigarette (Garber 155-157) in hand, to sing "Quand l'amour meurt," a song written for a man. Even Dietrich admitted the power of this scene: "[T]hat's an interesting scene," she said, with typical un-derstatement, more than 50 years later in the documentary made about her, *Marlene.*

What happens in this scene is considerably more than "interesting." At the conclusion of her song, Jolly/Dietrich straddles a railing separating her from the audience, takes a swig of champagne from a man's glass, and then removes a gardenia from a woman's hair. Dietrich sniffs the flower and then impul-sively kisses the woman on the lips. This is an action that Sue-Ellen Case might describe as "high camp" (304), acceptable to the audience because of its artificiality, for, as Susan Sontag has famously argued, "Camp is a solvent of morality. It neutralizes moral indignation, sponsors playfulness" (290). Dietrich again breathes deeply from the flower and then tosses the bud to Gary Cooper's Tom Brown, who puts the flower behind his right ear, exactly where the woman had originally worn it.[1] Echoing Butler, Garber comments, "The question of an 'original' or a 'natural' cultural category of gender semiotics is immediately put *out* of question. There is in the nightclub in *Morocco* nothing *but* gender parody" (338; italics in original).

But what makes this scene "interesting," as Dietrich describes it– and one of the most enduring in cinema? It is not simply the audience's introduction to Dietrich in drag, playing directly to a lesbian in-crowd by her both kissing the woman and inhaling the scent of her flower. What makes the scene interesting is Dietrich's asserting her power, granted to her by her tuxedo (Weiss 35), over an entire audience, men and women, straight and gay. As Andrea Weiss points out, in transcending both class and gender by wearing a tuxedo–by combining butch clothing with femme performance–Dietrich thus renders herself attrac-tive to both the men and the women in the audience, whether the nightclub's audience or the movie theater's (35). Nevertheless, the entire scene is performed in a way that makes light of its homoeroticism and thus allows the audience to quite literally laugh it off. As Case argues about butch-femme roles in theater performance, describing just the sort of camp moment that is presented as high art in this scene in *Morocco*: "The point is not to conflict reality with another reality, but to abandon the notion of reality through roles and their seductive atmosphere and lightly manipulate appearances. Surely, this is the atmosphere of camp, permeating the *mise en scène* with 'pure' artifice. In other words, a strategy of appearances replaces a claim to truth" (304). That the kiss–and the entire scene–is intended as camp and not to be taken seriously is punctuated by the laughter of the woman and of the audience. But for all its campiness, it is the sheer sexual power of this double-drag performance that provides one of the most enduring images of Dietrich, more than 60 years after it was filmed. Dietrich's studio photographs for *Morocco* are justifiably famous (see *http://www. bombshells.com/gallery/dietrich/marlene_gallery.shtml*). She strikes a very "male" pose, right hand in her trousers pocket, left hand holding a lighted cigarette, legs crossed in a distinctly "unladylike" manner, hat at a jaunty angle–but in the blonde hair tumbling from beneath the hat and the seductive directness of the gaze, a smile playing around her lips, Dietrich is all woman.

For the film *Blonde Venus* (1932), Dietrich built even further on the look she was developing for her own personal drag act. In *The Blue Angel*, that look had been symbolized by a garter and white top hat; in *Morocco*, by a black top hat and tails; now it became a white top hat and tails. At the beginning of the scene in which she appears dressed in that white tuxedo, Dietrich, as Helen Faraday, suggestively brushes her hand across the breast of a chorus girl before going onstage in Paris. Although the song she then sings ("I Couldn't Be Annoyed") is rather mediocre, the performance– and the outfit–are unforgettable. As in the scene in *Morocco* in which Dietrich kisses the woman, an action rendered harmless by her character's devil-may-care attitude, what made this scene in *Blonde Venus* acceptable to the audience, as Weiss points out (44), is that Dietrich's character, already declared an unfit mother and abandoned by her husband, is merely confirmed in her degeneracy by her cross-dressing. Nevertheless, the white tuxedo created such a durable image that Dietrich used it quite often in her stage show 20 years later.

Dietrich began that second career in 1953, coming full circle in a fashion, since she had started her career onstage as a cabaret singer. For the next 20 years she performed in nightclubs, first in Las Vegas and then on enormously successful world tours. By this time, she had already firmly established her public persona, not so different from her private one. On stage, flashy and revealing "nude dresses" (Bach 368-369; see Dietrich 228) in the first half of the show gave way in the second half to tuxedos so that she could sing "men's songs" such as "Lili Marlene," a soldier's song she had made famous in her

USO shows during World War II. "If I have often appeared in tails," Dietrich writes in her autobiography, "it was for the reason that the best songs are written for men. . . . That's the reason I changed my costume with lightning speed and exchanged my dress for a tuxedo" (179; see also 244). This change in outfit was very much calculated to appeal to both the men and the women in her audience, as her daughter Maria Riva makes clear: "In her glitter dress, she sang to men; in her tails, to women" (661). Like Madonna, who has continually satirized her own sartorial statements (Kellner 197), Dietrich often parodied her now-trademark tuxes for maximum dramatic effect (Riva 622, 696). Sometimes the tuxes were black, sometimes white; the pants sometimes became shorts; the stockings, fishnet. Small wonder, then, that Dietrich's double mimesis–her copy of a copy–inspired a double drag of its own. Almost all drag queen acts, as Hanut observes, now include a "Dietrich." Hanut continues: "Her appearance was brilliantly effective in assimilating her to the 'third sex.' And her sartorial reality has become a dramatic reality. Or an everyday reality, which is practically the same thing" (118).

Although disguised as campy drag, in every performance and every outfit, Dietrich exuded sexuality, what Sternberg called her "sensual appeal" (qtd. in Martin 68). It is that, more than any one costume and more even than all her costumes combined, for which she is known. Butler observes that "sexuality always exceeds any given performance, presentation, or narrative. . . . That which is excluded for a given gender presentation to 'succeed' may be precisely what is played out sexually, that is, an 'inverted' relation, as it were, between gender and gender presentation, and gender presentation and sexuality" ("Imitation" 315). Perhaps Dietrich's affectational double drag accomplishes this in her own performances of gender, resulting in a sexuality that exerted the kind of power Colette observed resides in just this sort of performance by "a person of . . . dissimulated sex" (76).

For both Dietrich and her modern-day successor Madonna, the relationship among gender presentation, sexuality, and power is quite clear. When Garber comments about the "*empowered* images of Marlene Dietrich, or Madonna, in garter belt and bustier" (271; italics in original), she both connects the two performers and reinforces the contention that power emanates not only from their "male" garb but also from their "feminine pieces," which both of them adopted and adapted from performances of gay male drag. Although Dietrich always denied that she was interested in power, Maria Riva's biography of her mother is full of descriptions of the authority Dietrich wielded both on and off the screen. As for Madonna, riffing off of Dietrich's shtick and as equally adept as her predecessor at adapting her style to bend gender, there is no question that her performances are assertive acts of power (Kellner 198-199; Garber 155) and of power redisposition. This can be seen particularly clearly in Madonna's music video of "Express Yourself" (see *http://www.sindrismadonnapage.com/Welcome/Welcome.htm*) and its reenactment on her Blond Ambition tour, intentionally modeled on Dietrich's enduring image and thus also in itself a kind of double drag (Martin 71): dressed in a double-breasted suit, monocle held to her eye, backed by two female singers also in pinstripes, Madonna "assertively claimed all possible gender space" (Garber 126). Dietrich did the same. Madonna's double-drag performances acknowledge this legacy of power, especially in her music video "Vogue," in which, Dietrich-like, she appropriated a gay male drag concept and turned it into haute couture.[2]

In their enduring performances of sartorial power, both Dietrich and Madonna seem to have furthered Butler's own project: "[P]ower," says Butler, "can be neither withdrawn nor refused, but only redeployed. Indeed, in my view, the normative focus for gay and lesbian practice ought to be on the subversive and parodic redeployment of power rather than on the impossible fantasy of its full-scale transcendence" (*Gender Trouble* 158). Whether she would admit to it or not, it was this sort of power–obtained through tux and top hat and through gown and garter–that Marlene Dietrich deployed.

NOTES

1. Writing to her husband, Dietrich admits to the suggestiveness of this gesture: "You know what *I* do in the tails? I go over to a pretty woman at a table and kiss her–on the mouth–then I take the gardenia she is wearing, put it under my nose, and in-ha-le it! Well . . . you know *how* and why I do it . . . like *that*. Good? Then I flick the flower to Cooper. The audiences go wild. Can you imagine if even Americans get that scene, what will happen once the film opens in Europe?" (qtd. in Riva 101; italics in original).

2. As recently as February 2001, Madonna's double-drag style from the 1980s was still having a profound effect on fashion: "This spring it's Madonna's masculine[-]meets[-]Monroe look from the Express Yourself video that's inspiring fashion. Just look at Gucci's current ads[,] which not only feature Kate Moss dressed in mannish trousers and shirt teamed with a corset, but show the super [model] striking a pose very similar to Madonna's famous vogueing dance. To get the cross-dressing Marilyn Monroe look, go for pinstripe suits and masculine cut separates feminized by corsets and high heels" ("Express Yourself").

WORKS CITED

Abelove, Henry, Michèle Aina Barale, and David M. Halperin, eds. *The Lesbian and Gay Studies Reader*. NY: Routledge, 1993.
Bach, Steven. *Marlene Dietrich: Life and Legend*. NY: Da Capo P, 1992.
Benstock, Shari. *Women of the Left Bank: Paris, 1900-1940*. Austin: U of Texas P, 1986.

Borch-Jacobsen, Mikkel. *The Freudian Subject.* Trans. Catherine Porter. Stanford: Stanford UP, 1988.

Butler, Judith. *Bodies That Matter: On the Discursive Limits of "Sex."* NY: Routledge, 1993.

_____. *Gender Trouble: Feminism and the Subversion of Identity.* NY: Routledge, 1999.

_____. "Imitation and Gender Insubordination." Abelove, Barale, and Halperin 307-320.

Case, Sue-Ellen. "Toward a Butch-Femme Aesthetic." Abelove, Barale, and Halperin 294-306.

Colette. *The Pure and the Impure.* Trans. Herma Briffault. NY: Farrar, 1967 [1941].

Dietrich, Marlene. *Marlene.* Trans. Salvator Attanasio. NY: Grove P, 1989.

Esterberg, Kristin G. " 'A Certain Swagger When I Walk': Performing Lesbian Identity." *Queer Theory/Sociology.* Ed. Steven Seidman. Cambridge, MA: Blackwell, 1996. 259-279.

"Express Yourself." 2001. *http://www.widemedia.com/fashionuk/news/2001/02/13/ news0001483.html* June 29, 2001.

Faderman, Lillian. *Odd Girls and Twilight Lovers: A History of Lesbian Life in Twentieth-Century America.* NY: Penguin, 1991.

Garber, Marjorie. *Vested Interests: Cross-Dressing and Cultural Anxiety.* NY: Routledge, 1992.

Hanut, Eryk. *I Wish You Love: Conversations with Marlene Dietrich.* Trans. Anne-Pauline de Castries. Berkeley, CA: Frog, 1996.

Haraway, Donna. *Simians, Cyborgs, and Women: The Reinvention of Nature.* London: Free Association Books, 1991.

Kellner, Douglas. "Madonna, Fashion, and Identity." *Women in Culture: A Women's Studies Anthology.* Ed. Lucinda Joy Peach. Malden, MA: Blackwell, 1998. 187-201.

Marlene: A Feature. Dir. Maximilian Schell. With Marlene Dietrich, Maximilian Schell, Karel Dirka, Bernard Hall, Anni Albers, Heidi Genee, and Dagmar Hirtz. Oko-Film, 1984.

Martin, W. K. *Marlene Dietrich.* NY: Chelsea House, 1995.

McLellan, Diana. *The Girls: Sappho Goes to Hollywood.* NY: St. Martin's, 2000.

Mistry, Reena. "Madonna and *Gender Trouble.*" *Theory, Gender and Identity Resources.* 2000. *www.theory.org.uk/madonna.htm.* June 27, 2001.

Riva, Maria. *Marlene Dietrich: By Her Daughter.* NY: Ballantine, 1992.

Solomon, Alisa. "Not Just a Passing Fancy: Notes on Butch." *The Passionate Camera: Photography and Bodies of Desire.* Ed. Deborah Bright. London: Routledge, 1998. 263-275.

Sontag, Susan. *Against Interpretation and Other Essays.* NY: Delta-Dell, 1966.

Thiem, Annika. "Narrative Performativity: Theorizing Desire and Memory in Subject Formation." Unpublished essay, 2001.

Thomas, Bob. *Liberace.* NY: St. Martin's, 1987.

Weiss, Andrea. *Vampires and Violets: Lesbians in Film.* NY: Penguin, 1992.

White, Patricia. *UnInvited: Classical Hollywood Cinema and Lesbian Representability.* Bloomington: Indiana UP, 1999.

The Suit Suits Whom?
Lesbian Gender, Female Masculinity,
and Women-in-Suits

Lori Rifkin

SUMMARY. This paper is an excerpt from a larger cultural study that reads the figure of a woman wearing a suit with pants as a "text" that functions discursively to reveal the production of our sex/gender/desire system. There I argue that the woman-in-a-suit isolates the power of the heterosystem and offers a subject position for making visible, contesting, and producing new meanings and relations of power. Here, I use the contemporary cultural figure of a woman-in-a-suit as a testing ground for asking questions about how current conceptualizations of lesbian gender and female masculinity affect and prescribe our reading of women ranging in genders and sexualities. *[Article copies available for a fee from The Haworth Document Delivery Service: 1-800-HAWORTH. E-mail address: <getinfo@haworthpressinc.com> Website: <http://www.HaworthPress.com> © 2002 by The Haworth Press, Inc. All rights reserved.]*

KEYWORDS. Lesbian, gender, butch-femme, female masculinity, cultural studies, suit, clothing

---

Lori Rifkin is currently a graduate student at New York University. Her academic background is in law, feminist and gender studies, social and political theory, and cultural studies.

[Haworth co-indexing entry note]: "The Suit Suits Whom? Lesbian Gender, Female Masculinity, and Women-in-Suits." Rifkin, Lori. Co-published simultaneously in *Journal of Lesbian Studies* (Harrington Park Press, an imprint of The Haworth Press, Inc.) Vol. 6, No. 2, 2002, pp. 157-174; and: *Femme/Butch: New Considerations of the Way We Want to Go* (ed: Michelle Gibson, and Deborah T. Meem) Harrington Park Press, an imprint of The Haworth Press, Inc., 2002, pp. 157-174. Single or multiple copies of this article are available for a fee from The Haworth Document Delivery Service [1-800-HAWORTH, 9:00 a.m. - 5:00 p.m. (EST). E-mail address: getinfo@haworthpressinc.com].

SUIT HER UP, SHE'S READY TO PLAY

Butch-femme is back–and those who theorize it and many who live it look to the reclamation and contextualization of the "old" butch-femme to speak a new discourse about what butch-femme is and does. Contemporary theorists, building on work establishing that lesbian butches-in-suits do not, in general, aspire to be men and that butch-femme does not, in general, aspire to heterosexuality (cf. Nestle 1987, 1992; Kennedy & Davis 1993) created a new concept to better capture what butches and femmes *are* doing: lesbian gender. "Lesbian gender" embodies the authenticity felt by lesbians who name butch or femme as their identities. Lesbian gender also emphasizes how both identities disrupt traditional gender categories, indicating their disavowal of a system in which sex uniformly predicts gender and sexuality. This paper explores lesbian gender in relation to women-in-suits, moving closer towards an understanding not just of who butches and women-in-suits are *not*, but also, of who they *are*. Throughout, I seek to expand beyond a discourse of the lesbian butch to all women-in-suits.

I begin with a discussion of the power of self-naming via 1950s butch-femme. Next I consider contemporary theorizing of female masculinity and lesbian gender and the transgressive potential of both. Using Halberstam's *Female Masculinity* (1998b)–considered *the* text of female masculinity–I show how queer theory's conception of female masculinity as lesbian gender is problematic; it reinforces rather than disrupts the heterogendered sex/gender/desire system, and it dismisses the potential for multiple versions of "masculinity" to be claimed as subversive subject positions by women of all sexualities.

WHAT'S IN A NAME? THE POWER OF SELF-NAMING

[W]e shall have to struggle for the right to create our own terms through which to define ourselves and our relationship to the society, and to have these terms recognized. This is the first necessity of a free people, and the first right that any oppressor must suspend. (Stokely Carmichael, 1966, 639)

We are named in and by language, and these names represent our lived relation to the material conditions of our existence, to those around us, and to ourselves (Weedon 1987, 26). Taking control of the linguistic process of naming is a means of repositioning oneself as subject rather than object. This intervention reconstitutes a subject's lived relation to her environment and offers the opportunity for agency in, though not necessarily authorship of, her own relations.

Although upwardly-mobile and affluent lesbians in the 1950s and 1960s felt that lesbians should not be open about declaring their identities (cf. Faderman 1991; Bender & Due 1994; Roof 1998), working-class butches saw the visible claim to identity as a powerful tool. Butches believed that through a visible break with the traditions of the past, they would be in a stronger position from which to fight. According to Nestle (1987):

> We were a symbol of women's erotic autonomy, a sexual accomplishment that did not include them [straight spectators]. The physical attacks were a direct attempt to break into these self-sufficient erotic partnerships. The most frequently shouted taunt was, "Which one of you is the man?" This was not a reflection of our Lesbian experience as much as it was a testimony to the lack of erotic categories in straight culture. (102)

The butch-femme couple disrupts the normative process of gender interpellation: as women, butches and femmes "should" instead be hailed as heterosexual and heterofeminine. Butches and femmes restructure and reorder the space around the female body. When 1950s lesbians proclaimed their identities through appearance, they made the radical and subversive statement that sex is not a one-way traffic sign, but is, instead, one of multiple factors fashioning one's identity. It is a statement that lesbian women increasingly declare today through butch, femme, and other nontraditional genders.

Introducing their book about butch women, Lily Burana, Roxxie, and Linnea Due (1994) write, "Dagger is about women wanting others to see, about women claiming a name, about all of us carrying on in our diversity. It is about every one watching us be ourselves" (13). For these authors, "lesbian gender" juxtaposes a claim of masculinity or femininity (gender) that refuses the invisible preface of "hetero" against a sexuality that also rejects this preface. By speaking the absence of heterogender and heterosexuality as well as the presence of lesbian gender and homosexuality, lesbian gender first references, then renounces, the existing heterosystem. From a Foucauldian perspective, the woman-in-a-suit performs a similar operation: she presents images (i.e., woman and suit) that simultaneously resonate with assumptions of the heterosystem and repudiate the contextualization of female femininity and male masculinity traditionally accompanying these meanings.

When a woman dons a suit, she alters her relation to the conditions of her existence, changing her occupation of space either by occupying it in a different way or by occupying a different space. She interpolates herself rather than being interpolated; although she remains marked by the preexisting gender discourse and thus does not control the terms in which she reinscribes herself, she still makes a new statement, (re)naming herself and her relative positionality

(De Lauretis 1987, 10). Her new locus–both inside and outside traditional understandings of gender–is a site of struggle from which she can contest and transform the conditions of her existence. In this vein, Sue-Ellen Case argues that "butch and femme, as a dynamic duo, offer precisely the strong subject position" required for claiming the position of female subject (1993, 295). Is this radical transformative potential available exclusively to lesbians by virtue of their apparent abstention from heteroculture? Or does this argument occlude a "reverse" hierarchy produced by queer theorists that unduly dismisses non-lesbian women as potential subjects?

WHO GETS TO WEAR THE PANTS?
ALL THE GAY GIRLS ARE DOING IT . . .

Though touted as more flexible and accepting, the new butch-femme has its own guidelines for who can belong to the butch club. First and foremost, a woman must be a lesbian. For example, Sherrie Inness and Michelle Lloyd (1996) present a number of rules for "butch" that "explain why the masculine straight woman is not a butch" (16). These "precepts of butchness" provide both a useful introduction to a popular view of butch and insight into the territoriality that comes with lesbian gender. First, a woman must consistently present herself as butch rather than attempting to draw butch identity on and off like an article of clothing. Second, a "real" butch never presents herself as traditionally feminine in order to appeal to a male gaze; "a woman whose appearance is designed to gain the sexual attention of men is not butch" (16). Third, butches present their butchness only for other women.

All understandings of butch as lesbian gender are not this strict, but flexibility is found only in the first regulation rather than in the latter two: in contemporary butch-femme, butches may acknowledge a "feminine" side, translating into a broader range in the expression of "masculinity." Some butches view being butch as *identity*, while others perceive it to be more playful, a way of *doing* one's lesbianism that is subject to change according to circumstance, context, and mood. "For over a decade the separate terms have been treated with amusing elasticity, like 'she's a femmy butch' or 'a butchy femme,' which prove what many have long suspected–the categories cannot hold the myriad ways in which we perform our lesbian genders" (Smyth 1998, 83). The constant throughout these different modes of gender performativity is the modifier "lesbian," linking the presentation of female masculinity to a sexual desire for other women.

"Butch," then, is explicitly denied to non-lesbian women; is the same true of "masculinity"? Inness and Lloyd deny the "masculine straight woman," claiming "real" female masculinity cannot exist within the heterosystem. Because their aim is to justify butch-butch relationships, they take pains to separate butchness from the specific requirements of butch-femme desire, but, even so, leave no room for masculine women who express heterosexual desire:

> We have shown that it is masculinity, not sexual desire and choice of sexual object, that should be the chief identifying trait of the butch. . . . Associating the butch with her masculine display, rather than with her choice of sexual partner, frees the butch up to have sex with whomever she wants in whatever way she desires, while still avoiding the trap of "infinite elasticity." (Inness & Lloyd 1996, 27)

This declaration seems, at first glance, to include heterosexual women in the sweep of butchness. But the authors' explicit statement that straight women are not butches (via the three axioms presented above) serves as a disclaimer. The passage should read:

> We have shown that it is masculinity, not sexual desire and choice of sexual object [*as long as it is still lesbian desire and a female sexual object*], that should be the chief identifying trait of the butch. . . . Associating the butch with her masculine display, rather than with her choice of sexual partner, frees the butch up to have sex with [*any woman*] she wants in whatever way she desires.

In fact, the "trap of 'infinite elasticity' " to which the authors refer–and attempt to avoid–is a trap door whereby the expansion of definitions of butch would allow heterosexual women to enter the club. Thus, although Inness and Lloyd conclude their article by announcing masculinity–"masculine display"–as the only requirement for butch, they do not include straight women in butch possibilities, implying that straight women are somehow deficient in their "masculine display." Writing in 1971, Rita Laporte addressed this relation of sexuality and masculinity directly: "An interesting side light in this connection is the masculine, apparently heterosexual, woman. . . . Many will insist that such a woman *is* heterosexual. No, this is an extreme case of denying one's self. So long as this woman was convinced of her heterosexuality, she was unaware of her masculinity" (9). The belief that a masculine woman cannot be straight and a straight woman cannot be masculine continues to background the writings of theorists today.

Considered by many to be *the* authority in these matters, Judith Halberstam's *Female Masculinity* (1998b) illustrates queer theory's lesbian fundamentalism. Halberstam states that the goal of her book is to address the "collective failure to imagine and ratify the masculinity produced by, for, and within women" (15). Crucial to this aim is the consideration of masculinity among women of *all* sexualities, or, at least, a reasoned argument for why masculinity cannot exist in all of them. Yet Halberstam skirts an exploration of the possibility of masculinity in non-lesbian women. In her introduction, she writes, "Often masculinity is the sign of sexual alterity, but occasionally it marks heterosexual variation" (9). Later, she observes that "we have a word for lesbian masculinity: butch" (120). Here, Halberstam uses "lesbian" instead of female, indicating the possibility of other female masculinities, but does not actually address the point in more detail. Although she seems to acknowledge the existence of masculinity in women regardless of sexual desire, giving a nod to the idea in both introduction and conclusion, Halberstam's silence speaks louder than her words as she fails but to elaborate in the pages in between.

Halberstam allows that "while much of this book has concentrated on the masculinity in women that is most often associated with sexual variance, I also think the general concept of female masculinity has its uses for heterosexual women" (268). "Has its uses" is noticeably not "is also applicable" or "also exists" or some other equivalent; it specifically does not imply the same identity, ownership, or authenticity in regard to masculinity that "butch" or "lesbian gender" does. Halberstam then suggests it would be useful for heterosexual women to acquire some masculinity to allow them to experience freedom from the "passivity and inactivity," "various forms of unhealthy body manipulations," and "girl problems" associated with femininity (268-9). Certainly Halberstam does nothing here to build up any credibility for the idea of masculinity for the heterosexual female.

In one of her few passages considering straight women, Halberstam describes the 1992 *Vanity Fair* cover showing Demi Moore wearing a man's suit painted onto her body (Liebowitz 1992; see *http://demimoore.org/mags/van92.html*). Halberstam cursorily compares this image with those of lesbian women and concludes:

> Moore's body suit fails to suggest even a mild representation of female masculinity precisely because it so anxiously emphasizes the femaleness of Moore's body. Whereas Opie's and Grace's portraits often make no effort to make femaleness visible, the Moore images represent femaleness as that which confers femininity on even the most conventional of masculine facades (the suit). The female masculinity in the work of Opie and Grace, by comparison, offers a glimpse into worlds where alternative masculinities make an art of gender. (40)

Halberstam does not consider that perhaps her reading of "femaleness" as the focal point in Moore's image rests more upon a deeply-ensconced cultural assumption–that a nude curvy woman's body epitomizes traditional "feminin-ity" and "femaleness"–than in any added feminization present in the picture. She reads femaleness only as femininity because she *expects* to find it in the image of a movie star and heterosexual beauty icon.

Moore's image, however, is polysemic: it exposes the "masculinity" of men as a painted-on, rather than natural, construction; it disrupts in the assumed correlation of sex and gender; it claims her own form of masculinity as a woman-in-a-suit. In summary, it critiques gender. Halberstam not only by-passes these readings, but also asserts they should not be taken seriously as challenges to the heterosystem, claiming instead that "female masculinity seems to be at its most threatening when coupled with lesbian desire" (28).

> I have no doubt that heterosexual female masculinity menaces gender conformity in its own way, but all too often it represents an acceptable degree of female masculinity as compared to the excessive masculinity of the dyke. (Halberstam 1998b; 28)

It seems here that Halberstam is not really referencing lesbian desire itself, but is reading signifiers of desire that are not as transparent as she intimates. Would Moore present a more authentic picture of female masculinity if she were flat-chested, short-haired, or more muscular? What is the test: can bisexual women be butch or is female masculinity restricted to bulldykes? Do large breasts disqualify women as subversive? Does long hair? If these signifiers are the criteria for knowing which women are "masculine enough," female mascu-linity becomes a shallow performance rather than the authentic identity claimed by theorists. If Moore had appeared in a painted suit with a shaved head and buffed body–as she had for *G.I. Jane*–would she have been a more acceptable representation of female masculinity? Ironically, Moore has appeared in drag on-stage in public, complete with suit (fabric this time) and facial hair, seeming as male–as butch–as some of the drag kings pictured in Halberstam's (1999) re-cent *The Drag King Book*. Halberstam's ready disregard of *Female* masculin-ity–or masculin*ies*–does not offer an adequate framework for assessing whether or not and in what ways non-lesbian women access Masculinity.

MEMBERS-ONLY?
THE LESBIAN CLUB AND FEMALE MASCULINITY

Female masculinity is linked historically and conceptually to butch lesbian sexuality. The development of butch-femme culture in the 1950s enabled les-bians to make space for themselves in a society that tried to squeeze them into the rigid constructs of heterosexual culture. Butch and femme were powerful positions of subjectivity and agency, and lesbians have invested much in the protection and defense of these identities in the face of opposition inside and outside lesbian communities. Butch identity is important as a strongly articulated site of subversion because this position is a source of strength, pride, and courage–three attributes indispensable to those who dare openly transgress social norms. As a lesbian gender, butch marks a source of power seemingly outside the patriarchal power hierarchy.

The signifiers that accompany and announce butch and femme identities are vital as "legible" symbols of lesbian existence and desire in a culture that tries its best to erase them. Katrina Rolley (1992), quoting Joan Nestle, writes:

> When we broke gender lines in the 1950s, we fell off the biologically charted maps. How else was a woman recognizable as a lesbian except through her body, her clothes, and the dialogue between the two? I loved my lover [Nestle writes] for how she stood as well as for what she did. Dress was a part of it: the erotic signal of her hair at the nape of her neck, touching the shirt collar; how she held a cigarette; the symbolic pinky ring flashing as she waved her hand. (38)

This link between female masculinity and lesbian desire is more than semantics: it did and does carry profoundly difficult and dangerous real-life implications for the women who live it. Butch lesbians are ridiculed, marginalized, stigmatized, and attacked–verbally and physically–for their expression of self (e.g., Feinberg 1993; Nestle 1987; Halberstam 1998).

The extension of female masculinity to non-lesbian women who may not identify closely with the specific historical discrimination and oppression of lesbians seems to risk making "butchness" less powerful and subversive–less valid as an identity. Thus, the "mainstreaming" of butch is feared as a mechanism that will dilute and trivialize butch identity: "Butch women on the covers of popular magazines are thus absorbed into the general culture to be cast aside as yesterday's icon, or 'mainstreamed'–stripped of sexuality and meaning, as if we were adherents to a quirky style, no more than a fashion statement" (Burana et al. 1994, 10). In contrast, securing female masculinity within lesbianism is thought to protect its disruptive and empowering potential: "Female masculinity within queer discourse allows for the disruption of even flows between gender and anatomy, sexuality and identity, sexual practice and performativity" (Halberstam 1998b, 139). Although these observations explain the reluctance of most queer theorists to admit non-lesbian women into the ranks of female masculinity, they do not justify a continued exclusion, especially one at least partially based in a lesbian fundamentalism seeking to designate who is "really" masculine, hence "really" lesbian.

In this regard, the restriction of butch and female masculinity to lesbians occludes a process that maintains the subjugation of feminine to masculine and preserves heteronormative connections between gender and sex. Butch-as-lesbian-gender does this first through its repeated conceptualization within the butch-femme partnership. Butch and femme are jointly referenced in lesbian gender and theoretical considerations of it. Sue-Ellen Case (1993), for example, suggests that "butch and femme *as a dynamic duo*, offer precisely the strong subject position" required for actualizing female subjectivity (295, emphasis added). As Biddy Martin (1994) persuasively argues, this practice of considering butch and femme as butch-femme erroneously reduces the femme's transgressiveness to dependency on the butch because butchness is often presented as "lend[ing] visibility to the femme." Halberstam points out that theorizing butch subjectivity within butch-femme as positive or transgressive does not, in theory, render femme subjectivity passive or conservative (1998b, 59). But in practice–in the context of theory that limits butch to lesbians–theorizing butch as powerful because of the butch's visible transgressions implicitly depreciates the femme's subversiveness. The result of theorizing lesbian gender in this dependent dyad–the butch-in-a-suit making the femme-in-a-dress visible as subversive–is that femme agency is often left out of theorizing about lesbian and feminist subjectivity.

From a feminist standpoint striving to conceptualize independent female agency, positing butch and femme as interdependent lesbian genders seems undesirable; if it *is* to imply agency, an individual's subjectivity should not rely upon her sexual partner. Furthermore, the coupling of butch-femme as subject makes it appear as though gender is the only force at work in the relation of desire between two women in a butch-femme context. Yet, "Butch, like any other gender identity, also relies heavily upon racial and class constructions [and these] may intervene in the primacy of the butch-femme dyad" (Halberstam 1998a, 60). Although these shortcomings of butch-femme as a coupled position may seem reminiscent of the 1970s-80s lesbian-feminist critiques of butch-femme as undesirable, I want to distinguish my *critique* of butch-femme from the lesbian-feminist *rejection* of it. I am not arguing against the existence of butch-femme nor against butch and femme identities; neither am I suggesting that by being masculine or appropriating parts of traditional masculine culture, butches are subjugating femmes and participating in misogynistic practices. I *am* contending that theorizing butch and femme *as inter-dependent lesbian-specific genders* unduly limits butch and femme and obfuscates the subversiveness of their separate existences. Moreover, it denies their existence outside butch-femme and lesbian cultures.

The second pitfall of equating female masculinity to butch lesbian gender is the naturalization of heterogendered desires such that masculine desires feminine and feminine desires masculine. The butch-femme construction focuses desire around the difference of gender between butches and femmes. Limiting female masculinity to lesbians ascribes femininity to all heterosexual women and masculinity to all heterosexual men by default. This gendering of heterosexual desire is also accomplished in the refrain that femmes can "pass" as straight women, but butches cannot. Heterosexual desire thus follows a strict heterogendered path, and femmes, who can pass because they are feminine, become interchangeable with heterosexual women as objects of heterosexual male desire. Once again, femme agency disappears while masculine subjectivities–butch and heterosexual man–are preserved.

Many discussions of bisexuality similarly reinforce heterogendered desire. It is always the femme who is bisexual, rendering desire for men necessarily feminine and men's desire for women necessarily masculine. Laporte minced no words in claiming "all heterosexual relationships are butch/femme" (1971, 7). Contemporary queer theory maintains Laporte's assumption. This fallacious logic reinforces one of the most debilitating myths of the heterosystem: "The heterosexual logic that requires that identification and desire be mutually exclusive is one of the most reductive of heterosexism's psychological instruments: if one identifies *as* a given gender, one must desire a different gender" (Butler 1993, 239).

The third misstep made by the lesbian fundamentalist construction of female masculinity is its reinforcement and naturalization of a formulaic connection of gender and sex. If butchness is exclusively lesbian, Masculinity is linked only with people who desire women. Thus, heterosexual males not only rightfully claim Masculinity, but Masculinity is naturalized and essentialized for them; Femaleness and Femininity are linked and naturalized for straight women. Both of these collapse and conflate sex, gender, and sexuality. A crucial assumption here is that men do not desire masculine women and that women do not desire feminine men–assumptions that do not resonate with lived relations of desire. Furthermore, if and when these "inverted" desires do appear, they are rendered pathological and dysphoric, once more preserving the strict binaries of heterogender. In Butler's words, this conflation of heterogender and heterosexuality "is precisely to fail to see what makes sexual seeing possible: prevailing regulatory norms of perception that confer ontological possibility on sexual subjects to the extent that they conform with prior normative expectations of gender, where there are men and there are women, and sexual desire is an exclusive function of their relation" (1998, 226). Sexuality becomes a prerequisite for breaking the assumed heterogender code, and even then it can only broken in specific binary-preserving ways.

Limiting "true" female masculinity to butch reinforces the link between Masculinity and butch for men as well as lesbian women. When we stabilize the heterosexual male, heterosexual masculinity, and the heterosexual male's sexuality as "butch" in this way, we do a disservice to all those who have worked to separate the language of gender from the language of sex and we deny the existence of desire outside hetero-binaries. Increasingly, individuals (of all sexes) presenting a multitude of genders self-identify under the rubric of Masculinity. But queer theorizing of lesbian gender and female masculinity unlinks sex and gender only in the context of lesbian desire, and fails at that: although lesbian gender and female masculinity prove that sex does not predict gender (i.e., woman equals feminine), both concepts still conflate sex and gender–albeit with a twist.

WHAT IF SHE DOESN'T LIKE GIRLS?

The recent return of butch-femme (cf. Munt 1998; Burana et al. 1994; Weston 1993; Nestle 1992) coincides with a heightened contemporary queer awareness of the interplay of sex, gender, and desire. Kath Weston (1993), for example, observes that "coming out to oneself as a gay person generally entails coming into a heightened consciousness of gender" (6). This consciousness, however, is not exclusive to lesbians; some non-lesbian women also challenge the gender-norming of the heterosystem. Although they do not intend to do so, Inness and Lloyd (1996) offer a starting point for a female masculinity that does not presume lesbian desire: "In this process of redefining the butch we explode the myth that the butch is characterized by the object of her desire . . . butch is a singular identity position, not a coupled one" (10).

Looking to the figure of the woman-in-a-suit as an example, we can see that Female Masculinity beyond the context of homosexual desire suggests a multidimensional spectrum of "masculinities." Some women-in-suits claim masculinity and pursue the maleness and male subject position that go along with it. Passing women and some female-to-male transsexuals are female-bodied individuals who wear the suit as part of their identity as men–Billy Tipton and Murray Hall are two examples. Another group of women-in-suits use the suit to break into male-dominated professions or to gain economic advantage. Dressed for success in a man's world, they may or may not associate their appearance with a "cross"-identification of sex, gender, or desire; poor women at the turn of the nineteenth century, women in the 1970s struggling to break into "male" professions, and contemporary corporate women are a few examples. A third group of women wear the suit because they identify with the "masculinity" that it symbolizes. They do not, however, claim to be men nor do they imitate men. Lesbian butches, celebrities such as k.d. lang and Katharine Hepburn, 1920s spinsters (Franzen 1996), and some heterosexual women fall into this group.

Narratives of women-in-suits who identify as "masculine" women are predominantly those of women who also identify as lesbian. Heterosexual and bisexual women-in-suits may make fewer public claims to masculinity than do lesbian women, but this is partially a result of the perception–pervasive in straight *and* queer communities–that masculinity cannot exist in women who are not lesbian. But not all masculine women-in-suits identify as lesbian; one woman, for example, identifies as heterosexual:

> A lot of the phase I went through in my adult life, the struggle with gender identity, was after putting on a man's suit and feeling at home for the first time . . . I felt COMFORTABLE. So I explored that for a long time. I think that I felt comfortable because suddenly the way that I moved–which has always been very "masculine"–became, it made sense. It looked like suddenly you were supposed to FIT in the world. (McGann 1999)

A fourth group of women-in-suits wear the suit as performance, moving beyond performativity in order to flaunt a crossing and potential deconstruction of the binary sex/gender/desire system. They don the suit as erotic play with gender, desire, and sex–Madonna is a prime example. These categorical descriptions of women-in-suits are neither mutually exclusive nor exhaustive. Marlene Dietrich, for example, used the suit as an on-screen erotic signifier, but also donned it in her personal life, perhaps as an embodiment of gender or sexual identification. Other women-in-suits, such as Billy Tipton, do not fall clearly into categories because the historical record does not offer conclusive evidence of their motives. Among this variation of women-in-suits, however, there *is* a universality in how a woman-in-a-suit interacts with both the suit and the cultural space she inhabits. Despite differing in degrees of intent, all women-in-suits reference a "crossing"–an appropriation of power accessed through a Masculinity that stands in for power. And thus, Female Masculinity is an identification available to all women and experienced by them in a variety of ways.

QUEERING THE HETEROSYSTEM: FEMALE MASCULINITY AND "STRAIGHT" WOMEN-IN-SUITS

> Loving masculinity in a woman differs crucially in one way from loving it in a man: In her it is a badge of standing out, not of fitting in. . . . Being

butch is not the same as masculinity–it's a version of masculinity reflected in a wavy mirror, masculinity where our culture tells us not to
look for it: in women, or in "macho" gay men, where a very male presentation throws a curve ball. . . . Loving butchness amounts to an attraction
to what's not "supposed" to be there. (Queen 1994, 21-23)

Note here that Queen does not use a modifier for "women" as she does for
"men" (" 'macho' gay"). This formulation makes sense because masculinity is
"not 'supposed' to be there" in *any* woman, whatever her sexuality. Theorists
who bypass considerations of the heterosexual "mannish woman" suggest that
masculinity in non-lesbian contexts either points to the false consciousness of
a woman who is "really" lesbian, or is not particularly transgressive–or at least
not transgressive "enough." Furthermore, these theorists also imply that recognizing masculinity in non-lesbian women detracts from its subversive potential for lesbians. To test these assumptions, we need to relocate butchness or
Female Masculinity within the context of desire–this time, heterosexual desire–to see if this indeed disqualifies–even "de-queers"–it. The argument behind both the defense of butchness as exclusively lesbian and Queen's
declaration of butch eroticism is that Female Masculinity itself is *queer*: it refuses to be interpellated by the heterosystem. But heterosexual relations do not
negate this queerness; in fact, one might claim that heterosexual butches are
queer-er because their masculinity is more unexpected. Who would win the
"best queer" superlative is not the point, however; my point is to show that
queerness can exist in "straight" frames. Butler (1990), discussing butch-
femme relations, writes:

As one lesbian femme explained, she likes her boys to be girls, meaning
that "being a girl" contextualizes and resignifies "masculinity" in a butch
identity. As result, that masculinity, if that it can be called, is always
brought into relief against a culturally intelligible "female body." It is
precisely this dissonant juxtaposition and the sexual tension that its
transgression generates that constitute the object of desire. (123)

Butler continues in a way that potentially locates queerness within heterosexuality:

[S]ome heterosexual or bisexual women may well prefer the relation of
"figure" to "ground" work in the opposite direction–that is, they may
prefer that their girls be boys. In that case, the perception of "feminine"
identity would be juxtaposed on the "male body" as ground, but both
terms would, through the juxtaposition, lose their internal stability and
distinctness from each other. (123)

Variations in the "figure" to "ground" relationship create desire, transgression, and queerness. Although Butler does not discuss it, her line of reasoning brings the possibility that some heterosexual or bisexual men may want their boys to be girls, juxtaposing the "masculine" identity on the "female body" as ground. Thus, a man in a "heterosexual" relationship with a masculine woman would agree with Queen's statement of butch eroticism. Heterosexuality then does not necessitate an acceptance of heterogendered heterosexual identity for women, but, instead, can itself be a queer space.

In their explication of being "butch," Inness and Lloyd (1996) note:

> [B]utch lesbians use clothing as a way to indicate membership in a group; butches are easily recognized as lesbians because both lesbian and heterosexual cultures typically interpret masculine appearance and clothing, particularly when combined with few feminine signifiers such as lipstick, make-up, long hair, and jewelry as indicators of homosexuality. (15)

Their statement is true, but the connection of primarily masculine signifiers and the absence of feminine ones with homosexuality is a conventional, rather than necessary, one. The woman-in-a-suit may present herself in an entirely masculine manner, wearing a man's suit with men's shoes, a tie, and short hair, without make-up or jewelry—and she may even *be* a lesbian. She might also be heterosexual or bisexual. She may combine a man's suit with long hair, dangling earrings, and lipstick. Or, she might don a suit tailored to a traditional woman's shape. The degree to which a woman-in-a-suit is legible as "masculine" varies. The woman wearing a suit shaped to fit her curves, with jewelry, makeup, heels and long hair is read differently from the woman wearing a man's suit with no jewelry, no makeup, men's shoes and short hair. But all are read through the same system in which the first woman references the image of the second even as she moves away from it. It seems then, that any woman-in-the-suit engages in reverse discourse, taking a symbol standardized for men by productive power, and destandardizing it by placing it onto a female body. And, expanding from Butler (1990), when she writes, "The replication of heterosexual constructs in non-heterosexual frames brings into relief the utterly constructed status of the heterosexual original" (31), we conclude that by repeating a heterogendered construct in a non-heterogendered—that is, *queer*–frame, the woman-in-a-suit engages in parodic repetition. The non-lesbian woman-in-a-suit parodies the construction of masculinity for men and for lesbian women as well, reminding us that masculinity *is* constructed for *both*.

Although butch lesbians have much at stake in exclusively claiming the identity of masculinity as essential and natural, heterosexual and bisexual women-in-suits ground us in the knowledge that this claim is one of lived experience rather than fact. Garber notes:

> Just as to ignore the role played by homosexuality would be to risk a radical misunderstanding of the social and cultural implications of cross-dressing, so to restrict cross-dressing to the context of an emerging gay and lesbian identity is to risk ignoring, or setting aside, elements and incidents that seem to belong to quite different lexicons of self-definition and political and cultural display. (1992, 4)

Sally Munt (1998), discussing butch and femme lesbian genders, observes, "We have adopted heterosexual iconography, but we reproduce it in masquerade, as a knowing copy, thus, as an analogy which cannot simply return to a reidealized, retrenched original" (11). Heterosexual women-in-suits have adopted male heterosexual *and* butch homosexual iconography, displacing the suit even farther from its once-entrenched place in the patriarchy. Martin (1994) observes:

> If it is true, to paraphrase Judith Butler, that the structuring presence of heterosexual roles in homosexual relations does not determine them, it is also true that the structuring presence of heterosexual roles in heterosexual relations does not determine them. It is not possible to reimagine gender configurations outside binary frames by sustaining an absolute division between lesbianism and heterosexuality. (113)

Although a more "feminine-looking" woman-in-a-suit may not be as transparently subversive as her butch counterpart, the potential to disrupt remains written in her appearance. The recognition of this potential often results in literal dress codes (McGann forthcoming) that discourage women from wearing suits or pressure women-in-suits to appear as feminine as they can.

It is useful here to (re)read an example of a woman-in-a-suit to see the expansion of possible readings. Halberstam cites a 1993 *Vanity Fair* photo series that pictures singer and butch lesbian icon k.d. lang in a suit with supermodel and feminine heterosexual icon Cindy Crawford in a bodysuit (Ritts 1993; see *http://www.kt.rim.or.jp/~majo/mag/VF0893/1.html*). The inside spread features Crawford lying on top of lang, faces close together, lang's hand on Crawford's buttock. Halberstam's reading:

> First, by positing a conventional heterosexual pinup as the object of butch lesbian desire, the photo-fantasy makes an unholy alliance between the male gaze and a more queer butch gaze. Second, the picture

flaunts stereotypes and by doing so explodes the tension between homophobic and queer representation. Finally, it calls for many different identificatory strategies from viewers: a heterosexual male must access his desire for Crawford only through the masculinity of a lesbian; a straight woman might identify with Crawford and desire lang; a queer viewer finds that dyke desire is mobile here and may take up butch, femme, masculine, or feminine spectator positions. (1998b, 175)

Halberstam does a good job pointing out different possibilities and the ironic repositioning that this photo produces through viewing strategies, but her labels of "heterosexual" and "straight" gloss over what she really means: heterogendered heterosexuality. Moving beyond this assumption proffers additional possibilities. Perhaps a man might desire lang's female masculinity; a woman might identify with lang as masculine and still desire lang's masculinity either as a stand-in for male masculinity or as female masculinity; a "straight" masculine woman might identify with lang's gender identity and desire Crawford. These crossings further blur the lines connecting gender, sex, and sexuality even as these moves are made available through a "standard" butch-femme set-up.

These kinds of interpretations help us recognize the range of resistance to traditional heterogender- and sexuality-norming, reminding us not to bypass or dismiss some women-in-suits as pandering to convention simply because of their real or presumed sexual orientation. The dismissal of so-called feminine women as straight and, therefore, unthreatening to the patriarchal order, has long been identified as a flaw of mass culture by queer critics as they look back to claim a lesbian history in popular and historical culture. Susan Sarandon points out in *The Celluloid Closet* (1996) that the pairing of two women in movies has not been taken seriously because at least one, and usually both, has always been presented as feminine, and, consequently, their interaction has been dismissed as "experimental" when noticed at all. I add to this charge of queer erasure the dismissal of straight women as necessarily feminine.

To ignore this possibility is to contribute to the re-alignment of sex and gender as deterministic of identity potential, limiting men to masculinity and women to either femininity or lesbian masculinity. By reading women-in-suits of all sexualities as accessing masculinity to some degree, we un-conflate sexuality and gender, rejecting the notion that sexuality must be a prerequisite for gender identification:

[The effect of] disjoining categories of gender from desire and recombining them in ways that disrupt and restructure the sexual field . . . is to dismantle the very edifice of heterosexual normativity, showing that its various "parts" do not always work in concert, that they may be appropriated and recirculated independently, and that, finally, the heterosexual center does not hold. (Butler 1998, 228)

With binary assumptions exploded, we start to grasp the multiplicity of possibilities open before us. Gender becomes comprehensible as a fluid category and Masculinity is exposed as one of Butler's iterative practices. Our dominant idea of Masculinity as a coherent formulation is the result of constant marking and remarking of boundaries and continual reaffirmation that sex, gender, and desire attributes converge along heteronormative axes. When this iteration of necessary coherence–even the subversive iteration in lesbian contexts–is disrupted by being referenced, performed, and read in a new way, we disrupt the circulation of heterosexuality and heterogender.

WORKS CITED

Bender, D., & Due, L. (1994). Coming up butch. In L. Burana, Roxxie, & L. Due (Eds.), *Dagger: On butch women* (pp.96-112). Pittsburgh: Cleis Press.

Burana, L., Roxxie, & Due, L. (1994). Introduction. In L. Burana, Roxxie, & L. Due (Eds.), *Dagger: On butch women* (pp. 9-14). Pittsburgh: Cleis Press.

Butler, J. (1990). *Gender trouble: Feminism and the subversion of identity.* New York: Routledge.

_____. (1993). *Bodies that matter: On the discursive limits of "sex."* New York: Routledge.

_____. (1998). Afterword. In S. Munt (Ed.), *butch/femme: inside lesbian gender* (pp. 225-230). London: Cassell.

Carmichael, S. (1966, Autumn). Toward Black liberation. *Massachusetts Review,* 639-651.

Case, S.-E. (1993). Toward a butch-femme aesthetic. In H. Abelove, M. A. Barale, & D. Halperin (Eds.), *The lesbian and gay studies reader* (pp. 294-306). New York: Routledge.

Celluloid Closet, The. (1996). R. Epstein & J. Friedman (Directors). [Film]. Columbia/Tristar Studios.

De Lauretis, T. (1987). *Technologies of gender: Essays on theory, film, and fiction.* Bloomington: Indiana UP.

Faderman, L. (1991). *Odd girls and twilight lovers: A history of lesbian life in twentieth-century America.* New York: Penguin.

Feinberg, L. (1993). *Stone butch blues.* Ithaca, New York: Firebrand Books.

Franzen, T. (1996). *Spinsters and lesbians: Independent womanhood in the United States* (The Cutting Edge Lesbian Life and Literature Series). New York: NYU Press.

Garber, M. (1992). *Vested interests: Cross-dressing and cultural anxiety.* New York: Routledge.

Halberstam, J. (1998a). Between butches. In S. Munt (Ed.), *butch/femme: Inside lesbian gender* (pp. 57-66). London: Cassell.

_____. (1998b). *Female masculinity*. Durham, NC: Duke UP.

Inness, S. A., & Lloyd, M. E. (1996). G.I. Joes in Barbie land: Recontextualizing butch in twentieth-century lesbian culture. In B. Beemyn, & M. Eliason (Eds.), *Queer studies: A lesbian, gay, bisexual, & transgender anthology* (pp. 9-34). New York: NYU Press.

Kennedy, E., & Davis M. (1993). *Boots of leather, slippers of gold: The history of a lesbian community*. New York: Penguin.

Laporte, R. (1971). The butch/femme question. *The Ladder* 15 (9-10), 4-11. At the Lesbian Herstory Archives, Brooklyn, NY.

Liebowitz, A. (Photographer). (1992, August). Cover photo (Demi Moore). *Vanity Fair*. URL: *http://demimoore.org/mags/van92.html*.

Martin, B. (1994). Sexualities without genders and other queer utopias. *Diacritics*, 24, (2-3), 104-21.

McGann, PJ (1999). Skirting the gender normal divide: A tomboy life story. In M. Romero, & A. Stewart (Eds.), *Women's Untold Stories*. New York: Routledge.

_____. (forthcoming). *The ballfields of our hearts: Tomboys, femininity and the gendered body*. Philadelphia: Temple UP.

Munt, S. (1998). Introduction. In S. Munt (Ed.), *butch/femme: inside lesbian gender* (pp. 1-11). London: Cassell.

Nestle, J. (1987). Butch-femme relationships: Sexual courage in the 1950s. *A restricted country: Essays & short stories*. London: Sheba.

_____. (1992). Flamboyance and fortitude: An introduction. In J. Nestle (Ed.), *The persistent desire: A femme-butch reader* (pp. 13-22). Boston: Alyson.

Queen, C. A. (1994). Why I love butch women. In L. Burana, Roxxie, & L. Due (Eds.), *Dagger: On butch women* (pp. 15-23). Pittsburgh: Cleis.

Ritts, H. (Photographer). (1993, August). k.d. lang cuts it close. [L. Bennetts (Author)]. *Vanity Fair*, pp. 94-95. URL: *http://www.kt.rim.or.jp/~majo/mag/VF0893/1.html*.

Rolley, K. (1992). Love, desire, and the pursuit of the whole: Dress & the lesbian couple. In J. Ash & E. Wilson (Eds.), *Chic thrills: A fashion reader*. London: Pandora.

Roof, J. (1998). 1970s lesbian feminism meets 1990s butch-femme. In S. Munt (Ed.), *butch/femme: Inside lesbian gender* (pp. 27-36). London: Cassell.

Smyth, C. (1998). How do we look? Imaging butch/femme. In S. Munt (Ed.), *butch/femme: inside lesbian gender* (pp. 82-89). London: Cassell.

Weedon, C. (1987). *Feminist practice & poststructuralist theory*. Cambridge, MA: Blackwell.

Weston, K. (1993). Do clothes make the woman?: Gender performance theory, and lesbian eroticism. *Genders* 17, 1-21.

Wilson, E. (1988). "Chic thrills." *Hallucinations: Life in the postmodern city*. London: Hutchinson Radius.

The Perfect Child

Karen Ripley

Karen Ripley has been teaching improvisation to children and adults for over twenty years at colleges, camps, festivals, and adult education centers. You can read her humor in *The Homo Handbook, Revolutionary Laughter, A Funny Time To Be Gay*, and *Multiple Sarcasm*. Her work is included on a CD called *The Best of Lesbian Comedy*.

Contact Karen Ripley by e-mail: <UmorMe@aol.com>.

[Haworth co-indexing entry note]: "The Perfect Child." Ripley, Karen. Co-published simultaneously in *Journal of Lesbian Studies* (Harrington Park Press, an imprint of The Haworth Press, Inc.) Vol. 6, No. 2, 2002, p. 175; and: *Femme/Butch: New Considerations of the Way We Want to Go* (ed: Michelle Gibson, and Deborah T. Meem) Harrington Park Press, an imprint of The Haworth Press, Inc., 2002, p. 175. Single or multiple copies of this article are available for a fee from The Haworth Document Delivery Service [1-800-HAWORTH, 9:00 a.m. - 5:00 p.m. (EST). E-mail address: getinfo@haworthpressinc.com].

175

Index

Anderson, J., 9-10
Androgyny, 147-156
Artifacts, cultural, 114-115
Audience prioritization, 13-14,16-17,
    20-23
Authentication, 92-94

Bisexuality, 166-167
Blonde Venus (film), 143-155
"Boy," concept of, 61-71
Boy-mommy dynamics, 80-83
Britain, eighteenth-century. *See*
    Historiography,
    eighteenth-century Britain
Bulgarian culture, lesbian
    communities in
    case studies of, 137-144
    future perspectives of, 144
    historical perspectives of, 135-137
    Internet, impact of, 137-138
    introduction to, 3-8,135
    rhetoric, importance of, 143-144
    self-identification and, 135-144
    terminology, importance of,
        142-144
Butch privilege, 90
Butches, stone, 11-24
"The Butch/Femme Tango" (M. C.
    Matthews), 59
Butler, J., 74,84,94-101,147-156

Califia, P., 62-71
"Case of Homosexuality in a
    Woman" (S. Freud), 61-71
Charke, C., 105-120
Chi, T.-W., 130-132

Chinese culture, contemporary
    introduction to, 3-8,123-125
    reference literature about, 132-133
    tongzhi politics and
        butch-femme identification and,
            130-132
        Crocodile's Journal (C.
            Miao-chin) and, 124-133
        cross-cultural studies and,
            128-130
        ethnographies, scattered, 125-130
        female traditions, resurgence of,
            129-130
        gender role-playing and, 125-126
        introduction to, 123-125
        Island's Edge (T-W. Chi, H. Ling,
            and T. Tang-mo) and, 130-132
        literary modulations and, 130-132
        Tomboy (TB) *vs.* Tomboy girl
            (TBG) roles and, 127-130
Clothing-related issues
    future perspectives of, 173
    introduction to, 3-8, 157
    reference literature about, 173
    women-in-suits, contexts of
        bisexuality and, 166-167
        butch, rules for, 160-163
        butch-femme theories and, 158
        Female Masculinity (J.
            Halberstam) and, 161-163
        female masculinity *vs.* lesbianism,
            163-167
        feminist theories and, 165-167
        fundamentalist lesbian constructs
            and, 166-167
        gender identification and, 160-163
        heterosexual constructs and, 164,
            168-173